WHERE CUSTER FELL

WHERE CUSTER FELL

Photographs of the Little Bighorn Battlefield Then and Now

James S. Brust, Brian C. Pohanka, and Sandy Barnard

University of Oklahoma Press : Norman

Library of Congress Cataloging-in-Publication Data

Brust, James S.

   Where Custer fell : photographs of the Little Bighorn Battlefield then and now / James S. Brust, Brian C. Pohanka, Sandy Barnard

     p.   cm.

   Includes bibliographical references and index.

   ISBN 0-8061-3666-9 (alk. paper)

   I. Little Bighorn Battlefield (Mont.)—Pictorial works.   2. Little Bighorn Battlefield (Mont.)—History—Pictorial works.   3. Little Bighorn Battlefield (Mont.)—Pictorial works. 4. Little Bighorn, Battle of the, Mont., 1876.   I. Pohanka, Brian C.,   II. Barnard, Sandy. III. Title.

E83.876.B89 2005
973.8"2—dc22

                                   2004062015

The paper in this book meets the guidelines for permanence and durability of the Committee on Production Guidelines for Book Longevity of the Council on Library Resources, Inc. ∞

2 3 4 5 6 7 8 9 10

Dedicated to our colleague and "Pard," Brian Pohanka,
who died as this book was nearing publication.
We will miss him as we walk and study the battlefield—no one did it better.

CONTENTS

MAPS ⁓

PREFACE ⬲

A PHOTOGRAPH FIRST drew me into the research world of Lieutenant Colonel George Armstrong Custer and the Battle of the Little Bighorn. The acquisition of a haunting early view of the Little Bighorn Battlefield in 1990 sent me scurrying to my books to see if it had been published before or if anything were known of its photographer, John H. Fouch.

In my inquiries, I located neither the newly found view nor any mention of Fouch. But my interest was piqued in the familiar battlefield images I had previously viewed only superficially. Additionally, I realized how confusing the photos were. Going from book to book, I might find the same early battlefield picture marked with three different dates and labeled as the work of two different photographers. I had not paid much attention before because these pictures were mere window dressing, with little analysis in the captions and no discussion of them in the text.

A camera records exactly what is in front of it, making a photograph the most objective and literal of historical documents. One early picture of a battlefield ought to be worth a thousand words of years-later reminiscence, but most historians and authors pay scant attention to the photographic record.

After research confirmed that the Fouch photo I had discovered was the earliest ever taken of the battlefield, I began to study other images related to the Little Bighorn fight. While at the archives of the Little Bighorn Battlefield National Monument two years later, I looked at a familiar image taken in

1886 at the tenth anniversary of the battle and spotted a detail in the sharp vintage print that I had never seen in its typical murky reproductions in books. A pile of rocks was visible below the monument on the southwestern slope of Custer Hill--could it have marked the site of George Custer's battlefield grave prior to the removal of his body to West Point in 1877? Armed with a photocopy of the photo, I raced up to Last Stand Hill and attempted to match the site of the 1886 rock pile to the modern landscape, but from outside the fence below the marble markers that now mark where the soldiers died, I was unable to do so.

After I returned home, I continued to think about that pile of stones visible in the 1886 view. How nice it would be if, all along, a picture of Custer's original burial site had existed. Would that spot match the position of the current marble stone for George Armstrong Custer? I called Douglas McChristian, then chief historian at the battlefield, and asked if I could attempt to shoot a precise modern comparison to that 1886 photo.

This project was born during that visit to the battlefield in the autumn of 1992. Doug and I spent only one day reshooting a few early photos. Because the placement of the rock pile in the 1886 photo did not match the location of any current marker, we were unable to confirm that it was Custer's original gravesite. We had greater success with several other historical views, some of which showed a wooden cross among the marble markers. That cross turned out to be in the same location as

Custer's current stone. The value of comparing historical photographs to the present landscape quickly became apparent.

So I continued to research early views of the battlefield, returning each autumn to reshoot those that I had located. This was not the kind of work to be done alone, however. In 1994, I invited Brian Pohanka to join me. With his knowledge of the battle and the field on which it had been fought, as well as his expertise in historical photos, this project advanced to a serious level of study. The following year Sandy Barnard became part of the team. We were further motivated by the work of photo researcher William Frassanito. His series of excellent books on Civil War photography have both underscored the value of photographs as historical documents and made effective use of modern comparison photos of early views.

As our research progressed, our admiration of the early photographers grew ever stronger. Often forgotten among those who chronicle history, these hard-working visionaries hauled their heavy equipment over the ground where the events actually occurred. With great effort, and even at risk of life, they gained a greater sense of the site than those who studied and wrote from a distance. The photographs they produced pass their experience on to us, and we hope that this book will not only spotlight the historical value of these images, but also serve as a tribute to the photographers who created them.

Happily, this is a never-ending project, as previously unknown early battlefield photos continue to surface, presenting new opportunities to walk the field and find the sites where they were taken, looking and learning as we go. But the time has arrived to share this work with other students of Custer's last battle. We hope this volume will stimulate interest in the study of photographs of the Little Bighorn Battlefield.

ACKNOWLEDGMENTS ⌒

A PROJECT THIS large requires a good deal of assistance, and we have been fortunate to have had the help of many knowledgeable people.

Douglas C. McChristian, the former chief historian at the then-named Custer Battlefield National Monument, was the first to actively support this work, and his encouragement, validation, and hands-on help greatly aided our early efforts. Subsequent Chief Historians Tim McCleary and John Doerner have likewise assisted. Our research has extended through the tenure of four superintendents of the Little Bighorn Battlefield National Monument: Barbara Booher Suteer, Gerard Baker, Neil Mangum, and Darrell J. Cook. Each has welcomed us and allowed us to go onto the field to make the modern comparison photos. Kitty Belle Deernose, former archivist at the Little Bighorn Battlefield National Monument, helped us over and over again throughout this project by identifying, retrieving, and copying photographs and other documents. Many other current or past members of the battlefield staff, including Michael Stops and Cliff Arbogast, have cooperated with us and offered their goodwill.

Curators at other institutions provided valuable assistance as well: Lory Morrow of the Montana Historical Society; Susan Rochester and Lesli Larson of the University of Oregon; Leslie Shores of the American Heritage Center of the University of Wyoming; William Vollmar of the Anheuser Busch Companies, St. Louis, Missouri; Anne Wilson and Dorothy Neuhaus of the Over Museum in Vermillion, South Dakota; and Michael Winey and Randy Hackenberg of the U.S. Army Military History Institute in Carlisle, Pennsylvania. Others deserving mention here are Peggy Albright, Steve Arnold, Casey Barthelmess Jr., Marilyn Bilyeu, Rocky Boyd, Gerald Davidson, Brian Dippie, Michael Donahue, Jerome Greene, Aubrey Haines, Ken Hammer, Paul Harbaugh, Paul Hedren, Vince Heier, Tom Heski, John Husk, Jerry Keenan, Bob Kolbe, Dan Martinez, Carl Mautz, Ron McCoy, Mary Ellen McWilliams, Milton Miller, Ron Nichols, Elaine Ooley, Thomas Robinson, Douglas D. Scott, Joe Sills Jr., Putt Thompson, Richard Upton, and Robert M. Utley.

A special note of thanks must go to those who, at times, walked the battlefield with us and helped to reshoot the photos: Mike Cowdrey, John Doerner, Dennis Fox, Richard A. Fox, Ralph Heinz, Paul Hutton, David Jurgella, Douglas McChristian, Jason Pitsch, and Glen Swanson. Finally, we wish to thank Gary Raham, who prepared our maps for this book. The authors offer a special note of thanks to their lovely and supportive wives, Kris Brust, Cricket Bauer Pohanka, and Betty Barnard, who understood and accepted our need to walk the Little Bighorn Battlefield each autumn.

To all of these people and many, many others, the authors are sincerely grateful.

WHERE CUSTER FELL ⤻

Part 1

THE LITTLE BIGHORN

I

HISTORICAL BACKGROUND ⌒

ON JUNE 25, 1876, Lieutenant Colonel George Armstrong Custer and five companies of the Seventh U.S. Cavalry perished in an epic clash with Sioux and Northern Cheyenne warriors on the banks of Montana's Little Bighorn River. The dust had hardly settled on the field when "Custer's Last Stand" assumed the status of legend. The event remains a fascinating challenge to those who pursue historical truth within a subject heavily mantled in mythology, recrimination, and dispute.

Colonel William A. Graham, author and dedicated student of Little Bighorn (whose 1953 compendium, *The Custer Myth*, remains an essential text within the subject's vast printed record), believed there is "no incident of American history that has been made the subject of more research, investigation, and speculation . . . and the end is not yet."[1] Indeed, during the century and more that has elapsed since warrior and soldier clashed on the sprawling landscape of southeastern Montana, many researchers have attempted to reconstruct the fate of Custer's command, but none can ever hope to know the actual sequence and course of events. George Custer, a major general of volunteers and brevet major general in the Civil War, offered in life a flamboyant, larger-than-life persona. Not surprisingly, the enigmatic details of the general's last fight remain a fertile ground for the endeavors of amateur and professional historians alike.

Just as many volumes, if not more, have been written on the topic of Little Bighorn as on far larger, bloodier, and more historically significant engagements, such as Waterloo, Gettysburg, Verdun, and Stalingrad. The literature of Custer's Last Stand runs the gamut from dime novel to scholarly tome, and the battle continues to spawn a copious outpouring from artists and illustrators as well—some of it as historically suspect as many literary endeavors. As frontier historian Don Russell concluded, "No single event in United States history, or perhaps even in world history, has been the subject of more bad art and erroneous story than Custer's Last Stand."[2]

While passionately subjective agendas and florid imaginations have served to obscure the literary and artistic path to the truth of June 25, 1876, the eye of the camera lens provides an objective glimpse of the place where Custer fell. As with recent archaeological investigations, the photographic images compiled in this volume are a vital part of the historical record, one more

Lieutenant Colonel George Armstrong Custer, 1876. Courtesy of Little Bighorn Battlefield National Monument, National Park Service

Hunkpapa spiritual leader Sitting Bull. Courtesy of Little Bighorn Battlefield National Monument, National Park Service

ingredient in the interpretive challenge and enduring riddle of the Battle of the Little Bighorn.

≈≈

THE CONTROVERSIAL circumstances and dramatic manner of Custer's death might make the modern reader forget that his regiment was but one part of a larger military operation. The campaign that resulted in "The Great Sioux War" was intended to compel so-called hostiles—principally Sioux (Lakota) and Northern Cheyenne—onto reservations, forcing them to forever abandon their traditional nomadic ways. Three columns of soldiers advanced on the area believed to be occupied by what were assumed to be scattered bands of these Indians. From the west marched Colonel John Gibbon's Montana Column; from the south came Brigadier General George Crook's Wyoming Column; and from the east, setting out on May 17, moved Brigadier General Alfred H. Terry's Dakota Column from Fort Abraham Lincoln. That force included Custer's twelve-company Seventh U.S. Cavalry, some six hundred strong. Terry was confident of success, informing General Philip Sheridan, "I have no doubt of the ability of my column to whip all the Sioux whom we can find."[3]

The army's foe, ultimately numbering as many as ten thousand men, women, and children, had coalesced under the leadership of the charismatic Hunkpapa spiritual leader Sitting Bull. On June 17, with Terry camped near the new supply depot at the confluence of the Powder and Yellowstone rivers and Custer awaiting the return of Major Marcus A. Reno's scout, Crook's column was attacked along the banks of the Rosebud River by a large Indian force. Although the warriors withdrew following a daylong battle and casualties on both sides were light, Crook curtailed his northward march, ostensibly to replenish his supplies and ammunition. His troops would be out of action for several weeks—a fact unknown to Terry, Gibbon, and Custer. Moreover, the fight at the Rosebud served to strengthen the confidence and resolve of the Lakota and Cheyenne.

Four days later, at the mouth of the Rosebud, Terry and his subordinates planned their next move. The just-completed, grueling nine-day scouting expedition with six compa-nies, led by Custer's second-in-command, Major Reno, had found indications that an estimated eight hundred warriors appeared to be headed in the direction of the Little Bighorn Valley. On June 22, Terry accorded Custer the task of pursuing the Indians south, up the Rosebud, then west to the Little Bighorn. Meanwhile, Terry and Gibbon would march west along the Yellowstone, then south along the Bighorn River to the mouth of the Little Bighorn. If all went well, Terry would arrive at that point on June 26, ready to block whatever Indians Custer had pressured from the south. Unfortunately for Terry's plans, Indian strength had grown considerably, and the loose coalition of tribes encamped on the Little Bighorn—known to the native peoples as the Greasy Grass—included at least fifteen hundred adult warriors.

Traveling light, Custer's regiment—597 soldiers plus 50 scouts and civilians—advanced rapidly up the Rosebud, hindered only by the laggardly mule-borne pack train.[4] By June 24, Custer's Crow and Arikara (or Ree) scouts had determined that the enemy were in all likelihood situated on the lower reaches of the Little Bighorn. Reconnoitering at dawn of June 25 from atop a ridge overlooking the bowl-like depression known as the Crow's Nest, the keen-eyed scouts spotted the unmistakable signs of a large Indian pony herd in the Little Bighorn Valley, some fifteen miles to the west. Following a night march, Custer rode ahead of the column and joined his scouts at the Crow's Nest. Although Custer could make out neither the massive pony herd nor the smoke of the enemy encampments, he accepted his scouts' information.

Concerned that his regiment had been spotted by outriding hunting parties and fearing that his elusive foe would escape, Custer decided to risk a daylight offensive rather than wait to strike at dawn as he had in the Battle of the Washita eight years earlier.[5] Soon after crossing the divide between the waters of the Rosebud and the Little Bighorn and beginning his approach down the valley of what today is known as Reno Creek, Custer made the first of several divisions of his command.[6]

He dispatched Captain Frederick W. Benteen and the 115 men of Companies D, H, and K with orders to ride southwest, over a succession of ridges, to the river valley and attack whatever Indians or outlying villages that might be located there. Should Benteen find no quarry, he was to countermarch to rejoin the rest of the command. Custer also assigned three-company battalions to Reno (A, G, M) and Captain Myles W. Keogh (C, I, L) and a two-company battalion to Captain George W. M. Yates (E, F). Two hours and several miles closer to the Little Bighorn, Custer ordered Major Reno to cross the river and charge what the Seventh's commander suspected was a foe in the process of breaking camp and scattering. Reno's battalion included 24 scouts and 140 soldiers.[7] Meanwhile, Custer, with Keogh's and Yates's battalions—some 220 men prior to the dispatch of 2 couriers, the departure of 4 Indian scouts, and the straggling of at least 4 troopers whose horses gave out—moved northward up the high bluffs east of the river. The pack mules, escorted by an estimated 135 men,

including Captain Thomas M. McDougall's Company B, lagged behind the other elements of the regiment and would rejoin the command only after the Indians had been engaged.

We will never know for certain what Custer intended when he turned his two battalions northward. Sergeant Daniel Kanipe, who soon after was sent back with a message urging on the pack train, thought the move was a reaction to the appearance of some fifty to a hundred warriors who had materialized on the high ground.[8] Perhaps Custer suspected that the presence of these warriors indicated that a hostile force had already sallied forth to engage the soldiers, or he may have intended to follow them into the village proper. Cheyenne accounts confirm the presence of a sizeable band east of the Little Bighorn, among them the warriors Wolf Tooth and Big Foot. Likely other parties, of

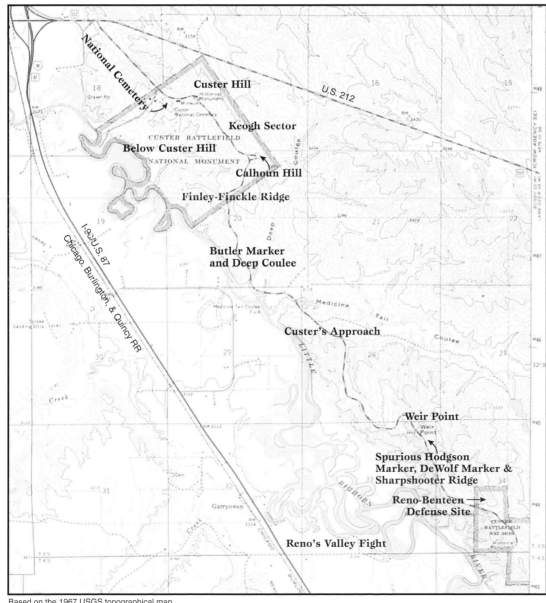

Based on the 1967 USGS topographical map

Map 1.1. The Full Battlefield

varying strength, were also east of the river.[9] Some historians think that Custer was endeavoring to cut off the supposed flight of his prey—interpreter Frederick Girard informed Custer that he had spotted one group of Indians "running like devils" from the vicinity of an abandoned camp on the lower reaches of Reno Creek. Other students of the battle believe that Custer planned to hit the village at its northern end in a classic pincer movement. As with many other aspects of Little Bighorn, the fatal move northward is shrouded in mystery and controversy.

Custer's hastily improvised plans soon began to go awry. Although the Indians had, in fact, been taken by surprise, hundreds of warriors—fiercely determined to safeguard their panicked families—rushed to confront Reno's advance. Alarmed at the growing numbers at his front and the vast village that lay to the north, Reno halted his battalion, dismounted, and formed a skirmish line. The led horses were taken into a belt of timber that lay along the river on Reno's right flank, and with Company G detached to safeguard the mounts, the major's slender line was in danger of being flanked and possibly surrounded.

After ten to fifteen minutes of fighting, Reno drew his exposed companies back into the cover of the trees. Although Custer had assured Reno that his advance would be supported, and the major had dispatched two couriers alerting his commander to the fact that the warriors were coming forth in strength to confront the soldiers' attack, Custer's battalions were obviously not within what his subordinate considered supporting distance.

Half an hour later, with Indian pressure increasing and warriors infiltrating Reno's tenuous perimeter, the major ordered his soldiers to mount, and they sortied from the timber in a disjointed charge. This fighting retreat quickly degenerated into a chaotic stampede—desperate troopers galloping for the river and the two-hundred-foot-high bluffs beyond with howling warriors in hot pursuit. By the time Reno's exhausted survivors had gained the summit, nearly 40 percent of the contingent were dead, wounded, or abandoned in the evacuation from the timber. In addition, about twenty scouts had absented themselves from the field of battle, placing the overall loss of effective combatants in Reno's force at more than 50 percent.[10]

Meanwhile, having called off his foray to the southwest, Captain Benteen followed the trail of the other companies, en route receiving two messages from Custer urging him to the scene of action. As the last of Reno's defeated troopers were gaining the crest of the bluffs east of the Little Bighorn, Benteen made his appearance. A little more than half an hour later, the first of Captain McDougall's pack mules began to arrive. While Reno and Benteen supervised the establishment of a defensive perimeter, the Indian pressure abated and heavy firing was heard to the north. Clearly Custer was engaged.

Disturbed that neither of his superiors seemed interested in riding to the sound of Custer's guns, Captain Thomas B. Weir started north from the defensive site, followed by his Company D. This unauthorized move eventually prompted a poorly coordinated advance by the remaining companies, several units joining Weir's troopers atop a conspicuous elevation known today as Weir Point. This position was one mile north of Reno's perimeter and three miles from the spot where Custer met his death. Weir's men likely witnessed the last stages of Custer's battle, although they could not have been certain about what the dust and movement to their north portended.[11]

The sight of approaching warriors caused the exposed companies to retire from Weir Point to their initial position on the bluffs. Only one man (Farrier Vincent Charley of Company D) was lost in the disorganized withdrawal, largely thanks to the efforts of First Lieutenant Edward S. Godfrey, who supervised a fighting retreat with the dismounted skirmishers of Company K. As Reno's and Benteen's men dug in for a protracted siege, some harbored misgivings about the fate of Custer's command, though most were convinced that he either was besieged in his own right or had pulled off to the north in the direction of Terry's forces.

For the remainder of June 25 and all through the 26th, the seven companies endured a deadly sniping fire that claimed a steady toll in killed and wounded.[12] Only partly sheltered from Indian fire in a swale at the center of the perimeter, acting assistant surgeon Henry R. Porter cared for the battalion's wounded amid the shambles of the pack train. When canteens were emptied, water could be obtained only by harrowing forays down the bluffs to the river below. Few warriors dared to attack the fortified position; on one occasion, those who did venture too close were charged and scattered by a detachment led by Captain Benteen. Benteen was instrumental in maintaining the unit's morale and overseeing the successful defense.

By the evening of June 26, the attackers had slowly faded away, and by dawn the surviving soldiers were able to breathe more easily. At 11 A.M. on June 27, Terry's and Gibbon's column came into view, marching through the detritus of the abandoned Indian village. But the rescued troopers' joy was short-lived: Custer's slain companies had been discovered downstream.

On June 28, the Seventh Cavalry buried its dead. The battlefield confronted the survivors with what Lieutenant Godfrey called "a scene of sickening, ghastly horror." Scattered over the sagebrush-covered ridges and coulees were the mute testimony of disaster—the bodies of all 210 men who had ridden into the final fight with Custer's contingent. Most were naked, bloated, and discolored, many had been terribly mutilated. Captain Walter Clifford of Gibbon's Seventh Infantry described the sight as "horrible in the extreme. . . . Here a hand gone, here a foot or a head, gaudy gashes cut in all parts of the body, eyes gouged out, noses and ears cut off, and skulls crushed in."[13]

In later years many survivors were understandably reticent about what they had found on Custer's battlefield. But it is from their testimony, interviews with Indian participants, and artifacts found on the site that historians have attempted to piece together the movements of the five doomed companies.

The last man to see Custer alive was a young Italian-born trumpeter named Giovanni Martini (or John Martin) who departed with a message for Benteen. Hastily scrawled by Custer's adjutant, the note read, "Benteen—Come on. Big village. Be quick. Bring packs. W.W. Cooke. P.S. Bring pacs [sic]." The trumpeter left Custer as the head of the column was about to enter the valley of Medicine Tail Coulee. Like Sergeant Kanipe, who had departed some ten to fifteen minutes earlier, Martin characterized Custer's troopers as enthusiastic, the men cheering, their horses moving at a rapid gait. The general himself appeared jubilant when he saw the village lodges standing and the targets of his offensive still vulnerable to attack.[14]

While his courier rode off with his message, Custer began to follow Medicine Tail Coulee toward the river and a ford opposite the Cheyenne encampment at the northern edge of the village, 1.6 miles to the west. Before Custer reached the Little Bighorn, the first engagement occurred between the Indians and his troopers. In the 1940s, battlefield Superintendent Edward S. Luce discovered a line of expended carbine shells on a ridge north of Medicine Tail Coulee, about halfway between the mouth of Cedar Coulee and the ford. Luce's findings seem to indicate a skirmish at this point (now known as Luce Ridge)—either with outriding warriors or possibly with fugitives fleeing east across the river as a result of Reno's attack.[15]

As Martin made his way southward, he passed Custer's younger brother Boston, who had ridden overland from the pack train to join Custer in the coming fight. We know that at some point Boston reached the command, for his body was later found on the slope below the site of the last stand. The younger Custer would surely have informed the general of the relative proximity of Benteen's column, which he had passed along the way.

Several Indian accounts describe an abortive attempt spearheaded by Company E (the Gray Horse Troop) to ford the river at the mouth of Medicine Tail Coulee, opposite the Cheyenne circle at the northern edge of the village. Other warriors testified that Custer's soldiers never gained the river proper, and military men who later went over the field were equally divided in their impressions of this action.[16] Some students of the battle believe that the movement of a portion of Custer's force to the ford was a feint, intended to pin warriors in place while the remainder of his command continued northward to flank the village from that direction. Others—including Richard Fox in his 1993 study, Archaeology, History, and Custer's Last Battle—postulate that because the encampment had largely emptied of fleeing noncombatants by the time Custer approached the ford, a movement north to intercept the fugitives made more sense than charging into a largely abandoned village. It might also be that the nagging presence of warriors to his flank and rear necessitated a deployment to deal with that threat, thus delaying an offensive movement across the ford and into the village.

In the years since the battle, artifacts indicating an action of some kind have been found in the vicinity of the ford, though their relative paucity seems to indicate that the fighting there was brief. However, since the 1920s, several hundred carbine shell cases have been found on high ground less than a mile to the north and east, scattered along a ridge that forms a northwestward extension of Luce Ridge, mentioned earlier. The discovery of this position, variously known as Blummer or Nye-Cartwright Ridge, indicates that a significant portion of Custer's command passed over this ground and was engaged there while en route to the final battlefield.

According to a number of surviving Seventh Cavalrymen, Custer had earlier divided his segment of the regiment into two smaller battalions, commanded by Captains Keogh and Yates. Quite possibly, while one battalion (generally assumed to have been Companies E and F under the command of Yates) approached the ford, the other three companies, under Keogh, moved northward along the crest of Blummer/Nye-Cartwright Ridge. Clearly some sort of engagement occurred there, possibly with the Wolf Tooth–Big Foot band. However, only a few slain soldiers were later found in the vicinity. Thus, the firing likely occurred at fairly long range. The decisive battle would be waged more than half a mile to the north.

Some historians assume that Custer's movement away from the ford was a beleaguered withdrawal under heavy pressure from counterattacking warriors. Others believe that at least a portion of Custer's command lingered on the ridge overlooking the ford, awaiting the arrival of Benteen's command, before riding to the fatal battleground. A more likely scenario, given Custer's aggressive temperament, interprets his northward progress as a continuation of his offensive strategy. Cheyenne oral tradition describes a movement by part of Custer's command, probably Yates's battalion, to the vicinity of another crossing point, northwest of the present-day museum and national cemetery.[17] From that position the soldiers were a potential threat to the many women, children, and old people who had sought shelter in the trees and brush on the river's west bank. According to this interpretation, only when warrior pressure began to mount against the three companies of Keogh's command (positioned near what is known today as Calhoun Hill) was Custer forced to call off his northern offensive and wage an increasingly desperate defensive battle.

Some Indian accounts credit the Cheyenne war leader Lame White Man with inspiring a charge that precipitated the decisive collapse of the defensive positions. This attack may have come in response to the deployment of Company C from the vicinity of Calhoun Hill to a site closer to the river, from where they attempted to check the growing numbers of warriors massing behind the cover of Greasy Grass Ridge. There the troopers became a vulnerable target for the counterattack spurred on by Lame White Man and other warrior leaders. Apparently only a portion of Company C had deployed in line when the Indians struck and drove the troopers back toward Calhoun Hill. The Brule Lakota Two Eagles recalled that "some of the soldiers were mounted and some were dismounted. Most of those dismounted had lost their horses."[18]

This sudden reversal turned the tables on Keogh's battalion and brought the soldiers on Calhoun Hill under heavy pressure from front and flank. Other Indians moved along the cover of ridges to the east and fired on Keogh's Company I before those soldiers could adequately react to the unfolding disaster. With every fourth trooper detailed as a horse holder for his own mount and those of three comrades, the dismounted company's skirmish lines were dangerously thin, while the led horses presented a vulnerable target to warriors attempting to stampede them. That point was not lost on Lieutenant Godfrey, who as a retired general wrote researcher Walter M. Camp, "It can be safely assumed that as soon as the horse holders discovered that the Indians were after them, the horse holders would make every effort to get to the command, even to the extent of letting go the led horses; it was a desperate situation as the horse holders can do little in self defense and maintain control of his charger."[19]

In his testimony before an army court of inquiry that in 1879 investigated Reno's conduct at Little Bighorn, Captain Benteen asserted that the scattered disposition of the dead on Custer's field showed the clash to have been "a rout, a panic, till the last man was killed."[20] Others shared this view. Private Jacob Adams later stated, "We came to the conclusion then and there that the fight had been a rout, a running fight."[21] Many of the Indian accounts reinforce this impression of chaos and annihilation. "Horses were running over the soldiers and over each other," the Cheyenne Wolf Tooth remembered. "The fighting was really close and they were shooting almost without taking aim."[22] Low Dog, an Oglala war leader, likewise recalled that his opponents "did very poor shooting." In an apparent reference to the horse holders, Low Dog noted, "Their horses were so frightened that they pulled the men all around, and a great many of their shots went up in the air and did us no harm."[23]

Benteen claimed to have counted some seventy dead cavalry horses on Custer's battleground and only two dead Indian ponies—not impossible given the fact that the Sioux and Cheyenne generally preferred stealthy infiltration on foot to head-on mounted assaults—but also, perhaps, lending credence to the view that the troopers were wiped out before they were able to assume a cohesive defensive position. Many scholars believe that no more than sixty Indians died in the battle against Custer, and some have set the figure at fewer than forty. That the Indians were able to remove their dead from the field has added to the continuing debate over the number of warrior casualties.[24]

However, the most intense and close-quarters combat may well have followed an extended period of tactical maneuver and seeming stability on the part of Custer's force. Many Indians had engaged Reno prior to turning north to meet the new threat posed by Custer, and it clearly took them some time to build their numbers against Custer's five companies. Once that strength had accumulated, the warriors lashed out in several sectors of the field more or less simultaneously. Custer was thus unable to concentrate his dispersed companies in the sort of tight defensive perimeter that might have enabled his

outnumbered force to hold off the warrior onslaught.

The first significant concentration of dead soldiers, found at the southwestern corner of the battlefield, included some fifteen troopers, among them Sergeants Jeremiah Finley and August Finckle of Company C. On the rise northeast of this position lay men of Company L, including Custer's brother-in-law, First Lieutenant James Calhoun, for whom the hill was later named. Witnesses reported that Calhoun's men appeared to have been deployed in skirmish formation, and around some bodies were scattered twenty-five to forty expended carbine shells. Clearly Calhoun's troopers had maintained tactical stability and put up a considerable fight before the hill was overrun.[25]

On the exposed eastern slope of battle ridge, halfway between Calhoun Hill and the site of "Custer's Last Stand," Captain Keogh's body was identified amid a pile of slain troopers. One of his trumpeters was sprawled across the captain's corpse, and his two sergeants, guidon bearer, and orderly lay nearby. Most of the dead men in this group seemed to have belonged to Keogh's Company I, though a few men from Companies C and L were among them. The remains of troopers from several companies—likely those constituting Keogh's battalion—were scattered up the slope from Keogh's position toward Last Stand Hill.[26]

Atop the ridge and strewn down its western face were the bodies of Lieutenant Colonel George Armstrong Custer, Captain Thomas W. Custer of Company C (the general's brother, who was likely serving as an aide that day), First Lieutenant W. W. Cooke (the regimental adjutant), and the bulk of Captain Yates's Company F. Yates and his subordinate officer, Second Lieutenant William Van Wyck Reily, were there, as was First Lieutenant Algernon E. Smith of Company E—whose presence, a considerable distance from the other men of his company, may indicate that Smith was an early casualty. Several witnesses noted that a body believed to be that of Assistant Surgeon George E. Lord was also among the corpses on the hillside. From all appearances Custer had chosen to make a "last stand" at this point.[27]

The only other large concentration of

dead was found several hundred yards south-west of Custer Hill in the upper recesses of a deep ravine leading to the river. Numerous witnesses counted twenty-eight bodies there, including those of First Sergeant Frederick Hohmeyer and seven others belonging to Company E, the "Gray Horse Troop." Four of the eight identified dead were noncommissioned officers of Company E. Several men from Company F were also tentatively identified in the vicinity of "Deep Ravine" though most of these bodies were logically assumed to be Company E men. Whether as the result of a tactical deployment gone awry or a desperate attempt to escape, these troopers had been cut off and forced to wage their own last stand in that narrow cul-de-sac.[28]

Near the foot of Custer Hill lay the commanding officer's brother, civilian Boston Custer, and his nephew, Harry Armstrong "Autie" Reed. Scattered bodies—Captain McDougall said no more than a dozen—were found between the hill and Deep Ravine. Some of those men may have been fugitives from the last stand, making their way toward soldiers holding out in the vicinity of the ravine, an event recounted by many Indian veterans of the fight. In an isolated area, likely north of Last Stand Hill, Colonel Gibbon discovered the body of reporter Mark H. Kellogg. Given the relative lack of mutilation inflicted on the slain correspondent, he probably was an early casualty rather than one of the last survivors, in which case he would have attracted more attention.[29]

Unfortunately for historians, no detailed, accurate maps were made showing the location of the dead men and horses or of the carbine shells scattered about the field. Indeed, no one was ever quite sure how many corpses were interred on Custer's battleground or how many were overlooked. Most witnesses seem to have shared the sentiments of Captain Clifford, who wrote in his diary, "Let us bury our dead and flee from this rotting atmosphere."[30]

For today's visitor the most obvious features of Little Bighorn Battlefield National Monument are the marble markers that dot the rolling landscape. These ostensibly show where the soldiers' bodies were found and originally buried and have provided a primary ingredient to many historical studies of the Last Stand, most notably Doctor Charles Kuhlman's 1951 opus, *Legend Into History: The Custer Mystery*. But how accurate are these markers?

Like many aspects of Little Bighorn, from the beginning the subject has been clouded in controversy. Contemporary records of the number of dead interred on Custer's battlefield vary from 202 to 212, with most estimates falling in the range of 204 to 208. The initial burials were hasty and inadequate at best, with the fallen officers generally receiving somewhat more attention than the slain enlisted men. In most cases the remains were either rolled into shallow excavations or covered where they lay with dirt scooped up from either side of the body. A wooden stake was pounded at the head of each shallow grave, and then the army departed.[31]

In early July 1877, a detail supervised by Captain Michael V. Sheridan, brother of General Philip Sheridan, returned to the battlefield with orders to disinter the remains of slain officers for shipment to their families. Even in Custer's case identification was difficult. Heavy rains, melting snow, and scavenging animals had opened many graves, and the bones of horses and men were exposed and intermingled. Eventually eight bodies were removed from the Custer portion of the field and three from the Reno-Benteen defense site. At his father's request, Second Lieutenant John J. Crittenden was reinterred on Calhoun Hill at the spot where he fell. The bodies of four other officers could not be identified. While part of the detail went about this grim task, others reburied the disinterred remains of enlisted men, again marking the spots as best they could. Shortly after the detail departed, photographer John Fouch arrived on the scene and took the earliest known image of Last Stand Hill.

Later that same July, General Sheridan led a party to the battlefield and discovered that his younger brother's efforts had had little effect. Describing the scene in his diary, Lieutenant John Bourke asserted, "It was hard to go ten yards in any direction without stepping on portions of the human anatomy and skeletons of horses, singly or mingled together. . . . Pieces of clothing, soldiers' hats, cavalry coats, boots with the leather legs cut off, but the human feet and bones still sticking in them strewed the field."[32]

Two years later, in April 1879, Captain George K. Sanderson led a detachment of the Eleventh U.S. Infantry to the field and remounded the eroding graves. The detail then gathered all the horse bones they could find and placed them inside a large stack of cordwood on the crest of Custer Hill. Some human remains discovered by the party were buried under the improvised structure. Photographer Stanley J. Morrow documented this 1879 expedition in a series of well-known though often misdated images.

In July 1881, First Lieutenant Charles F. Roe supervised the erection of an eighteen-ton granite shaft bearing the names of the soldier dead, at the site of the former cordwood marker atop Custer Hill. In a trench surrounding the monument, Roe's detachment interred as many human remains as they could locate, exhuming the bones from their original burial sites and placing them in the mass grave. Before the detail departed, a civilian scout named James A. Campbell reportedly restaked the original gravesites to preserve the locations where the troopers had fallen five years before.

In early May 1890, with Campbell's guidance, a company of the Twenty-fifth U.S. Infantry marched to Little Bighorn from their station at nearby Fort Custer. Their commanding officer, Captain Owen J. Sweet, supervised the installation of the marble markers that now dot the battlefield. Unfortunately, the detail erected 246 stones on the Custer portion of the field, where 210 men had perished; with the exception of two markers (for First Lieutenant Donald McIntosh and Acting Assistant Surgeon James DeWolf), the stones intended to designate the former burial sites of Reno's and Benteen's companies were in fact placed on Custer's field. "Several headstones were set near the graves previously marked where indications led to the possibility that more than one body rested," Sweet reported but said this course of action was "resorted to only at the end of the work."

According to Sweet's report, the captain seems to have been under the impression that he was marking actual graves, not the locations of previous exhumations. In fact, Sweet's contingent did find human bones at many of the marker sites—an indication that the earlier reburial detail had overlooked portions of soldiers' remains. "But few skulls were found unbroken and comparatively few pieces were found with the remains," Sweet reported, describing "the many pieces of broken skulls, hand and feet bones etc., that were found scattered in all directions."[33] "In erecting the markers," Sweet informed Walter Camp in 1912, "each grave was dug into to see enough of the skeleton to determine which was the head to thus be sure in placing the headstone at the head. If the head was not found at all then search was continued to find the shoulders, etc., thereby [to] avoid placing the markers at the feet."[34]

Over the years the placement of additional markers for Custer's contingent raised the total number of marble cenotaphs to 259. Among the more obvious examples is Custer Hill, where today 52 stones occupy a site where 42 bodies were initially buried. Similarly, the more than fifty markers between Custer Hill and Deep Ravine give the appearance of a substantial soldier deployment although observers noted only a dozen or so bodies in that vicinity. This so-called South Skirmish Line has been one of the most hotly debated features of the Custer battle.

Perhaps the most baffling error, however, is one of omission. Sweet placed no stones in Deep Ravine, where many contemporary witnesses had described a concentration of twenty-eight or more dead. At least some of these bodies may have been removed from the depression, but a strong case can be made that the remains of the Gray Horse troopers have yet to be discovered in the confines of the ravine. In any case the markers for those soldiers must be added to the tally of spurious stones erected by Sweet's 1890 expedition. The end result is that about seventy markers now stand where no body was found.

The abundant photographic record of the Little Bighorn Battlefield chronicles the timeless face of that historic landscape and the changes wrought by our ongoing endeavor to memorialize, interpret, and comprehend what transpired there. These images cannot solve the mystery, but they do elaborate upon it, and perhaps they can guide us a little closer to the unknowable truth.

2

ARCHAEOLOGICAL DIGS ⤷

I N 1983, many people who felt a special bond with the Custer Battlefield National Monument in southeastern Montana were initially distressed when on August 11, fire swept across its deep coulees and high ridges.[1] Fortunately, no one was injured, none of the National Park Service buildings or the historical monuments were destroyed, and, as time would show, the battle ground itself was rejuvenated as nature intended. More important for our interest in history, that conflagration led to a series of archaeological studies that have had a profound effect upon our understanding and our interpretation of the great clash of cultures that began on that hot Sunday afternoon in June of 1876.[2]

The August 1983 fire stripped away decades of prairie grasses, prickly pear, sagebrush, and undergrowth. A preliminary field study that month by archaeologist Richard A. Fox provided the impetus for further exploration by archaeological teams under the overall direction of Douglas D. Scott of the National Park Service's Midwest Archaeological Center in Lincoln, Nebraska. They combed the battlefield during major investigations in 1984, 1985, 1989, and 1994 as well as during a number of smaller inquiries on other occasions. In each of his major projects, Scott was assisted by a team of archaeological and other scientific experts and a dozen or more volunteers who offered expertise not only in archaeology, but also in history, frontier weapons, and military gear.

SURVEYS AND EXCAVATIONS

In 1984, the team scoured the hills and ravines of the main battlefield, breaking new ground archaeologically by relying on metal detectors to locate artifacts used by combatants from either side. In 1985, their quest for battlefield debris shifted to the Reno-Benteen Defense Site (four miles south of Custer's own battlefield), where Major Reno and Captain Benteen and about 350 of their troops successfully withstood a two-day siege.

During both years another activity on the main battlefield involved excavation of thirty-seven of the marble field markers that designate where soldiers fell during the battle. During these excavations, partial skeletal remains of twenty-one men were recovered. All in all, the team's forensic experts (first Clyde Snow and later P. Willey) would study the fragmentary remains of thirty-four men. Soil studies were also conducted around one of the main battlefield's most significant geographic features, Deep Ravine, where an estimated twenty-eight men, mostly from Company E, may still be buried.

In 1989, Scott's archaeological team focused on excavating what was believed to be an equipment disposal site, or dump, used by the Reno-Benteen troopers after they were relieved by the Terry-Gibbon column on June 27, 1876. History records that the men gathered unserviceable equipment, broke it apart, and burned it. Located during the 1985 metal-detecting survey at the Reno-Benteen Defense Site, this area was marked for later exploration. In 1989, the dump was excavated to recover artifacts and to protect it from relic collectors. When the archaeological work was completed, a metal grid was installed over the area to make future metal-detecting more difficult for looters.

In 1994, the first week of May once again found Scott surrounded by eager volunteers, armed with their metal detectors and their enthusiasm for searching the rugged countryside in and around the renamed Little Bighorn Battlefield National Monument. Procedures for the battlefield dig of 1994 operated much the same way as previous searches. During the inventory phase the field crew relied on metal detectors, visual survey methods, and piece-plot recording techniques, all similar to the methodology followed in the 1980s. The professional metal detector operators aligned themselves at three-to-five-meter intervals. They walked precise routes while maintaining their intervals, but the rough terrain often forced deviations. All the while they listened for the telltale pings that signaled the presence of a metal object beneath the surface of the battlefield. Pin flags were inserted at the site of a "hit."

Another group, or recovery team, carefully used hand tools such as spades, trowels, and dental picks to expose an object's positioning in the ground as well as its specific location, as both these aspects provided clues to the

archaeologists. If Scott or another project expert made a field determination that the object likely had ties to the battle, electronic gear recorded its exact placement on the field.

As in the earlier digs, recording data was important in the 1994 survey. Each artifact was assigned a sequential field-specimen number beginning at 8,000. While records were coded in a SDR33 data collector, Scott and company took no chances—a handwritten field-specimen catalog was also kept as a backup. The information was transferred daily from the SDR33 to a laptop computer.

The method of recording data was also similar to earlier projects. The instrument was set up at a known location on the ground, or datum point. Distance, azimuth, and coordinate point readings for each artifact's location were recorded electronically. Its distance was read to the nearest millimeter; the north and east coordinates were read to the nearest second of a degree.

Once out of the ground, objects were cleaned by brushing and washing. Metallic items were treated in diluted glycolic acid to remove oxides built up during years in the ground. Each object was placed in a self-sealing clear plastic bag that bore its field-specimen number and other identifying data. Eventually, the artifacts were shipped to the Midwest Archaeological Center for further study. Today, the thousands of objects collected during the various projects are housed in the archives at Little Bighorn Battlefield National Monument.

Given the combat situation inherent at Little Bighorn, the procedures for firearms analysis were crucial in 1994, as in the earlier projects. As Scott noted, "Firearms, in their discharge, leave behind distinctive metallic fingerprints or signatures on the ammunition components. These signatures, called class characteristics, allow the determination of the types of firearm (i.e., model or brand) in which a given cartridge case or bullet was fired."[3]

Continuing, Scott explained the value of a comparison microscope in analyzing ammunition. That instrument has two separate microscope tubes joined by a bridge with prisms mounted over the tubes. It transmits separate images to the center of the bridge, where additional prisms transmit the images to central eyepieces. The latter are divided so that each image appears on one-half of each eyepiece. From this visual comparison, the number and the kinds of weapons can be determined and individual weapons can even be tracked across the battlefield.

Scott concluded: "This capability is very important because coupled with the precise artifact locations, identical signatures can be used to identify specific combat areas. This can be done with cartridge cases and bullets even though actual weapons are not in hand. With this information, patterns of movement can be established and sequences of activity can be more precisely interpreted." His last statement sums up a critical ingredient attesting to the value of the scientific investigations at the battlefield over the years. As Fox, who was Scott's codirector of the early battlefield digs, once said, "Archaeology is the physical evidence; history is the eyewitness testimony. Together they can solve a mystery."[4]

Beyond the increased sophistication of equipment, the 1994 dig also exhibited a more profound difference from the major projects of earlier years. It was the first to explore contested ground of 1876 that lay outside the boundaries of the modern National Park Service administrative site. Earlier digs had focused on government-held property on the main battlefield and at the Reno-Benteen Defense Site. In 1994, such privately held areas as Medicine Tail Coulee, Weir Point, and some 295 acres near the battlefield's entrance road underwent formal archaeological review. In all, 780 acres in four separate areas were inventoried during the two-week project.

Fox's belief that archaeology and history can assist in solving the mysteries of the Little Bighorn battle has proved insightful, if not yet fully realized. Archaeology has helped unravel some of the confusion surrounding what proved to be the final military engagement of George Armstrong Custer's career. Although the majority of the soldiers under Reno and Benteen survived—thus ensuring a more complete historical record of that engagement—archaeology has added to our knowledge of what these men were like and how their own battles unfolded. As Fox has stated, "Archaeology provides a new data base, a new atmosphere in which the historical record can be sifted."[5]

The most important result of the digs in Scott's opinion is how the National Park Service has incorporated the scientific data into the interpretation of the battle that is offered to those who visit the site. He added, "They have integrated history and archaeology and ethno-history—telling a more complete story to the public."[6]

PERTINENT FINDINGS

Number of Firearms in Use

In *Archaeological Perspectives on the Battle of the Little Bighorn,* Scott stated that at least 371 firearms of all types may have been used by both sides, but that figure is low because not every recovered cartridge case and bullet was examined. From the artifact sample he projected that the number of firearms the Indians used against Custer himself may have amounted to as many as 414. He calculated that the men under Custer's command had been outgunned about two to one. At the Reno-Benteen defense site, he suggested that according to statistical projections based on the findings, the Indians had used between 259 and 300 firearms. In both engagements, repeating weapons—Henrys or Winchester Models 1866 or 1873—were the most numerous guns used against the soldiers. Scott concluded, "When all the firearm data are taken into account, it becomes readily apparent that Custer and his men were outgunned, if not in range or stopping power, then certainly in firepower."[7]

Location of Indian Positions

Scott's field teams located at least seven positions where the volume of cartridge-case types suggested that these had likely been manned by the Indians.[8] Two on Greasy Grass Ridge had long been known, but the other five had been previously unknown. One off the Calhoun Hill position manned by Company L was dubbed "Henryville" because of the large number of .44 Henry cartridges located there. The second was a knoll some 660 feet northeast of Last Stand Hill; at this site the crews found a variety of nongovernmental cartridges as well as split .45-55 government cases, which Scott believed represented captured government ammunition fired in

.50-caliber weapons. The other three warrior positions were found on the lower end of Greasy Grass Ridge and on the upper portion of Deep Ravine.

Soldier Behavior

In *Archaeology, History, and Custer's Last Battle,* Fox unleashed a storm of controversy with his suggestion that the Custer battalion had "disintegrated" in the face of the Indian onslaughts. This ran counter to the so-called Fatalistic view of the battle, in which the Sioux and Cheyenne had forced the battle action to conclude in the more celebrated heroic last stand on Custer Hill. Fox relied on both the archaeological database and Indian accounts of the fighting to shape his theories. He was concerned by the relatively small numbers of cartridges fired by the soldiers that were found during the dig projects. He concluded that the Seventh Cavalrymen's fighting spirit may have wilted prematurely in the face of superior numbers and firepower.

Spurious Burial Markers

Among the more haunting features of the Little Bighorn Battlefield are the markers that denote where soldiers fell and were initially buried after the fighting ended. Surprisingly, prior to the archaeological projects, no precise count of the number of markers on the field had been made since their installation in 1890. Also, questions circulated about their accuracy—an important consideration, as many students of the battle, professional as well as amateur, have relied on the markers' placement to formulate theories about the flow of battle.[9]

The problem became evident after the project research concluded that 252 markers stood on the Custer field even though only 209 men had died with him. Since then, 7 more have been erected. In addition, the field study determined that 43 pairs of markers were scattered over the battlefield; Scott and the other experts concluded that the majority of paired markers represented the burial sites of only a single fallen soldier instead of the two indicated. Using statistical projections, they postulated that the number of spurious markers could be as high as 72.[10]

Human Remains

The historical record documents that burial or reburial of the dead troopers of Custer's command occurred on four occasions. The first took place a few days after the fighting ended, when on June 28, 1876, troops under the command of Major Reno and Captain Benteen covered over the dead the best they could. In 1877 and again in 1879, military details were sent to the battlefield to rebury the remains that had become exposed. Finally, in 1881, a detail erected the granite memorial shaft that stands on Last Stand Hill and around its base placed the remains of soldiers that had been recovered from the battlefield. Even in 1890, the party under the command of Captain Sweet that erected the marble markers reported finding unburied remains.

Thus, the archaeologists were not surprised to discover human remains on the battlefield, especially during their excavations of the markers. In 1984 and 1985, partial remains of some thirty-four individuals were studied. Most were remains excavated from the field during the projects, but others were in the battlefield's archives. Subsequently, bones from seven more soldiers were found in museum collections, and in 1989, a partial skeleton of a soldier was found eroding from the bank of the Little Bighorn River at the Reno retreat crossing. Additionally, the archaeologists exhumed unidentified remains of ten soldiers in the Custer National Cemetery. They estimated that all the remains represented some forty-four men.[11]

Using a multidisciplinary approach to the subsequent study of the human remains, Scott and forensics expert P. Willey noted that they were able "to create detailed pictures of the men of the Seventh Cavalry and their last moments." Additionally, four individuals were identified from the examination and analysis of the human remains: Sergeants Miles O'Hara and Edward Botzer, Farrier Vincent Charley, and scout Mitch Boyer.[12]

The scientific studies of the skeletal remains determined that the soldiers' mean age was twenty-eight, and they ranged from seventeen years old to forty.[13] In height, they averaged 5'7". Interestingly, many of the remains displayed spinal disk degeneration, undoubtedly caused by the soldiers' many hours in the saddle and exacerbated by equipment including Springfield Model 1873 carbines and McClellan saddles. As Scott put it, "When the heavy carbine and hard saddle were combined, the butt-jarring ride across rugged trails must have resulted in excruciating pain. As the compression squeezed the intervertebral disks, the disks deteriorated and back pain became chronic. It is amazing considering the frequency and severity of the changes, that some of the cavalrymen could function. Nearly all the riders must have suffered and some men must have been nearly incapacitated."[14] Other degenerative changes also were noted in other parts of their bodies. In addition, a number had problems with their teeth. However, the physical remains of the cavalrymen seemed to indicate general health that was no worse than other frontiersmen of the time.[15]

In *They Died with Custer,* Scott quotes Elizabeth Bacon Custer's description of the health of the Seventh Cavalrymen as excellent, but his findings led him to a different conclusion: "For a group of men so young, an undue number had back problems, arthritis, and other pathologies and injuries that are infrequent among the young today. By present standards the incidence of injury and back problems is very high, and the dental health is atrocious."[16]

NEW INTERPRETATIONS

Enough time has passed for both professional historians and battle buffs to assimilate the findings from the various dig projects, to think long about them, to debate them at countless public gatherings or over pizza and beer in private discussions, and, finally, to lay out new thoughts and interpretations. The projects varied from broad surveys to focused investigations designed to answer specific questions. Together they yielded a substantial body of information about both the battle and the events that followed. As Scott noted, "In the course of the archaeological projects we have had the opportunity to study the Custer fight, the Reno-Benteen defense, movements to and from Weir Point, the fight in Medicine Tail Coulee, the actual remains of some of the soldiers who fought the battle, and one of the Seventh's pre-battle camps."[17]

The archaeological research and analysis resulted in "thousands of artifacts, reams of notes and other records, and a pile of reports, monographs, and books." Yet Scott conceded that the participants have not learned all that there is to know about Little Bighorn. The investigations confirmed some aspects of the historical record and oral tradition, while simultaneously uncovering artifacts and assessing their patterns of distribution to provide completely new insights. As Scott has argued, "The Little Bighorn archaeological record is not better than the others; rather it should be viewed as another set of information to be compared, contrasted, and correlated with the other information sources."

3

IMPORTANT PHOTOGRAPHERS

John H. Fouch (1849–1933).[1] To Ohio-born John Fouch, a resident of northern Minnesota, falls the honor of being the first to photograph the site of Custer's last stand. For many years, the Little Bighorn was a most inhospitable place to reach and make photographs. At the time of the battle, no permanent settlements existed on the plains of eastern Montana Territory. Only the nomadic encampments of the native tribes dotted the countryside. That changed quickly after the Battle of the Little Bighorn with the establishment of military bases in the area. The first of these was Cantonment Tongue River, the forerunner of Fort Keogh, which was established at the confluence of the Yellowstone and Tongue rivers in late August 1876, two months after Custer's defeat on June 25, 1876.

Fouch arrived at Cantonment Tongue River in December 1876. His initial stay was brief, and by March 1877, he was back in Minnesota for the birth of his first child. Tragedy struck as his young wife, after miscarrying the baby, died of a fever. Fouch soon returned to Montana Territory, where he became Fort Keogh's first photographer. Fouch had barely settled into his new job when opportunity knocked. The army sent Captain Michael V. Sheridan, younger brother of General Philip Sheridan, to the Little Bighorn to exhume and retrieve the bodies of Custer and the other officers slain the previous year. Perhaps anticipating difficulty in completing his assignment, Sheridan forbade any press coverage, so if Fouch had entertained hopes of joining that expedition, they were quickly dashed. But the photographer's fortunes changed nine days later when Philetus W. Norris stopped at Cantonment Tongue River on his way to Yellowstone National Park to assume his duties as the newly appointed superintendent.

John H. Fouch, circa 1883.
Courtesy of James Brust

Norris planned to travel by way of the Custer battlefield for two reasons. He doubled as a reporter for the *New York Herald,* and he wanted to cover Captain Sheridan's expedition and learn what he could about the battle. He also had a more personal mission. On his earlier trips west,

Stanley J. Morrow, 1871. Courtesy of W. H. Over Museum, #289

Norris had befriended scout Charlie Reynolds, who had perished with Custer at the Little Bighorn. Norris was determined to recover Reynolds's remains. Norris took Fouch and another man along and hurried toward the Little Bighorn. Eventually traveling ahead of his slower-moving companions, Norris managed to reach Custer's battlefield despite Sheridan's press ban, mapped the area, and retrieved the scant remains of Charlie Reynolds. A short time after departing, he encountered Fouch, "anxious yet to visit the Custer field."[2]

That Fouch successfully reached and photographed the battlefield remained unclear for more than a century, and the image did not surface until 1990, 113 years after it was taken. Fouch's July 1877 view, titled "The Place where Custer fell," is now recognized as the earliest photograph of Custer's battlefield. A second Fouch photo of the battle site, "View Down the Ravine on the Custer field," is listed among the preprinted titles on the reverse of Fouch's stereo cards. This photo, potentially of great historical importance if it shows Deep Ravine a year after the battle, remains undiscovered.

All of John Fouch's frontier photographs are rare. His ability to market and distribute his images did not match his extraordinary energy and skill in making them. But to him does fall the honor of being the first photographer on Custer Hill, and it seems fitting that the earliest photograph of the mystery-filled Little Bighorn remained a mystery for so long.

Stanley J. Morrow (1843–1921).[3] Born in Richland County, Ohio, on May 3, 1843, Stanley J. Morrow later moved to Wisconsin, where he enlisted in the Seventh Wisconsin Infantry in 1861. He entered the Civil War as a drummer boy and later saw hard fighting when his regiment was part of the famed "Iron Brigade." When the conflict was over, Morrow emerged as a photographer. For reasons still

unclear, he was transferred to the Veteran Reserve (or Invalid) Corps in April of 1864. While stationed at the Point Lookout Prison in Maryland, he reputedly acted as an assistant to none other than Mathew B. Brady, the best-known photographer of that time.[4] Until his discharge from the army five months later, Morrow studied the cameraman's art.[5]

Married the following year, Morrow and his wife moved to Yankton, Dakota Territory, in 1868. That location would remain his base of operations for fifteen years as he traveled and photographed the frontier. By the fateful summer of 1876, Morrow was well established on the northern plains.

Over the years, a number of myths and misconceptions have arisen about Morrow and the Battle of Little Bighorn. Elmo Scott Watson, early historian of frontier photography, wrote that Morrow was at Fort Abraham Lincoln in the spring of 1876 and had received permission to accompany the Seventh U.S. Cavalry on the summer's campaign. He was thwarted, however, when a shipment of photo supplies failed to arrive from Chicago on time and Custer's regiment marched off without him.[6] John S. Gray, a photo historian of no less repute, mentioned this tale, citing Watson, but made no attempt to verify or refute it.[7]

This is a wonderful story, but is it true? Unfortunately, the evidence is slender. Watson likely relied on an account of Morrow's career written by his seventy-nine-year-old widow, but her story is confusing, as it speaks of Morrow planning to join Custer as he marched from Yankton, Dakota Territory, not Fort Lincoln.[8] Morrow's biographers, Wesley Hurt and William Lass, made an extensive study of the Yankton newspapers. The local press covered Morrow's activities closely in the spring of 1876, reporting even such minor events as Morrow photographing a wagon train or a stagecoach leaving town.[9] No mention, however, is made of a trip to Fort Abraham Lincoln or an attempt to accompany Custer. Rather, the papers reported in early July 1876 that Morrow was heading for the Black Hills, which is exactly where he ended up.[10] Morrow became the only photographer to record part of the 1876 campaign when General Crook's command struggled into the area near Deadwood, Dakota Territory, after the Battle of Slim Buttes in September at the conclusion of their "starvation march."[11] But the story of Morrow almost marching to the Little Bighorn with Custer and the Seventh U.S. Cavalry appears to be fanciful.

Journeying to Montana Territory in the fall of 1878, Morrow established photographic studios at both Fort Custer and Fort Keogh, remaining in the area for some seventeen months as post photographer at both bases, replacing Fouch at Fort Keogh. During this time, Morrow visited Custer's battlefield and recorded his famous views. Perhaps it is a measure of their importance that historians, including his own biographers, tended to date them to 1877 or even 1876, far earlier than they were actually taken.[12]

In fact, not until early April of 1879 did Morrow accompany an expedition from Fort Custer to the Little Bighorn Battlefield. Led by Captain George K. Sanderson, a company of the Eleventh U.S. Infantry was assigned the task of tidying up the graves and clearing the field of exposed bones. So well did Morrow's photographs document their activities that Sanderson attached a number of them to his official report.[13] Though Morrow reached the site almost two years after Fouch, his photos became well known while Fouch's remained obscure.

When Morrow returned to Yankton at the end of 1879, his Fort Keogh gallery was taken over by L. A. Huffman, who acquired a number of Morrow's glass-plate negatives. These included some of the Custer battlefield series, which Huffman went on printing under his own name for half a century, leading to the common misattribution of these pictures to Huffman.[14]

David F. Barry (1854–1934).[15] Born in New York State to parents who had emigrated from Ireland, D. F. Barry moved to Wisconsin with his family in the early 1860s. He eventually arrived in Bismarck, Dakota Territory, as an assistant to O. S. Goff, who had established himself as photographer not only for the town, but also for nearby Fort Abraham Lincoln, home of the Seventh U.S. Cavalry. Goff, in the area since 1873, had photographed Custer and others who later died at Little Bighorn. Barry, who would later claim

to have arrived in 1874, printed the Custer images under his own name. In fact, the famous general was long dead by the time of Barry's arrival in 1878.

Barry was talented in his own right, and even though he never photographed Custer, he did take pictures of the scene of Custer's last battle. Several early Barry views show the granite monument that had been placed atop Custer Hill in 1881. Barry's most enduring photographic legacy of the Little Bighorn Battlefield, however, is a series of pictures taken at the tenth-anniversary observance in 1886. Almost all are included in this book.

David F. Barry. Courtesy of Thomas M. Heski

Frank Jay Haynes (1853–1921).[16] Frank Jay Haynes was born in Michigan and learned photography while living in Wisconsin. 1876, the year of Custer's defeat, proved important for young Haynes, as he established a photo studio in Moorhead, Minnesota, and began to travel the frontier making views for the Northern Pacific Railroad. By 1879, he was the railway's official photographer. In a long and distinguished career, he made pictures throughout the west, Alaska, and Canada. In 1881, Haynes first visited Yellowstone National Park, eventually becoming a concessionaire there. In time, Haynes's name would be synonymous with photographs of Yellowstone.

Haynes visited Little Bighorn at least twice. He seems to have gone there first in 1882, when he produced a number of stereographs of the newly erected granite monument on Custer Hill. These, along with those of Barry, are among the earliest photos taken of that landmark.

F. Jay Haynes, 1880. Courtesy of Montana Historical Society, H-323

Laton A. Huffman, circa 1880. Courtesy of Montana Historical Society, #981-599

In 1894, Haynes made a more extensive series of views of the battlefield. Although many photographers went to the Little Bighorn in that decade, none produced images more sharp and clear than Haynes's. In 1890, Captain Sweet's expedition placed the individual markers that still dot the field. The locations of these stones have heavily influenced theories of how the battle was fought, and thus an accurate record of the original marker locations is of great historical importance. Haynes's technically superb photographs have helped to establish and maintain that record.

Laton A. Huffman (1854–1931).[17] Born and reared in Iowa, L. A. Huffman, as did his father before him, left farming to take up photography. In 1878, he made his way to Moorhead, Minnesota, where he was employed at the Haynes photographic studio. In December 1879, he arrived at Fort Keogh, where he took over as post photographer, the position held first by John Fouch and then by Stanley Morrow. Unlike his predecessors, Huffman remained in the area for the rest of his life and enjoyed a long and successful photographic career.

Huffman's contribution to Little Bighorn photography was twofold: as a businessman and as a photographer. Soon after his arrival at Fort Keogh, he acquired a number of Morrow's glass-plate negatives. Huffman went on printing those images, including some of Custer's battlefield, under his own name for the next half-century. Though this created confusion in attribution, Huffman's successful marketing of these photos kept them in the public eye, and he, more than anyone else, is responsible for their wide recognition.

A fine photographer in his own right, Huffman added his own set of Little Bighorn photos to the record in 1916. In that year, Brigadier General Edward S. Godfrey, a respected veteran of the battle, traveled to Montana for the fortieth-anniversary observance. Accompanied by Walter Camp and others, Godfrey retraced the Seventh Cavalry's route and then toured the battlefield. Huffman went along as photographer, documenting the entire trip, including scenes of Godfrey pointing out to Camp various highlights of the encounter. The most important of these fascinating images are included in this book.

Lee Moorhouse (1850–1926).[18] Lee Moorhouse of Pendleton, Oregon, has been a virtual unknown among the ranks of early Little Bighorn photographers. Born in 1850 in Marion County, Iowa, he crossed the plains with his family and settled in Washington, near Walla Walla, in 1861. Moorhouse initially worked as an engineer and clerk. At the beginning of the 1878 Bannock War, Moorhouse was called to be the field secretary for Governor Chadwick in northeastern Oregon. Moorhouse was appointed assistant adjutant general of the Oregon state militia, with the rank of major. He held that commission for only four years, but for the rest of his life he referred to himself as "Major Moorhouse."

Moorhouse was among the first to settle in the Pendleton area and became one of the region's most respected citizens. He passed the bar exam and served in a number of civic positions including court clerk and city treasurer; he also maintained an insurance office. In 1889, Moorhouse was appointed agent at the Umatilla Reservation, and he maintained a close association with the Indian people of eastern Oregon.

Moorhouse was well into middle age when he took up photography in 1897, initially learning the skill from a friend and going on to teach himself. He made thousands of images of Umatilla, Cayuse, and Nez Perce people, and after the Pendleton Round-Up started in 1909, he began to record that event as well. Photo postcards of his Indian portraits and Round-Up pictures became popular.

Moorhouse appears to have made only one trip to Little Bighorn, in September 1901.[19] His series of views of the historic battlefield are of fine technical quality, and up to this time, they have been virtually unknown in the Custer battle literature. A number of these fine photographs appear in this book.

Edward S. Curtis (1868–1952).[20] Edward S. Curtis is arguably the most famous man ever to turn his camera on the Native American people and their cultures. Based in Seattle, Washington, Curtis undertook what would become a thirty-year project, creating *The North American Indian,* in twenty illustrated volumes, each with an accompanying large-format photo portfolio. He made about 40,000 photographs in the process. Despite the fact that he had documented all the tribes involved, had visited Little Bighorn several times, had interviewed participants, and had written an account of the battle, until recently he appeared to have made almost no photographs that showed the battlefield itself.

In early 1996, the Museum of New Mexico in Santa Fe acquired a group of previously unknown Curtis glass-plate negatives. These were "outtakes"—photos taken as part of the *North American Indian* project but not used in the publication. Thirteen of these images show three of Custer's Crow scouts, who were present on the day of the battle in 1876 and who accompanied Curtis around the field when he visited in 1907. Since their discovery a few years ago, these photographs have been studied and published several times, and a number of them appear in this book.

❧

MANY OTHER talented photographers have contributed to the historic photographic record of the Little Bighorn Battlefield.

Christian Barthelmess (1854–1906)[21] served in the U.S. Army as both a bandsman and a photographer. He had worked in Arizona Territory, New Mexico Territory, and Colorado before arriving at Fort Keogh in 1888 as a member of the Twenty-second U.S. Infantry band. While best known for his views of the post and portraits of Indians, Barthelmess did visit and record Custer's battlefield. His Little Bighorn views have not been widely circulated, but a number of them appear in this book.

❧

Two photographers actually lived in Crow Agency, Montana, site of the Little Bighorn Battlefield, so it is only natural that they recorded the field. **Richard Throssel (1882–1933)**[22] was of Cree descent although he lived on the Crow Reservation from 1902 to 1911 and was an adopted member of the Crow tribe. Throssel took up photography after his arrival in Crow Agency. Enjoying a high degree of acceptance among the Crow people, he produced sensitive portraits, artistic landscapes, ethnologically important images of religious ceremonies, excellent health-related documentary photographs, and romanticized images of the earlier days of Indian life. **Fred E. Miller (1868–1936),**[23] already a professional photographer when he became chief clerk at Crow Agency in 1898, worked in the area for more than a decade. Throssel and he were related by marriage and lived next door to one another. Like Throssel, he concentrated more on portraits of Crow people, but both photographers made views of the nearby battlefield.

H. R. Locke[24] of Deadwood, South Dakota, did a series of seven views of Custer's battlefield that were published by the Black Hills and Montana Railroad in 1894 and 1895. These large-format prints are of excellent quality.

William R. Cross (1839–1907)[25] of Hot Springs, South Dakota, issued both full-plate and stereo photos of the battlefield, some of which were used by the railroad to promote tourism in the 1890s.

❧

Of a later era but certainly worthy of mention is Kansas-born **Kenneth Roahen (1889–1974).**[26] First a county and then a state game warden in Washington, Roahen entered federal service in 1924, serving for many years as a Fish and Wildlife agent. His encounters with poachers and bootleggers, many of a violent nature, left Roahen with a number of scars and a heroic reputation. Roahen took up photography while still a federal agent. Starting in late 1930, he spent the final years of his career in Montana, and after retiring from government service in 1955, he continued to live in and photograph in Billings.

Elsa Spear, far left, 1912. Courtesy of Paul and Teresa Harbaugh Collection

In addition to wildlife photography, at which he became accomplished, he did scenic work and Indian portraits, and he was a pioneer in aerial photography. Roahen's views of the Little Bighorn Battlefield, issued in the form of real-photo postcards from the 1930s to the 1950s, are of exceptional quality; despite their relatively late date, we have included some in this study, along with an even later nonpostcard image.

Also of a more recent era was **Elsa Spear** (1896–1992),[27] known at times by her married names, Elsa Spear Edwards and Elsa Spear Byron. Born near Big Horn, Wyoming, she was the daughter of Willis Spear, a successful cattle and dude rancher, who later became a state senator. Elsa Spear had a camera by age twelve and took pictures throughout her life. According to her daughter, she carried a Brownie strapped to her saddle.

She is best known for her scenic photos and Indian portraits, which she began selling professionally in 1923. Spear also photographed historic sites, which complemented her role as a historian of the Sheridan area. Fortunately, she tended to caption and inscribe her photographs. Eventually, she began writing about them, producing several books.

Despite her justly deserved reputation as a photographer and historian, she has never been known for her views of the Little Bighorn Battlefield. She did take a number of pictures at the fiftieth anniversary of the battle in June 1926, including a magnificent image of General Godfrey and Sioux chief White Bull shaking hands across the still-open casket of the unknown soldier after "burying" a symbolic hatchet inside.[28] But Elsa Spear was taking pictures at the Little Bighorn Battlefield as early as 1912, and we have included a number of her early views in this book.

Part 2

THEN AND NOW
PHOTOGRAPHS

4

The Approach to the Valley ∽

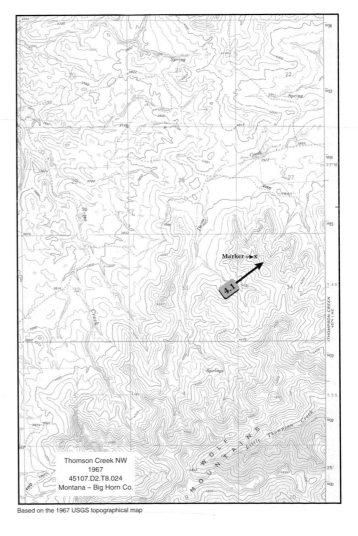

DEPARTING THE Rosebud Valley amid increasing signs of a strong Indian presence ahead, and with a growing conviction that his forces had been discovered, General Custer led the Seventh U.S. Cavalry toward the valley of the Little Bighorn River. They had no idea what awaited them. Their fate that day would become the source of legend, enigma, and controversy. The endless fascination with Custer's last battle has led generations of students to pick over every detail of the command's movements that day. In the pages that follow we will use historical photographs and their modern comparisons to help shed a little more light on the mysteries of the Little Bighorn, which will never be fully solved.

THE CROW'S NEST

From the Crow's Nest, first Custer's scouts and later the general himself glimpsed the Little Bighorn Valley early on the morning of June 25, 1876. Despite the importance of the spot, its exact location was uncertain for many years and even now remains the subject of debate.[1] Only one historical photograph documents the whereabouts of the Crow's Nest, and that image, reproduced here, played a large role in relocating the site.

This 1919 amateur snapshot shows General Hugh Scott, a former officer of the Seventh Cavalry and later U.S. Army chief of staff, accom-

RIGHT: *Map 4.1. The Crow's Nest*

OPPOSITE TOP: *4.1A. General Hugh Scott at the Crow's Nest, 1919. Courtesy of Tim McCoy Collection and Glen Swanson.* OPPOSITE BOTTOM: *4.1B. 2000.*

Based on the 1967 USGS topographical map

Walter M. Camp. Courtesy of John Husk

panied by Colonel Tim McCoy, who later became a popular western film star. They were guided by White Man Runs Him, one of the Crow scouts who had originally led Second Lieutenant Charles A. Varnum of Custer's command to this spot just before the battle. First published by Colonel William A. Graham in 1953,[2] this image was used by local rancher Henry Weibert to establish the Crow's Nest location in recent times.[3]

The observation point revealing the Little Bighorn Valley is higher up the hill on which the 1919 visitors stand, behind the camera position. The line of trees crossing the view in the low point of the depression is Davis Creek, the route followed by Custer's command on its way from the valley of the Rosebud (toward the right in the photo), to the divide and on to the Little Bighorn Valley (toward the left). The divide separating the Rosebud and Little Bighorn valleys is about a quarter-mile farther to the left and hidden from view in this picture. The term "Crow's Nest" may refer to the bowl-shaped depression seen in the middle background of both photos. Lieutenant Varnum later said that the depression was on the Rosebud side of the Crow's Nest and estimated that the distance from the observation point to the divide was

a quarter to half a mile.[4] Both of Varnum's observations fit this scene. Without this 1919 photo, the exact location of the Crow's Nest would still be unknown.

THE MORASS

The morass was noted by various members of Custer's command, some of whom watered their horses there as they advanced down Reno Creek toward the Little Bighorn, but their accounts leave a good deal of uncertainty about its location.[5] Only two historical photographs, both taken by Walter Camp, purport to show the spot. Neither has received much attention.[6]

Known for his objectivity, Camp interviewed or corresponded with many battle participants and visited the field with a number of them. A capable amateur photographer, he used photographs to augment his battlefield studies.[7] Sergeant Kanipe accompanied Camp to the battlefield in September 1908 and August 1909.[8] Kanipe, who as a messenger from Custer had avoided the deadly fate that befell the others of his company, would have passed the morass three times during the initial advance, his ride back to the pack train, and the return to the battlefield. He must certainly have been the one who pointed out the morass location to Camp. Although Kanipe's memory may have dimmed over the third of a century that had elapsed between the battle and his visits with Camp, it would be hard to find a more qualified witness to the morass site than he was.

Thanks to the photos, we know exactly where Kanipe said the morass was. The roadbed has been built up in the modern comparison photo, and the road has been graded, but despite the heavier vegetation, a study of the hills on the horizon shows this to be the same spot.

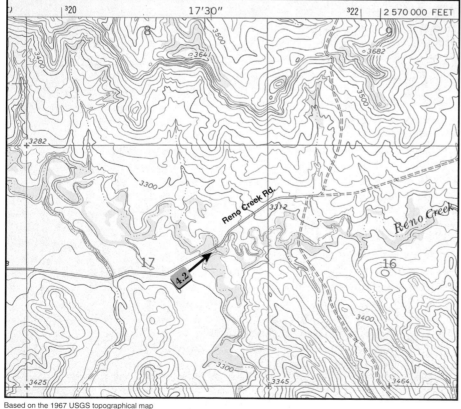

Based on the 1967 USGS topographical map
USGS Quad: Lodgegrass NE Montana (image enlarged)

5

RENO'S VALLEY FIGHT ⬛

ARGUABLY, CUSTER'S most important decision on June 25, 1876, occurred after he concluded that his regiment likely had been discovered by his Indian foes. He would attack their camp that day instead of following his original plan of waiting until the next morning. Another critical decision came a little later and may have had as much impact as the first on the battle that followed.

Custer divided his command into four combat-maneuver elements, assigning Companies D, H, and K to Captain Benteen; A, G, and M to Major Reno; C, I, and L to Captain Keogh, and E and F to Captain Yates (see chapter 1).

Company B, commanded by Captain McDougall and reinforced by men from the other eleven companies, guarded the slow-moving pack train. Custer then sent Benteen's forces to the southwest to engage any enemy warriors who might approach from the rear. That left the commander with five companies as his own attack force.

According to First Sergeant John Ryan's account of the events of June 25, 1876, shortly after the troops left the divide, "[Second] Lieutenant [Benjamin H.] Hodgson, who was assigned as adjutant to Reno's battalion, rode from front to rear of the battalion, giving orders to ride a little off from the preceding company so that we would not raise a large dust cloud, which would warn the Indians of our approach."[1] Custer's and Reno's commands rode on either side of the stream known today as Reno Creek, toward the Little Bighorn River. In a few miles, they came across what traditionally has been described as a lone tepee, containing the body of a warrior. It was learned later that that man had been slain June 17 in a fight between the Indians and another army column under Brigadier General George Crook along Rosebud Creek. Whether Custer's troops came across one tepee or more has been a matter of discussion among students of the battle over the years.

In his memoirs, Sergeant Ryan, for one, suggested that the Seventh Cavalry had encountered more than a single tepee: "After crossing the divide, we moved down through a small valley and around the foot of the bluff. We saw a few abandoned lodges, with the fronts of them tied up, and it appears that General Crook's command had an engagement on the 17th with some of these

Indians, and some of their chiefs were killed, and their bodies were in these lodges, which accounted for the front of them being tied up, although we did not know what they contained at the time. I think Custer had preparations made to charge that camp, believing it was the Indian camp."[2]

Ryan added: "When we got as far as there, we could look down through this little valley and see objects ahead of us. We could not tell whether they were Indians or buffaloes. At this point, I understood that Custer gave the command to Reno to overtake those Indians and he would support him, although I did not hear that order given myself."

According to most accounts, the soldiers had spotted a band of warriors dashing for the Little Bighorn. Most prominent among the spotters was interpreter Fred Girard, who had ridden up a nearby knoll. Seeing the Indians, he waved his hat and hollered to Custer, "Here are your Indians, running like devils!"[3] Crow scout White Man Runs Him also informed Custer that the distant dust clouds suggested that the Sioux were running away.

Custer was concerned that his foe might escape from the valley before his troops could reach them. That spring, Custer and other senior officers shared a common fear that the Indians would flee and disperse, making their capture by the more ponderous army columns nearly impossible that season. Now, beyond the bluffs that blocked his view to the north, Custer could see dust rising. Not able to see the village yet and having at best skimpy information about his foe's intentions, Custer incorrectly surmised that they were scattering. His immediate reaction: Attack!

Having decided to engage the Indians as quickly as possible, Custer sent Regimental Adjutant Cooke forward to Reno with the commander's orders. These were the only concrete orders Reno would receive that day from Custer. Reno recalled that Cooke told him: "General Custer directs you to take as rapid a gait as you think prudent and charge the village afterwards, and you will be supported by the whole outfit."[4]

The ambiguity of what Cooke had actually promised Reno by his statement that "you will be supported by the whole outfit" has been debated ever since 1876. At that time, and certainly in the years that followed, Reno clearly adopted a literal interpretation of Custer's orders and intentions: The major expected Custer's command to follow his own down the valley toward the Indians.

Reno led his three companies along the creek to the Little Bighorn River, where they paused to water their horses and make last-minute preparations for the battle that might await them down the valley. Despite Custer's belief that his foe was hurrying to flee before his troops, Girard and other scouts reported that the Indians were coming out to meet Reno's command. Girard relayed the information to Cooke, who promised to pass it to Custer.

About the same time, Custer learned from his scouts and officers that another group of Indians had been seen on the nearby bluffs to the north. Despite his perceived promise to support Reno—directly, as the major believed—Custer apparently decided either to chase them or to move north to attack the Indian camp from that direction. His revised strategy was similar to what had worked for him at the Washita some eight years before, when he had surrounded the Cheyenne village of Black Kettle and simultaneously launched his attack from several directions. However, the circumstances in 1876 were appreciably different. In 1868, a blizzard had virtually imprisoned the Indians in their camp, enabling Custer to approach the bluffs and surround the village without being spotted. As the Seventh Cavalry prepared to attack at dawn, the Indians remained asleep in their tepees. None of that was true in 1876. First, this camp along the Little Bighorn was far larger than Black Kettle's. Also, this time bluffs not only blocked Custer's view of the village, they denied him crucial intelligence that would influence the outcome of the battle. Thus, in issuing his orders, Custer had little idea about the lay of the land, the camp of his foe, or even the number of inhabitants. Worse, the warriors outnumbered his forces, they were well armed, and they were already aroused and preparing to meet Reno's command head-on.

After watering their horses in the three-foot-deep river, Reno's troopers moved forward at a trot and then increased their pace to a slow gallop. Company M under Captain Thomas H. French moved on the left, while

Regimental Adjutant First Lieutenant W. W. Cooke. Courtesy of Steve Arnold

Company G under First Lieutenant Donald McIntosh was on the right; Company A under Captain Myles Moylan rode behind the two lead companies. After advancing nearly two miles, the soldiers saw warriors riding out from the still barely visible village to meet them, as the scouts had claimed. Twice, the major dispatched messengers to Custer, alerting him that the warriors were standing before the troops, not fleeing as the commander had supposed. No further word was received from Custer, and the bodies of the two messengers were found with Custer's dead a few days later.[5]

THE SKIRMISH LINE AND TIMBER FIGHT

According to Ryan's account, the troops rode down an embankment into a dry channel that was probably twenty feet lower than the prairie. They dismounted in haste, the number four trooper of each set of fours holding all the horses. The other three men rose out of the channel and formed a skirmish line on the prairie, stretching from the timber on the right toward the bluffs on the left. They faced downstream, in the direction of the Indian camp. Some men lay down while others knelt. Some ducked behind mounds of a prairie dog village, using them as temporary breastworks. Before them lay the huge camp, with about five hundred well-mounted and well-armed warriors massing for a charge.[6]

Ryan recalled, "They tried to cut through our skirmish line. We poured volleys into them, repulsing their charge (my troop being on the extreme end of the line) and emptying a number of their saddles. Lieutenant Hodgson walked up and down along the line, encouraging the men to keep cool and fire low. Finally, when they could not cut through us, they strung out in single file, lying on one side of their ponies from us and commenced to circle. They overlapped our skirmish line on the left and were closing in on our rear to complete the circle."

Several men were lost, including Private James Turley, whose rambunctious horse carried him to his death in the village. Sergeant Miles O'Hara likely was shot down on the line, although remains recovered elsewhere and examined by archaeologists in the 1990s were

identified as his.[7] How long this opening engagement lasted is a matter of debate. Estimates range from a few minutes to about half an hour.

The locations of the sites associated with Reno's opening actions in the battle have been debated for years.[8] Theories of three earlier researchers about where the actual locations of the skirmish line and the timber line were have received particularly close study.

In the 1930s, Fred Dustin believed that the river's Garryowen Loop had been dry in 1876, only to be naturally refilled with water between 1876 and 1891. In 1923, this loop was cut off intentionally by the Northern Pacific Railroad. Dustin theorized that the timber fight site had been part of the then-dry Garryowen Loop. Researchers today place little faith in this notion because early maps—including those of Philetus Norris in 1877, Oscar Long in 1878, and John T. Blake in 1883—clearly show an active Garryowen Loop. In 1951, researcher Charles Kuhlman advanced his theory that placed the timber one loop back—upstream (or southeast) of the Garryowen Loop. Finally, in 1966, J. W. Vaughn used a metal detector to search the countryside and to align artifactual evidence with that of history and geography. He believed that Reno's first skirmish line had been aligned east to west, with the east end of the line resting on what later became the site of the old Garryowen store. However, he positioned the timber fight behind the old Garryowen store and the Albert Caplett house, in an area that now is essentially steep-banked riverbed and swampland. With that view, he was closer to Dustin than to Kuhlman in his thinking. Until recently, Vaughn's views have held sway about the presumed location of the timber fight of Reno's troops.

According to Vaughn's interpretation, Reno then retreated from the timber through the open field north of the access road to the modern property formerly owned by the Pitsch family. In that field are markers to three individuals killed on the retreat: white scout Charlie Reynolds, interpreter Isaiah Dorman, and Lieutenant Donald McIntosh. In the 1990s, family member Jason Pitsch lived on the historical ground and spent considerable time metal-detecting for artifacts related to the battle. Pitsch's research on his property led him to believe that Kuhlman—although often given less credence by students of the battle—may have been the most accurate of the three. According to Pitsch's theory, on Reno's approach to the village, the major reined in his troops and established a skirmish line that began essentially in what became the Pitsch family's field near a log building that for a brief time in the mid-1990s housed Pitsch's now-defunct Reno Battlefield Museum. From there, it likely stretched west across modern Interstate Highway 90 and the service roads as well as the railroad tracks. As warriors poured from the village, Reno moved his line forward perhaps two hundred yards and angled this advanced skirmish line so that it faced in two directions—toward the Indians, advancing from the low hills to the west, who were attempting to turn the left end of the skirmish line, and toward the village. As pressure mounted on his troops, Reno had them shift position while maneuvering toward the timber, located well to the east.

Today, a monument to Charlie Reynolds stands just outside a spacious, sunken, arena-like field that Pitsch believes is where Reno's troops took refuge in the timber. In its openness, this area looks nothing like what one would imagine for a timber area. However, in this field, particularly along its western edge, Pitsch uncovered large numbers of artifacts, including bullets and cartridge cases, during his metal-detecting. A couple of hundred yards to the east, the Little Bighorn River flows. The field is likely smaller than it had been in 1876, because a section on the east collapsed into the river during a 1978 flood.

Perhaps equally important, Pitsch identified what are considered two new sites of Indian encampments on the day of the battle in 1876. The first, north of the area of the present-day Conoco gasoline station (formerly the Garryowen Post Office) may well have been the location of the Hunkpapa camp circle. The second area is located on the east side of the river below Weir Point. Between May 10 and May 14, 1993, National Park Service archaeologist Doug Scott conducted a project that mapped Pitsch's findings for future reference. In his report, Scott concluded that the location of the second Indian encampment east of the river was significant because no historic accounts had identified any Indian camps there.

Scott noted, too, that Pitsch had found numerous fired cartridges, apparently Indian-related, on a bench just east of the second village site. He concluded that the cartridge cases and a few army bullets may indicate the position of warriors firing on the soldiers at Weir Point. He added that the locating of this new Indian combat position was an important contribution.

In the fields west of the old post office area, Pitsch found eleven .45-55 cartridge

Map 5.1. Reno's Valley Fight

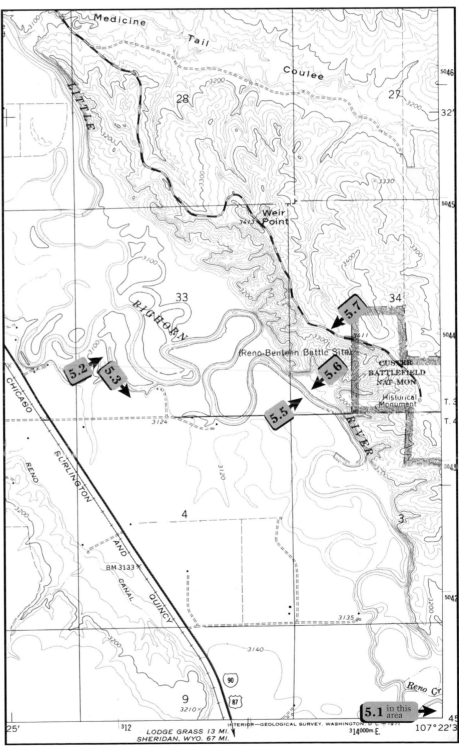

Based on the 1967 USGS topographical map

Major Marcus A. Reno. Courtesy of Little Bighorn Battlefield National Monument, National Park Service

cases in a roughly linear alignment from northwest to southeast. Scott concluded that these cases marked Reno's first skirmish line and noted, "The angled alignment is more in keeping with an attack on the village site at Garryowen than an east-west alignment as postulated by Vaughn [in 1966]." He added, "A due east-west alignment would cause the soldiers to face obliquely away from the now identified camp sites." He further suggested that the Hunkpapa camp had sat close to the river, which flows northwest, and thus the troops would have established their line at an angle to meet the warriors.

As further support for their belief that the northwest-southeast line represented Reno's skirmish line, Scott and Pitsch noted that the latter found some twenty-five .44 Henry, .50 Spencer, and .50-70 cases while metal-detecting on a bench to the west of the line, indicating an Indian firing position in a location "consistent with the fact that Reno's line was outflanked and forced to fall back." They believed that farming activities had likely disturbed the exact positions of these cartridges but not the general linear alignment.

On a terrace above the Hunkpapa village site, Pitsch found seven .45-55 cases mixed in with seven .44 Henry cases, five .50-70 cases, a Spencer case, and a round ball. Inasmuch as the positions of the cartridge cases seemed to lack a definite pattern, Scott concluded that their disposition was consistent with the more irregular fighting patterns of the Indians.

In the field that Pitsch considers the timber area, Scott mapped only the perimeter rather than individual artifact locations because the soil, particularly along a slough, had been disturbed by heavy equipment. However, his report offers an important conclusion: "If this is the timber fight area and if Vaughn and others are correct that the so-called Garryowen bend was active during the battle, then Reno's timber fight area was protected by the river on two sides. This may shed some light on comments by witnesses at the Reno Court of Inquiry that the timber area was defensible."

As pressure from the attackers mounted and no support from Custer appeared, Reno grew increasingly concerned. (His critics say he became panicky.) Several men, including Second Lieutenant Varnum, First Lieutenant Charles C. DeRudio, and Girard, reportedly saw Custer's command on the bluffs moving north in the vicinity of Sharpshooter Ridge and Weir Point, but no one passed this intelligence to the major. From his position in a clearing in the center of the timber, Reno ordered his soldiers to mount, but clearly not all received the word. After the scout Bloody Knife was shot dead beside him, Reno issued conflicting orders to dismount and remount. With Reno in the lead, the companies poured out of the timber, startling the warriors, who momentarily gave way. Nearly twenty men were left behind, although all but four later rejoined the command on the bluffs.

As the Indians recovered their fighting composure, they swarmed in among the stampeding soldiers. Clusters of cases and bullets in other areas, including in the fields where the Reynolds, McIntosh, and Dorman markers are located today, mark the Reno retreat route and also support the historical record.[9]

Although Pitsch's work seems to clarify the otherwise murky picture of exactly where the events associated with Reno's troops occurred in the valley, one caution must be applied. After the battle, relief troops under Colonel Gibbon camped there. Later, troops from Fort Custer crisscrossed the area during haying operations. Modern intrusions, including farming and road construction, have also significantly affected the site.

Reno has both detractors and supporters for his actions prior to leaving the timber, as well as for his decision to pull out. However, almost everyone criticizes his conduct of the retreat to the river. Many men never received the word to leave, and no steps were taken to ensure a proper defense as the troops headed for the crossing point. As the Indian combatants later suggested in their own accounts, striking down the fleeing soldiers proved as easy as killing buffalo. Moreover, once at the river, horses and riders plunged into the swiftly running stream without any regard for anyone's safety. By the time Reno's men reached the relative safety of the bluffs, his command had lost three officers and twenty-nine enlisted men as well as three civilians and two Arikara scouts.

RENO'S FIRST CROSSING

The exact point at which Reno's men forded the Little Bighorn to begin their charge toward the Indian village has never been clearly identified. Early maps differ—even the original manuscript 1891 USGS map and its 1908 printed counterpart, otherwise nearly identical, show Reno's first crossing in significantly different spots, with no explanation.[10] Battlefield researcher Henry Weibert, usually quite firm in his conclusions, likewise hedged on the issue, stating that the route he theorized was "the crossing that Reno *most likely* used in 1876" (emphasis added).[11] Thomas Bookwalter, another careful student of the Seventh Cavalry's route to the Little Bighorn, could give only an approximate location of Reno's first crossing.[12]

No nineteenth- or early-twentieth-century photographs document Reno's first crossing site, but an interesting image taken in 1970 (which has recently surfaced) may shed some light on the question. This 8 x 10-inch black-and-white print, hand lettered and marked with pencil and marker, is one of four battle-related views purchased in 1999 by Dennis Fox at a used book store in Billings, Montana. The other three were clearly marked as the work of photographer Kenneth Roahen, and on that basis we attribute this image to him as well. Titled across the top "Reno's 1st Crossing," and hand dated 9/23/70, it is a view of the Little Bighorn River near the mouth of Reno Creek, looking northeast from a ridge that used to be part of the Weibert ranch. Pencil lines indicate access to the river through a dry ravine. We do not know who originally owned or inscribed this photo, but whoever it was noted the evidence on the print: "See Sgt. O'Neil and Young Hawk."

Thomas F. O'Neill, also known as Thomas Dean, was a private in Company G at the time of the battle. Left behind in the valley after Reno's frantic retreat to the bluffs, O'Neill and three others, including Lieutenant DeRudio, eluded the Indians for a day and a half before finding their way back to Reno's lines on the night of June 26. In a later description of the battle, O'Neill wrote, "I belonged to Major Reno's battalion, and we were marched down an old dry creek-bed which debouched into the river nearby. Here we crossed the Little Bighorn."[13]

O'Neill gave a more detailed description of Reno's first crossing to Walter Camp in a 1919 interview. "He [O'Neill] remembers the ford where Reno crossed as at a high bank. The trail split and went around a little rise of ground on which some of the Rees were sitting holding a council and discussing the numbers of the Sioux. . . . He [O'Neill] went to the left of this knoll and down to the river through a dry ravine."[14] O'Neill's descriptions of the crossing place are supported by the statements of Arikara scout Young Hawk, who said that the soldiers and scouts "crossed at the mouth of a dry coulee."[15]

The terrain in the 1970 photograph seems to match these descriptions.

TOP: 5.1A. *"Reno's 1st Crossing,"* photo attributed to Kenneth Roahen, 1970. Courtesy of Dennis Fox.

BOTTOM: 5.1B. 2001.

Reno Creek runs along the line of trees in the middle distance, meeting the Little Bighorn River a little downstream of the area shown. High banks rise on either side of the dry ravine. Cattle occupy the knoll on which the Arikara scouts held their council. The pencil lines show access to the dry coulee from either side and an easy entrance to the water at its mouth.

In the modern photo, taken thirty-one years later, the course of the river has changed. This loop is no longer part of the flowing course of the river, though the section farthest from the camera is partly backfilled. The little island seen in the earlier view appears as a raised area in the present dry bed. With the actual fording area now dry, we can see how shallow and easy a crossing place this was.

One final note—the inscription on the 1970 photo includes the words "Burkman blazed tree," and a tree at the mouth of the dry ravine is indicated with an arrow in red marker. Private John Burkman of Company L served as Custer's striker but was assigned to the pack train the day of the battle.[16] As a battle veteran who lived nearby, Burkman visited the battlefield with a number of interested parties traveling in the area. We have found no exact reference to him blazing a tree at the first crossing site, but the tree marked in the 1970 photo is still present and does have unusual markings on it.

So was this dry ravine upstream from the mouth of Reno Creek the site of Major Reno's first crossing of the Little Bighorn River? Obviously, by 1970, no eyewitness was still living. Ken Roahen had been in the area since 1930, and he, or whoever else might have marked the photograph, could have had information acquired before this print was inscribed, but we have no knowledge of that. Nevertheless, given the fit between this spot and O'Neill's accounts, this is as likely a site for Reno's first crossing as any.

MEMORIAL MARKERS
Charlie Reynolds

Somewhat mysterious, though a dashing figure and crack shot, "Lonesome" Charlie Reynolds was Custer's chief scout. Reynolds went into action with Major Reno's battalion. When Reno withdrew into the timber, Reynolds

fought on the far right of the line along with several other scouts. Reynolds was killed just after leaving the timber, during the disorganized retreat. A number of eyewitnesses described Reynolds's death,[17] but despite the fact that his friend Philetus Norris claimed to have recovered Reynolds's remains in 1877, the spot was not well marked.[18]

In 1908, a four-inch pipe and a brass plate were placed at the Reynolds death site, followed in 1926 by a painted and lettered cross, wired to a taller iron pipe, erected by writer-researcher Earl A. Brininstool.[19] A number of amateur photos document this cross, including the one shown here (5.2A).[20]

On August 18, 1938, a group of dedicated students of the Custer battlefield—including Brininstool, Fred Dustin, Charles Kuhlman, and Robert Ellison—placed a more proper memorial to Charlie Reynolds, a granite marker with a brass plaque.[21] Presumably they placed the monument in the same spot the wooden cross had been and removed the latter at that time. But this was not the end of the odyssey of the Charlie Reynolds marker. Evidently it interfered with plowing, and at some point it was moved out of the field it had been in and was placed next to an irrigation ditch some distance away. The original spot, no longer marked, was lost again. Finally, in the late 1990s, Jason Pitsch and Glen Swanson replaced the Reynolds marker

"Lonesome" Charlie Reynolds. Courtesy of Little Bighorn Battlefield National Monument, National Park Service, #1304

LEFT: *5.2A. Charlie Reynolds grave marker, 1926. Courtesy of Edward S. Godfrey Collection, U.S. Army Military History Institute, RG48S, box 2.71.*

BOTTOM: *5.2B. 1998.*

at what they felt to be its original location, a site in front of the timber fight line and some two hundred yards from the line's far right edge.[22]

Our 1998 modern comparison photo tends to support this placement, showing the Reynolds stone resting approximately where the original wooden cross marker had been.

Lieutenant McIntosh

First Lieutenant Donald McIntosh commanded Company G in the valley. McIntosh was overtaken by the Indians, knocked from the saddle, and killed along the line of Reno's retreat. His body was buried where it was found on the field. A marble marker was

Mc Intosh – original marker

erected at the site in 1890, replacing the wooden headboard that had originally designated the spot. When agriculture came to the area, the McIntosh marker interfered with plowing, and it was moved from its original location in the field to a spot alongside the adjacent road. No record was kept of where it originally stood.

Fortunately, a couple of early-twentieth-century photographs show the marker, complete with a white picket fence around it.[23] The one we have matched was taken about 1912 by Elsa Spear (5.3A). The photo bears the inscription "McIntosh's original marker." Spear is known to have added later captions to prints of her earlier images, and likely she inscribed this one after the McIntosh stone had been moved from this spot in the field. Her handwritten title, though, tells us that this white picket fencing contained Donald McIntosh's marble marker at the spot where it was first set. Like the Charlie Reynolds marker, the McIntosh marker was placed back in its original location by Jason Pitsch and Glen Swanson in the late 1990s. Our modern com-

parison photo indicates that they approximated the spot well. The view is to the southeast. The Little Bighorn River runs beneath the bluffs visible in the background. In their hectic retreat from the timber, the men of Reno's command rode by this spot, warriors to their front and right pushing them toward the left (east). The actual retreat crossing is out of view on the left side of these photographs.

Also shown is an earlier photograph (5.4) of the white-fenced McIntosh marker taken by Edward Curtis when he toured the battlefield in 1907 with White Man Runs Him, Hairy Moccasin, and Goes Ahead, three of the Crow scouts who had been with Custer on the day of the battle. The three pose in this view, taken toward the northeast with Weir Point and the Little Bighorn River in the background. Note that the camera position is rotated 90 degrees in this picture, and we are looking at a different, and shorter, side of the rectangular white fence.

OPPOSITE TOP: *5.3A. "McIntosh's original marker," photo by Elsa Spear, circa 1912. Courtesy of Paul and Teresa Harbaugh Collection.*

OPPOSITE BOTTOM: *5.3B. 1998.*

ABOVE: *5.4. Crow scouts White Man Runs Him, Hairy Moccasin and Goes Ahead at the McIntosh marker, photo by Edward S. Curtis, 1907. Courtesy of Museum of New Mexico, Neg. No. 160458.*

THE RETREAT CROSSING

In this historic view (5.5A), taken in 1886 at the tenth anniversary of the battle, photographer D. F. Barry documented the site of Reno's retreat crossing. The camera is on the west bank of the Little Bighorn at the spot where Reno's column reached the river in their hurried withdrawal from the valley.

The steep banks, a major hazard to the fleeing men, leave the water barely visible in either the original or the modern view. A group of mounted visitors calmly pose on the ground frantically crossed by the 1876 cavalrymen as they raced from the fury at the river to the relative safety of the bluff tops. The mouth of the ravine they used is seen just to the right of center. Their route took them toward the right as they ascended the bluffs to the area they would later defend.

At least one of the guests at the anniversary observance, Doctor Henry R. Porter, had been in the valley fight, so Barry had an eyewitness to the events.[24] Despite lingering

LITTLE BIG HORN RIVER,
WEST SIDE RENO CROSSING,
CUSTER BATTLE FIELD.
JUNE 25th 1886.

debate about the crossing site and the route Reno's men took to the top,[25] Barry's photo would seem to leave little doubt that these landmarks are correctly marked at the battlefield at present.

Plate 5.6A is the reverse view of the previous one. Here, Barry stands on the east bank looking west at the same group of mounted visitors, now gathered at the point where Reno's men entered the river on their retreat. Large cottonwood trees currently growing on the west side of the river make modern comparison of this view difficult, but the several-tiered nature of the west bank, highlighted in the original photo by nine horsemen behind and above the larger group, can be seen in the recent view. At times this image has been misidentified as Reno's first crossing site, where he crossed the Little Bighorn River before his attack on the village. However, the terrain in this photo does not match that of the first crossing area near the mouth of Reno Creek (see plates 5.1A and B).

TOP: *5.6A. "Little Big Horn River, West Side Reno Crossing," photo by D. F. Barry, 1886. Courtesy of Little Bighorn Battlefield National Monument, National Park Service, #425.*

BOTTOM: *5.6B. 1999.*

5.7A. Photo of Reno's retreat crossing from the bluffs by Lee Moorhouse, 1901. Image courtesy of the Division of Special Collections and University Archives, University of Oregon Library System, #2264.

Lee Moorhouse took this 1901 view (5.7A) from the bluffs at the Reno-Benteen defense site, looking down at the section of the Little Bighorn River crossed by Reno's men as they retreated from the valley. Reno's command, galloping in a southeasterly direction (right to left in the photograph), swept around the prominent river bend in the center middle ground of Moorhouse's view (white X). Pressured by their foes, they turned toward the steep-banked straight stretch of river seen at the base of the bluffs in the picture. (This is the same section of the river seen in the preceding two photo pairs.) A few of Reno's men did not go all the way around that bend but cut across the loop instead.[26] The modern comparison photo reveals that the prominent

river bend in the 1901 view is now dry, cut off when flooding caused a natural change in the course of the stream in 1978. A thick stand of trees outlines where the river ran.

Other landmarks of Reno's valley fight are visible in these views, though on a very small scale. In the 1990s, relic collecting by local landowner Jason Pitsch led to a revised theory as to the site of Reno's timber position. The area indicated by Pitsch's most concentrated artifact finds, which also coincides with the earlier thought of Charles Kuhlman, can be seen in both of these photos taken one hundred years apart.[27] Most of the trees and brush had been removed, even by 1901, and what had once been a timbered position appears only as an embankment visible

between the single arrows in the vintage photo. Increased vegetation in other parts of the valley floor partly block the area in the modern picture, but a small section of that embankment can be seen between the arrows.

5.7B. 2001.

6

Reno-Benteen Defense Site ✑

As Second Lieutenant George D. Wallace splashed across the Little Bighorn River on the afternoon of June 25, 1876, with warriors in close pursuit, he somehow had the presence of mind to glance at his watch, noting that it was 4 p.m.[1] Within minutes, he had scrambled to the top of the steep bluffs and found himself among the demoralized remnants of Reno's command. They numbered only seven officers and eighty-four enlisted men. The Indian scouts who had accompanied the soldiers had scattered; most, if not still fighting in the valley below, were driving off ponies captured from their enemies.

The military predicament should have been cause for great alarm among Major Reno and the other officers. The total casualties in the valley probably numbered forty men killed and thirteen wounded. Several men were still missing, although fortunately most would turn up either later that day or the next. In the valley below some warriors remained engaged, looting the army's dead, killing the wounded, and occasionally firing up at the soldiers on the bluffs.

Among the soldiers, one question stood out: Where had their commander, Custer, gone? Additionally, where was the rest of the command, including Captain Benteen's battalion and the pack train under Captain McDougall? Even though Reno's men occupied the high ground, their barely defensible position made their military situation precarious at best. A makeshift picket line was established on the downslope of the bluffs away from the river. Doctor Porter, the command's only surviving medical officer, set up a hospital station to tend to the wounded men who had attained the bluffs.

Fortunately, about 4:20 p.m., Benteen arrived on the scene. He had approached the Little Bighorn ford at Reno Creek and glimpsed for the first time the Little Bighorn Valley. The sight must have astounded him, inasmuch as he had probably figured the fighting would be over before he could arrive. A message from Custer earlier that afternoon had left the captain with the impression that the Indians were on the run, but to his experienced eye that clearly was untrue. A group of Arikara scouts on a knoll to his right gained his attention. Beyond them, on a hilltop about a mile away, Benteen claimed to have spotted soldiers, the surviving men of Reno's battalion. He quickly headed in their direction. (His critics ever since have suggested that it was the first time all afternoon that he had picked up his pace.)

On his arrival, Benteen immediately encountered the understandably agitated major. Each of the two men gave the other an incomplete summary of what he knew. Trumpeter John Martin, standing nearby, recalled later that Reno blurted out, "For God's sake, Benteen, halt your command and help me. I've lost half my men." (At another time, Martin recollected the wording as, "Well, I have lost about half of my men, and I could do no better than I have done.")[2] Benteen showed Reno the message he had received from Custer, but the two officers felt no compulsion to move on immediately, even though firing could be heard to the north.

Their failure to act immediately has led to controversy and debate ever since. Some critics have suggested that Benteen, who personally disliked Custer, was unconcerned about what might be happening to Custer and his men, but, of course, at the time, the captain could not have realized what their true situation was. Reno, for his part, was likely dispirited as a result of his rout on the valley floor. Neither officer could have completely grasped Custer's predicament. However, their critics say that the two were obligated to comply with Custer's written order to Benteen to respond immediately. Despite the gunfire that many men later said they heard to the north, the two senior officers held their position on the bluffs. Perhaps they were waiting for the extra ammunition to arrive with the pack train; certainly they had to be concerned about the wounded, who would have been difficult to move immediately.

Below them, their attackers could be seen rushing toward the north, yet Reno inexplicably felt compelled to return to the river's edge, either to retrieve the body of his dead adjutant, Lieutenant Hodgson (who had been killed as he reached the east bank of the river) or at least to confirm Hodgson's fate. Reno's departure with Sergeant Ferdinand Culbertson and ten or twelve troopers left Benteen in temporary command of their troops on the hill, and he began to organize the defensive position, adding his own men to Reno's along the skirmish line. As the firing grew louder from downstream, the major dispatched Second Lieutenant Luther R. Hare on a twenty-minute ride to the pack train, requesting that

ammunition mules be rushed to the combined battalions' forward position. Two mules soon arrived, followed by the rest of the pack train starting about 5:15 P.M.

During this period, another significant event occurred, precipitated by Captain Weir, who may have become disturbed by his superiors' failure to respond directly to Custer's message or to move toward the sounds of the guns firing north of their position. Apparently without orders, Weir led his own Company D to the north. About fifteen minutes later, Benteen followed with Companies H, K, and M. Reno moved northward still later with the remaining troops, but their progress was slowed by the wounded and the pack train.

About a mile and a half ahead, Weir and Benteen had posted their companies around a high elevation that would come to be known as Weir Point. Perhaps two or three miles farther to the north, they observed large groups of Indians milling about or occasionally firing toward the ground. The action must have puzzled them, as none of them could have imagined that they were watching the final demise of Custer's companies. Such a thought would have been foreign to them; after all, Custer's force was larger than Reno's, and yet the major's command had managed to retreat and regroup.

When the focus of the enemy returned to the battalions of Reno and Benteen, the two officers determined that their original position on the bluff was better for a defense. Unfortunately, for the second time that day, Reno failed to organize his men for an effective retreat. Lieutenant Godfrey, commanding Company K, took action with his own company to safeguard the retreating soldiers. Surprisingly, only one man was lost on this retreat: Farrier Vincent Charley—badly wounded in the hips[3]—was told to hide himself until the others could rescue him later, but he had no place to do so. After returning to the bluff area, Lieutenant Winfield Scott Edgerly reportedly was forbidden by Weir to return for the wounded man. Charley paid for this decision with his life.

Soon, the rest of the command had taken up their positions, forming an elliptical defense perimeter on the crest of the ridges on what has become known as the Reno-Benteen Defense Site (map 6.1). In the center, protected

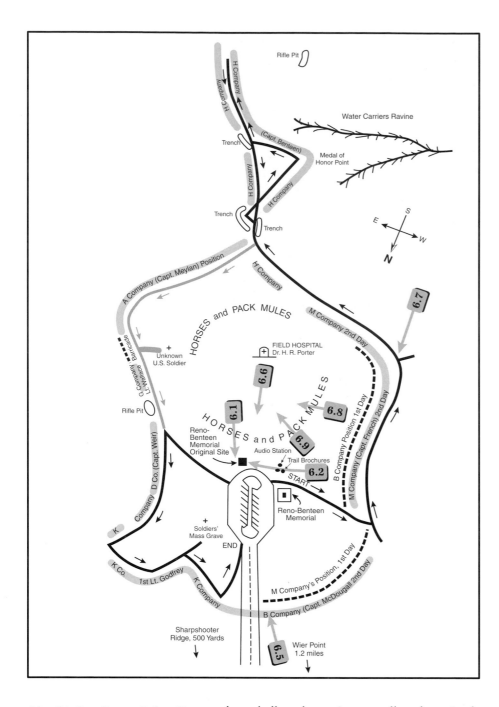

Map 6.1. Reno-Benteen Defense Site

expectation that the attacks would come from that direction from the village. The position was far from impregnable. A high bluff to the north that became known as Sharpshooter Ridge gave the Indians virtually unimpeded positions from which to look down on and to fire into the cavalry's lines. The animals and the wounded could not be protected from enemy fire. Most important, the soldiers' position on the bluffs was too far from the village's encampments and posed no threat to the warriors or their families.

The attackers soon took possession of the high ground around the defensive site, and the battle raged until dark. Fortunately, the Seventh Cavalry's odds were much better than at any other time on the afternoon of June 25, 1876, as Reno and Benteen may have had as many as 367 individuals—including 14 officers, 339 enlisted men, and 14 scouts or other civilians—under their command. Ammunition and food boxes provided makeshift breastworks, and the men dug in as best they could. Only another 6 men would be killed and 21 wounded before the day's fighting ceased.

Under the cover of darkness, some men may have speculated about Custer's whereabouts. Some, including a number of the officers and senior enlisted men, such as First Sergeant John Ryan, had fought at the Washita nearly eight years earlier and may have recalled the controversy over whether Custer had abandoned Major Joel H. Elliott and seventeen other soldiers by pulling out of the captured Indian encampment without ascertaining the whereabouts of the major's missing detachment. But in 1876, no man on Reno Hill could have known the truth at that moment—that Custer and 209 of his men lay dead on their own battlefield four miles to the north. Even in his report, Reno expressed the consensus within his command that "the awful fate that did befall [Custer] never occurred to any of us as within the limits of possibility."[5]

History has treated the memory of Major Reno's actions at Little Bighorn unkindly. Several episodes that may have occurred that night continue to stir heated debate and argument between the major's supporters and his detractors. Some assert that Reno entertained thoughts of abandoning his own wounded

by a shallow depression as well as the animals from the pack train and the soldiers' picketed horses, Doctor Porter set up his hospital. On the river side to the west, the high bluffs afforded reasonable safety, but on the east the gentle slopes offered the soldiers less protection. Benteen's Company H protected the high ridge on the south perimeter. On the east, Captain Moylan's Company A covered the swale housing the hospital and corral for the animals. Next to A was Company G under Lieutenant Wallace. Company D followed, with K and M in that order on the northern perimeter. McDougall's company came next, resting on the high bluffs and facing west toward the Little Bighorn River.[4] More men were assigned on the north, perhaps out of the and striking out under cover of darkness for the Powder River depot at the Yellowstone River. Others, including Lieutenant Godfrey and Captain French, claimed that Reno remained all but hidden that night, although Benteen credited Reno with being cool and collected.[6] Two mule packers, who testified at the Reno Court of Inquiry in 1879, stated that the major was drunk both during the afternoon fight and throughout that night on the bluffs. Lieutenant Edgerly, though, maintained that if Reno had been drunk, he would not have been allowed to retain command. Whatever the full truth of these episodes, the Seventh Cavalry's survivors certainly slept fitfully, if at all, the night of June 25.

Close to dawn on June 26, perhaps as early as 3 A.M., the Sioux and Cheyenne resumed their heavy fire on the soldiers' exposed positions. As was common in their manner of fighting, they relied on every bush, stone, and depression for cover in edging ever closer to the military's lines. Marksmen from such positions as Sharpshooter Ridge picked off troopers unlucky enough to appear in the open. Individual Indians launched attacks in unsuccessful attempts to overrun areas of the defense perimeter. One warrior, Long Robe, undoubtedly demonstrating the depth of his courage, charged the Seventh's entrenched line by himself to count coup on a body, but he paid for his display with his life.

On the south perimeter, Benteen's Company H was the most seriously threatened by these encroachments on the defenders' positions. Benteen, who may have seemed initially disinterested in the combat the day before, demonstrated his capability and courage by leading a countercharge. The maneuver so surprised the enemy that they scattered to safer positions and never again menaced the Seventh's positions on the bluffs.

On the northern perimeter, the warriors clearly had an advantage by manning a high ridge whose point aimed directly at the heart of the Seventh Cavalry's defensive line. Sergeant Ryan reported that several men were killed or wounded by warriors firing from this high ground on both days of the siege. Fortunately, Ryan was armed with a Sharps carbine outfitted with a telescopic sight, which he had had specially made for himself. As he stated about the June 26 action, "This

Captain Frederick W. Benteen.
Courtesy of Brian Pohanka

rifle cost me one hundred dollars. I fired a couple of shots until I got the range of that group of Indians, and then I put in a half dozen well directed shots in rapid succession into that group, and the Indians soon scampered away from that point of the bluff and that ended the firing from the Indians in that memorable engagement, and the boys set up quite a cheer."[7]

Later in the morning, lack of water proved to be a serious problem, especially for the many wounded being cared for by Porter in his hospital. Groups of men carrying camp kettles, canteens, and pots crept down the ravines under enemy fire to the river's edge. Protected by covering fire, they dashed to the stream, filled their receptacles with water, and struggled anew up the steep slopes of the ravines. For their heroic action, nineteen men were awarded the Medal of Honor.

About midday, the enemy fire began to slacken, and by late afternoon, the warriors were pulling back. Reno sent out scouts to try to link up with General Terry, but the men soon returned. Why he dispatched them to Terry and not to Custer remains an intriguing question, perhaps suggesting that Reno believed that his commander had been killed. As the soldiers watched from atop the bluffs, an enormous parade of warriors and their families, led by the Cheyenne, made their way

with loaded travois toward the southwest, leaving the valley to the army.

Four more of Reno's men, including Lieutenant DeRudio, all missing since the valley fight twenty-four hours earlier, made their way safely up the bluffs. The Battle of the Little Bighorn had ended and the enemy had seemingly retreated from the field, but no one in the Seventh Cavalry was in a mood to celebrate. Custer's command remained unaccounted for, and Reno's casualties had risen on that last day by another nine men killed and thirty-four wounded. In the two days of fighting on the hilltop, he had lost about fifteen men killed and fifty-six men wounded. Five of the wounded would later die.

THE DEFENSE PERIMETER

This view (6.1A) from D. F. Barry's well-known series taken during the tenth-anniversary observance in 1886 shows a group of visitors posed on the north end of the Reno-Benteen Defense Site. The slope of Sharpshooter

TOP LEFT: *6.1A. Visitors at the Reno Benteen defense site on the tenth anniversary of the battle, photo by D. F. Barry, 1886. Courtesy of Little Bighorn Battlefield National Monument, National Park Service, #6042.*

CENTER LEFT: *6.1B. 1996.*

BOTTOM LEFT: *6.2A. General Edward Godfrey and White Man Runs Him placing a cross at the site of a proposed marker at the Reno-Benteen defense site, 1926, photo by Edwin L. Wisherd. Courtesy of Edward S. Godfrey Collection, U.S. Army Military History Institute.*

BOTTOM RIGHT: *6.2B. Cricket Bauer Pohanka (l.) and Sandy Barnard (r.), 2000.*

Ridge is barely visible in the left background. On the right is what appears to be an early, primitive marker for the site, its origins and fate now lost to history. The spot is more flat now, having probably been graded when the walking trail was constructed.

The primitive marker seen in the 1886 view (6.1A) likely did not last long, and for more than fifty years after the battle, no permanent monument marked the Reno-Benteen defense site. At the fiftieth anniversary, a move was initiated to commemorate the spot. Image 6.2A shows battle veteran Edward Godfrey and Crow scout White Man Runs Him placing a lettered cross that reads, "This cross marks the site for a proposed monument to the 7th Cav., June 26, 1876, June 26, 1926."

Some people, including Custer's widow, Libbie, opposed allowing Reno's name to appear on any memorial. Bills were introduced in 1926 by members of the Montana congressional delegation but required several years for passage. Finally, a memorial shaft was set in place on August 14, 1929. It read, "This area was occupied by troops A, B, D, G, H, K, and M, Seventh U. S. Cavalry, and the pack train when they were besieged by the Sioux Indians June 25th and 26th 1876." Like Godfrey's wooden cross, it contained neither Reno's name nor that of any other individual. The Reno-Benteen site was purchased from the Crow tribe and taken over by the battlefield superintendent in August 1930.[8]

The 1929 engraved granite shaft still memorializes the Reno-Benteen defense site, but few current visitors realize that it has been moved from its original location. Plate 6.2B, with Cricket Bauer Pohanka and Sandy Barnard standing in for the 1926 participants, shows that Godfrey and White Man Runs Him placed their cross in a spot just south of the present paved parking loop. The current granite marker, which was at that time within a fence, was initially placed in the same or a very similar spot, as can be seen in the 1940s postcard view (6.3). The fence was removed in 1963.[9] In the fall of 1965, as part of a series of improvements at the battlefield, the parking loop at the Reno-Benteen defense site was constructed. Although the authors have been unable to

Views 6.5A and B are looking south toward the Reno-Benteen defense site with the Wolf Mountains in the background. Evident in the vintage photo is the earliest "road," which was little more than a pair of wagon ruts. The granite marker, surrounded by the early fence, is just to the west of the road as it existed then. The modern photo, its field of vision extended to the right past that of the vintage picture, shows the current road and parking loop. The man standing at the far end of the loop is on the bed of the old path and near the spot where the marker was first located. The relocated granite shaft stands without the fence and to the west of the parking loop.

In pair 6.6A and B, on page 51, the view is to the north. The wagon ruts extend south through the Reno-Benteen defense site. Sharpshooter Ridge is in the left background. As previously noted, the granite marker has been moved to the west (left) of its initial location. In the modern comparison photo, a traffic cone atop a trash can marks the original monument site.

ABOVE TOP: *6.5A. "Reno Monument Looking South," from Edward S. Godfrey Collection, U.S. Army Military History Institute, RG48-S, box 2.35.*

CENTER: *6.5B. 1998.*

BELOW LEFT: *6.7A. "Benteen Hill looking toward Sharpshooter Ridge," photographer and date unknown. Courtesy of Little Bighorn Battlefield National Monument, National Park Service, #11285.*

BELOW RIGHT: *6.7B. 2000.*

locate written documentation of the marker movement, a series of photographs in the battlefield archives shows the work at the Reno-Benteen area. The two views reproduced here show the granite monument at its original site at the start of the construction (plate 6.4A) and in its current spot after the parking loop was completed (plate 6.4B).[10]

Plate 6.7A, an early anonymous photo, shows horse bones atop a rifle pit dug during the siege at the Reno-Benteen defense site. The view is to the north, with Sharpshooter Ridge in the left background. The hastily dug rifle pits erode over time, making views like this one difficult to recreate. The breastworks at Reno-Benteen were restored in the 1990s, and the modern photo shows a current rifle pit that matches the one in the vintage picture.

LEFT: *6.6A. Reno-Benteen monument, photographer and date unknown. Courtesy of Little Bighorn Battlefield National Monument, National Park Service, #7763.*

BELOW: *6.6B. 1998.*

Moorhouse's 1901 view (6.8A), taken under a brooding sky, shows the old wagon road running through the middle of the defensive perimeter. Twenty-five years after the battle, numerous horse bones still dot the landscape, some gathered into discrete piles—a far cry from the tidy appearance of the modern view.

View 6.9A, taken under the same dark sky as the preceding one, shows the ruts of the old wagon road even more clearly. The horse bones, singly and in piles, provide a grim reminder of what had happened at this spot twenty-five years before.

HODGSON'S BURIAL SITE

Second Lieutenant Benjamin H. Hodgson, a personal favorite of Reno's who was acting as the major's adjutant, was wounded and unhorsed during the chaotic crossing of the Little Bighorn River but managed to reach the east bank by grabbing the stirrup of a passing trooper. Moments later, Hodgson was again shot and instantly killed on the flats below the bluff. When Reno learned of his adjutant's fall, he descended the bluff to ascertain Hodgson's fate and retrieved a ring and a watch chain from the lifeless lieutenant. The major then dispatched a detail to either recover or bury the slain officer but soon called them back.

Students of the battle, primarily on the basis of statements later made by Captain McDougall, have long assumed that Hodgson's body was later carried to the top of the ridge and buried there. Reno also indicated that Hodgson was buried on the heights, in or near the main defense position.[11] This information lends credence to a bluff-top marker location for Hodgson, even though he was actually killed near the river. However, reexamination of the accounts left by McDougall and others leaves doubt about a hilltop burial.

At the Reno Court of Inquiry less than three years after the battle, McDougall testified: "On the night of the 26th of June 1876, I took privates Ryan and Moore of my company, and we went and got Lieutenant Hodgson's body, and carried it to my breastworks, and kept it there until the next morning on the 27th. After sewing him up in a blanket and a poncho, I proceeded with those two men to bury him." He further stated that this occurred after the fight and that Hodgson's body lay "near where Major Reno crossed [the river] from the woods. On the side where we made our stand, the right-hand [east] side."[12]

Contemporary newspaper coverage of the Reno Court testimony in the *Chicago Times* (more widely available for researchers than the court transcript until recently) gives a somewhat different version of McDougall's testimony.[13] In the newspaper's account, McDougall and the two privates carried Hodgson's body "*up* to [McDougall's] breastworks" (emphasis added).[14] Both versions seem to imply that Hodgson's body was recovered near the river, then carried up the hill and buried atop the bluff. But the absence of the word "up" in the official transcript makes a ridge-top burial less certain.

McDougall gave another description of the recovery and burial of Lieutenant Hodgson's body in an 1878 Medal of Honor recommendation for Private Stephen Ryan of McDougall's Company B: "When [Ryan's] company [B] changed its position on the evening of the 26th to the banks of the river, he volunteered to secure the body of Lieutenant Benjamin Hodgson which was a quarter of a mile away, which he succeeded in doing, carrying the body over all this distance over a rough, unbroken country after which he dug a grave and buried the body."[15] Here McDougall clearly states that Company B was repositioned near the river on the night of the 26th and was no longer on top of the bluffs. Where were they?

In a third statement given to Walter Camp in 1909, thirty-three years after the battle and months before his own death, McDougall said that the company's position was changed on the night of June 26: "Cos. A and B went down on the bench just above the river, B on [the] south side and A on [the] north side of a gully running straight down from H Co.'s line. There Hodgson was buried."[16] An examination of the terrain does reveal a bench downhill from Company H's position on the south end of the hilltop siege perimeter. The gully McDougall mentioned is now called Water Carrier's Ravine. While this position is off the bluff top, it is still a good distance from the river. Nonetheless, Companies A and B likely did relocate on the night of June 26.

Confirmation of this move comes from Lieutenant Varnum, who wrote, "Looking from there [the southern end of Reno-Benteen Ridge] towards the river is where A and B troops moved on the night of the 26th."[17] Varnum also told Camp that "there was a full circular intrenchment [sic] just above [the] river when McDougall dug [the] trench [on the] night of June 26. Hodgson grave was near this, just up the bluff."[18] Again the description "just above the river" is confusing, as the new position is still a good distance uphill from the water. Moreover, despite the statements of McDougall and Varnum, the route from Hodgson's death site at the retreat crossing to the Company B position on the night of the 26th would have been so arduous that carrying a dead body that distance strains belief.

Balanced against McDougall's and Varnum's stories are an impressive number of witnesses who reported that Hodgson's body had been recovered alongside the river on June 27. Observers who had been there for the battle include Privates Thomas Coleman and August DeVoto and First Lieutenant Francis M. Gibson. Two additional officers, Second Lieutenant Richard E. Thompson (Sixth Infantry) and Captain Henry B. Freeman (Seventh Infantry),[19] were with the Terry-Gibbon column and did not arrive until June 27. One possible resolution of the conflicting reports on Hodgson's recovery and burial would be if McDougall had been mistaken on the date. If McDougall and his men had laid Lieutenant Hodgson to rest on the 27th, and not the 26th, no disagreement would exist with those who claimed to have seen the body on the later date. More important, any camp or lines to which they carried the fallen officer would be off the bluffs and closer to or in the valley by June 27, reconciling any confusion about their positioning away from the hilltop defense site. McDougall has been taken to task by at least

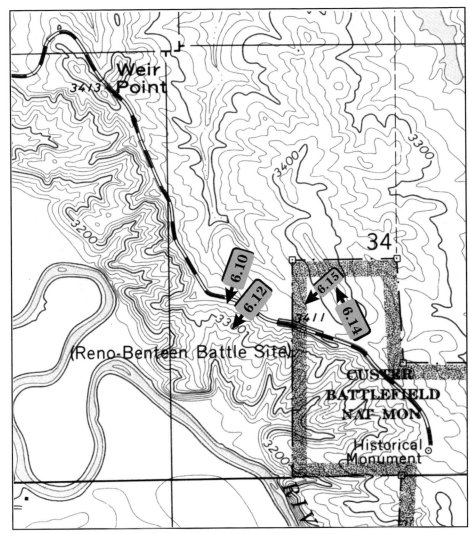

Based on the 1967 USGS topographical map

one researcher for his apparently contradictory accounts of which troopers recovered Hodgson's body;[20] it is not so far fetched that he might be off on the date as well. Certainly a bluff-top burial of Hodgson must be questioned, and if his body had been moved any appreciable distance uphill, it would have been to the bench below the south end of the siege perimeter.

SPURIOUS HODGSON MARKER AND DEWOLF MARKER

Regardless of the true location of Hodgson's initial burial, the marble stones on the battlefield are supposed to note the place where a given soldier actually fell. Originally some sort of marker for Hodgson (likely a wooden stake) did stand beside the river near the site of his death; General Godfrey reported that it was there in 1886.[21] Perhaps that marker eventually disappeared, creating confusion as to the actual spot where Hodgson perished. In

Map 6.2. Spurious Hodgson Marker, DeWolf Marker, and Sharpshooter Ridge

ABOVE: *6.10A. View from the bluffs near the Reno-Benteen defense site below Sharpshooter Ridge, photo by L. A. Huffman, 1916. Courtesy of Montana Historical Society, #981-1228.*

RIGHT: *6.10B. 1995.*

1910, four spurious markers were placed on the battlefield.[22] Three were for officers whose bodies had never been identified, and they were set at approximate locations. The fourth was for Hodgson, and though the site of his death was well documented, his 1910 marker was set up on the bluffs, far from where it belonged.

This 1916 photo by L. A. Huffman (plate 6.10A) shows the spurious 1910 Hodgson marker clearly, as does the close-up amateur vintage photo from a slightly later date (plate 6.11). Edward Luce stated that in 1939 he had the Hodgson marker moved back alongside the river near the actual site of the young lieutenant's death.[23] Luce's tenure as battle-

field superintendent did not begin until 1941, so he may have been a bit off on the date, but the Hodgson marker was likely relocated near the riverbank about that time.[24] In the left middle ground of our 1995 photo (plate 6.10B), a cut is visible through the flat plain, leading to the river. Hodgson's stone now sits at the high point on the right edge of that cut, where the terrain begins to slope down to the river.

A number of other noteworthy features are also visible in Huffman's 1916 image. The marker for civilian contract surgeon James DeWolf can be seen on the rounded knoll on the left, just below the high bluffs. DeWolf, retreating from the valley with Reno's command, had made it across the Little Bighorn safely. In ascending the bluffs, however, he took a route more to the left (north) than most of the others. Some warriors appeared on the heights, and before he could change

course, DeWolf was killed.[25] A stone was set for him at the site when the marble markers were placed on the battlefield by Captain Sweet in 1890.[26] In the modern photo, though a little less distinct because of the lighter color of the grass, the DeWolf marker is seen in the same spot it occupied in 1916. (The marker to the right of DeWolf's in the modern photo is discussed in detail with the next photo pair.)

Huffman's view also shows the sweeping loop of the Little Bighorn River around which most of Reno's command galloped on their way to the retreat crossing. It is visible to the left of the thick stand of trees in the background, seen over the top of the Hodgson marker. That loop has been dry since 1978. Our reshoot of Huffman's view shows the stand of trees clearly, but at present no water flows around it.

The original DeWolf marker appears

6.11. "Hodgson Monument Northern End of Reno Entrenchments on Reno Hill," 1928, from the Albert W. Johnson Album, Elizabeth Custer Collection. Courtesy of Little Bighorn Battlefield National Monument, National Park Service.

RIGHT: *6.12A. DeWolf marker,
photo by Lee Moorhouse, 1901. Image
courtesy of the Division of Special
Collections and University Archives,
University of Oregon Library System,
#2278.*

BOTTOM RIGHT: *6.12B. 1995.*

OPPOSITE: *6.13. Slaper and
Brininstool at the DeWolf marker in
1926. Courtesy of the Camp
Collection, Lilly Library, Indiana
University.*

clearly in Moorhouse's 1901 view, sitting by itself atop a small knoll overlooking the retreat crossing (plate 6.12A). It had already been chipped by souvenir hunters just eleven years after it was placed. The same damage to the upper right portion of the stone is visible in the 1926 photo of battle veteran William Slaper, posed next to the DeWolf marker with author and researcher Earl A. Brininstool at the fiftieth-anniversary observance (plate 6.13). The original DeWolf stone mistakenly referred to the civilian acting assistant surgeon as "Lieutenant,"[27] an error that has been corrected on the current marker.

Prominent in the modern photo is a second marble marker to the right of DeWolf's (see plate 6.12B). It was placed at that spot to commemorate the death site of Private Elihu Clear, assumed to be DeWolf's orderly and to have been killed alongside him in the ascent of the bluffs. The accuracy of that story is in question, however. The source of the DeWolf-Clear association seems to have been Godfrey, who identified the enlisted man as the doctor's orderly. According to one account of Godfrey's, Clear was killed about the same time as the doctor, and according to a second version, the two perished near each other but on opposite sides of a ravine.[28] No other primary source agrees with this assertion. At the 1879 Reno Court of Inquiry, Lieutenant Hare testified that Clear was his orderly, a fact confirmed by Sergeant Edward Davern.[29] Clear did perish in the retreat, though accounts of the location of his death vary from the timber to the river to the bluffs.[30] To add to the confusion, Hare at one point said that Clear was killed coming out of the timber and at another time implied that he was killed near the river.[31]

To further complicate the story, one witness, Lieutenant Varnum, asserted that DeWolf's orderly rejoined the column after the doctor's death.[32] Since it seems almost certain that Clear was in fact Hare's orderly, not DeWolf's, the surgeon likely had a different man assigned to him. A possible candidate is Private Harry Abbotts of Company E, who was DeWolf's orderly when he left Fort Totten to accompany the Seventh Cavalry on the 1876 campaign and was assigned as hospital attendant.[33] Abbotts survived the battle. All told, the evidence that Elihu Clear died next to Doctor DeWolf is not strong, but the placement of his marker on that little knoll has brought him to the attention of battlefield visitors.

TOP: *6.14A. "Gen'l. Godfrey and the late W. M. Camp searching Rocky Ridge near Reno's Hill for Cartridge Shells, 1916," photo by L. A. Huffman, 1916. Courtesy of Montana Historical Society, #981-182.*

RIGHT: *6.14B. 1995.*

SHARPSHOOTER RIDGE

In this 1916 photo (6.14A) by L. A. Huffman, Godfrey looks for artifacts in a piled-up group of rocks while Camp scans the ground along a little trail nearby. This image was taken on top of Sharpshooter Ridge, looking north toward the Custer section of the battlefield. Weir Point, partly obscured by Godfrey's horse, is visible in the center middle distance, and in the far background, just to the left of Camp, the Stone House can be seen. The modern view shows a few rocks still present at the spot where Godfrey searched. Weir Point is seen in the middle distance in the center of the image. In the background to the right of Weir Point, a stand of trees marks the location of

TOP: *6.15A. General Godfrey and Walter Camp at the Custer Battlefield, photo by L. A. Huffman, 1916. Courtesy of Montana Historical Society, #981-1225.*

LEFT: *6.15B. 2001.*

the Stone House and national cemetery. This well-known image was issued as a postcard by Huffman sometime after Camp's death in 1925.

In this panoramic 1916 view (6.15A) by L. A. Huffman, looking toward the west, Godfrey (on the left) and Camp descend from Sharpshooter Ridge toward the line of bluffs overlooking the Little Bighorn Valley. The spurious Hodgson marker (arrow) stands all by itself on the ridgeline. To the left, the view extends as far as the Reno-Benteen defense site. In the modern comparison photo, the Hodgson marker is gone, of course, and the auto road runs along the bluff tops, creating a horizontal line through the middle of the picture.

7

WEIR POINT ⌇

NOTHER OF THE complex and debatable episodes that pose a continuing challenge to students of Little Bighorn involves the advance by soldiers of Reno's and Benteen's battalions to the elevation known as Weir Point—named for the captain whose foray precipitated the deployment. With the benefit of hindsight comes the realization that had the movement been more aggressive and better coordinated, some portion of Custer's command might, perhaps, have escaped annihilation. But to view the abortive sally as a relief expedition is to fall prey to the bias of what we now know, and what those involved in the incident eventually came, all too tragically, to realize. Despite a wealth of testimony and recollection by participants, historians have been unable to reach a consensus as to how long troops were on Weir Point and what they saw or suspected of Custer's predicament.

The construction of a theoretical timeline is a problematic undertaking at best, complicated by the fact that Lieutenant George Wallace, the acting engineer officer (whose duties included the compilation of a chronology), seems to have set his watch some two hours ahead of the actual, or sun, time.[1] But a sense of the comparative duration of events is vital to an understanding of the Weir Point phase of the battle—particularly since those events paralleled but ultimately failed to intersect with the fatal drama unfolding on Custer's field.

Most of the survivors of Major Reno's shattered battalion seem to have reached the crest of the bluffs by 4:05 to 4:10 P.M. Some ten minutes later Captain Benteen arrived on the chaotic scene with his battalion.[2] Lieutenant Varnum thought that Benteen arrived about twenty minutes after Reno got to the bluffs, but of course some men gained the crest sooner than others, and stragglers were still coming in when Benteen's troopers rode up.[3] Enemy pressure had largely abated, as most of the warriors had turned north to engage Custer's force. Some individuals and small groups did continue to fire on Reno's retreat.

One enemy band opened fire on Reno's and Benteen's men from the cover of rocks on a rise of ground to the north—most likely the feature later known as Sharpshooter Ridge. Company D dismounted, formed a skirmish line, and secured the position. "We then stood to horse," Lieutenant Edgerly recalled, "and waited for the order to advance, which we felt sure would be given."[4] The sound of distant gunfire indicated that Custer was engaged. Edgerly said that Company D "was for a long while standing to horse, every man apparently anxious to move down to the firing." The lieutenant told his commander, Captain Weir, "We ought to go down there."[5]

At the 1879 Reno Court of Inquiry, Lieutenant Hare stated that soon after the rendezvous with Benteen's force he heard "two distinct volleys" from Custer's direction, observing, "I thought he was having a very warm time."[6] Reno and Benteen, conversely, testified to having heard little, if any, firing downstream. However, in his after-action report of July 5, 1876, the major wrote, "We had heard firing in that direction and knew it could only be Custer."[7] In any event the accounts of numerous participants make plain the fact that the sounds of battle were clearly audible and that the vast majority of their attackers had shifted northward.

Within ten minutes of Benteen's arrival on the bluffs, Hare was dispatched to bring up Company B and the pack train—and, more immediately, a fresh supply of ammunition. His own horse having been wounded, Hare borrowed Lieutenant Godfrey's mount and set out, presumably around 4:25 to 4:30. It would seem that Reno wished to reunite all the elements of his force before making any move in Custer's direction. In the meantime the major absented himself from his command, embarking on his mission to determine the fate of his adjutant and friend, Lieutenant Hodgson. Accompanied by Sergeant Ferdinand Culburtson and ten or twelve troopers, the major made his way to the riverbank, replenished empty canteens, searched for and eventually located Hodgson's body, recovered some personal effects, then made his way back to the summit. Along the way the group rescued a soldier of Company G who had been hiding on the slope.[8]

Given the rugged terrain and the uncertainty of the situation, not to mention the possible presence of warriors along the way, the major's journey clearly took some time. At the court of inquiry Reno stated that he was gone for half an hour; it might, in fact, have been closer to forty or forty-five minutes. If so, the commander would have returned to his troops at 5 P.M. at the earliest.

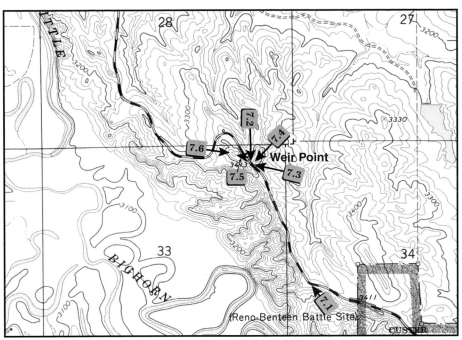

Based on the 1967 USGS topographical map

Map 7.1. Weir Point

In the meantime Lieutenant Hare had reached the pack train and hastened forward the mules carrying ammunition, with the remainder of the contingent arriving as quickly as the animals could be driven. Sergeant Culburtson recalled that "part of the train was up" when the Reno party regained the bluff.[9] Captain McDougall noted that when he reported his arrival to Reno, the major remarked, "Bennie is lying right over there"—an indication of Reno's continued preoccupation with his fallen adjutant even as the sound of Custer's battle sounded in the distance.[10]

Lieutenant Hare remembered his round trip as having taken about twenty minutes, which would put his return, followed by the lead elements of the pack train, in the 4:45 to 4:50 time frame. The mission might have taken him several minutes longer, and in any event the rest of the mules would be some time in arriving—the last of them perhaps as late as 5:30. Hare noted the sound of distant volleys and also observed a significant development: Captain Weir's Company D was riding toward a conspicuous crest a mile north of the Reno-Benteen position.

Weir had acted on his own initiative. In one of several accounts of the affair, Lieutenant Edgerly recalled his captain saying, "Are you willing to go down with only me and D Troop, if the rest of them don't go?"

"I most certainly am," Edgerly replied.

Captain Thomas B. Weir. Courtesy of Little Bighorn Battlefield National Monument, National Park Service

Initially intending to ask permission of Reno and Benteen, Weir instead called his orderly and rode toward the high point to reconnoiter without giving instructions to his lieutenant. Edgerly ordered the company to mount and followed his commander. "He [Weir] kept to the left along the ridge," Edgerly remembered, "and I swung off to the right and followed a ravine [probably Cedar Coulee] which led to the Custer field. I think we had gone about a mile when he saw the Indians start for me and waved his hand so as to swing me completely around and head for him."[11] Although Edgerly assumed that Weir had gotten permission for the movement, the captain later told him that "he hadn't spoken to Reno or Benteen, but rode out on the bluff hoping to see something of Custer's command."[12]

Edgerly testified that Company D moved out "about 30 or 35 minutes" after the union of Benteen's and Reno's battalions,[13] or about 4:45 to 5 P.M. This time frame fits with Hare's recollection of seeing the deployment under way when he got back from hastening up the pack train. It is even possible that Major Reno had not yet returned from his trek to Hodgson's body when Weir sallied forth. This possibility was skirted at the court of inquiry, although at one point Benteen was asked, "Where was Major Reno during that time when the movement started down?"

"I don't know whether he had gone to Lieutenant Hodgson's body or not," Benteen replied."[14]

Reno was on hand soon after Hare's return, for he ordered the lieutenant to ride out to Weir and direct the captain to open communication with Custer's force, if possible. Afterward, the major again turned his attention to his late adjutant, dispatching Lieutenant Varnum on a mission to bury Hodgson's remains. Varnum obtained some shovels from the pack train and started out; but after encountering scout George Herendeen and a group of survivors from the valley fight, the lieutenant and his companions came back to the bluff top. According to his recollection, Varnum was gone twenty or twenty-five minutes, and on his return he discovered additional elements of the command beginning to move toward Weir Point.[15]

Weir and his orderly likely reached the high ground about 5:10 P.M., while Edgerly and the troopers of Company D continued along a ridgeline or series of hillocks that descended toward South Medicine Tail Coulee. Dust clouds, galloping horsemen, and gunfire indicated an engagement in progress some two and a half miles to the north.[16] When Indians materialized to his front, Edgerly dismounted the troop and opened fire, eventually pulling back closer to Weir's position. In the meantime, three more companies—M, H, and K—rode out to join Weir. Benteen, the senior officer present, asserted that the move had been conducted without orders from Reno, which, if true, would further indicate that a vacuum in command existed at this crucial point in the battle.[17] The reinforcements probably arrived at Weir's position by about 5:45 P.M.[18] Lieutenant Godfrey believed that a stand was going to be made there.[19]

Soon after the additional troopers took position at intervals along the high ground at what would come to be known as Weir Point, Major Reno started to move the remainder of his force northward to join them, shepherding the pack train and carrying the wounded men in blankets. The latter task fell to Captain Moylan and the survivors of his Company A, who had a hard time keeping up with the rest of the command. Moylan asked Captain McDougall for assistance, and a platoon was detailed for that purpose.[20] McDougall stated, "The pack train merely got started before it was ordered to fall back."[21] Lieutenant Wallace and a handful of men from Company G fell in with the force on Weir Point, but Companies A and B and the pack train turned around prior to reaching the position.

The decision to abort the movement seems to have been made by Reno following a consultation with Benteen, whose view of the situation was recalled by Lieutenant Gibson.

"This is a hell of a place to fight Indians," Benteen remarked. "I am going to see Reno and propose that we go back to where we lay before starting out here."[22] The major clearly agreed with Benteen's assessment, although Benteen later maintained, "If he gave any orders, I did not hear them."[23] Godfrey testified at the Reno Court of Inquiry that Lieutenant Hare brought him word to fall back, while Reno asserted that Hare took the responsibility upon himself, although the major concurred in the decision.[24] In any event, the end result was a disorganized and haphazard retirement to the position where Reno's and Benteen's forces would subsequently be besieged.

Lieutenant Edgerly—commanding Company D in the absence of Weir, who had gone to confer with Reno—saw Benteen's Company H pull off the ridge. Captain French of Company M told Edgerly that orders had been given to retreat. "I said to him I thought not," Edgerly remembered, "that I [had] heard of no such order." Five minutes later French "said the order had been given to go back, and he was going. He mounted his men and moved off at a gallop."[25]

As Company D joined the hasty retirement, a band of warriors closed on Edgerly's troopers, their fire narrowly missing the lieutenant and his orderly and dropping Farrier Vincent Charley from the saddle. Unable to get the badly wounded soldier remounted, Edgerly told him to lie quiet and they would come back for him.[26] Later, when Edgerly informed his captain of Charley's plight, Weir "said he was sorry but the orders were to go back on the hill."[27]

"That was the thing that I regretted more than any other," Edgerly wrote his wife after the battle, "for I had promised that wounded man I would get him out and wasn't able to raise a finger for him."[28]

Lieutenant Godfrey endeavored to keep the troopers of Company K in formation as a rallying point, but the other units "came pell-mell" past his position.[29] Undaunted, Godfrey ordered his men to dismount, sent the led horses to the rear, and, assisted by Lieutenant Hare, formed a skirmish line some five hundred yards north of Reno Hill. Harangued and inspired by their commander, who "threatened to kill any man who ran away," the twenty-two troopers held the Indians at bay and retired on the remainder of the command without loss.[30] What Edgerly later described as Godfrey's "brave and fearless manner" stood in sharp contrast to the less-than-stellar performance of many other officers in the Weir Point episode.[31]

Just how long were troopers present on or near Weir Point? In an account written some twenty years later, Edgerly recollected that he was "out there about two hours," which would place the retreat sometime after 7 P.M.[32] On another occasion, Edgerly noted that it was half an hour after Company D took position with Benteen's three companies that the force fell back.[33] If Benteen arrived about 5:45, this would seem to put the withdrawal at about 6:15 P.M. Varnum thought it was "about two hours" after Reno arrived atop the bluff that the force withdrew from Weir Point, which would be in the 6:10 to 6:15 time frame.[34] Godfrey believed that everyone was back at their starting point "about seven o'clock."[35]

The period of heaviest firing was heard from Custer's field from the time Reno's force arrived on the bluffs until about 5:35 P.M. This would imply that Weir's men were in their advanced position for about the last twenty minutes to half an hour of the organized portion of the Custer fight. When Benteen arrived at Weir Point with his three companies, command and control of Custer's force had likely collapsed, although combat probably continued at least until 6 P.M., if not some minutes longer.

Just what Reno's and Benteen's men saw, suspected, or realized of their comrades' fate remains a murky and debatable issue. Most evidently chose to believe that Custer's command had been either driven off to the north or pinned down in a defensive position—though the diminution of firing and the subsequent siege of Reno's and Benteen's battalions by numerous well-armed warriors ought to have argued against the latter possibility. At the Reno Court of Inquiry, Lieutenant Varnum stated, "The idea of the command being cut up and wiped out as it was, I didn't think of such a thing. . . . The idea of Custer being killed never struck me, it never entered my mind."[36]

WEIR'S VIEW

Lee Moorhouse took this photo (7.1A) in 1901 from a position south of Weir Point, looking north toward Custer Hill. This would have been the view seen by Captain Weir and the men of Reno's command as they advanced from the bluff-top defense site to briefly occupy this point on the late afternoon of June 25, 1876. The picture was taken before the auto road from Last Stand Hill to the Reno-Benteen defense site was constructed. That road runs through the middle of Weir Point. In the 1901 photo, a central area of lower elevation is seen between the two humps on the left (west) side of Weir Point and the broader elevation on the right (east). The road placement has changed the configuration of Weir Point considerably. Grading

deepened that central notch to about twice its original depth.[37] The earth that was removed seems to have been piled up on the southwestern side of Weir Point, creating what almost appears to be a third hump, though it is lower and less prominent than the other two. The road winds through the landscape and is visible in the left foreground of the modern photo, which was made from a camera position on the pavement.

The two photo pairs on this page clearly demonstrate the extent to which the notch separating the east and west sides of Weir Point has been deepened by the construction of the road. In both vintage images (7.2A and 7.3A), taken by L. A. Huffman in 1916, General Godfrey and Walter Camp are on horseback in the swale between the two sides of Weir Point. The modern comparison photos are "off" in both the one facing toward the southwest (plate 7.2B) and the one facing toward the northwest (plate 7.3B), because the spots where the photographer stood and the places where the men posed no longer exist. Those sites would now literally be in thin air, as the ground surface has been lowered considerably by the road grading.

This terrain change can mislead the modern viewer. The deep cut made for the roadbed and the placement of the interpretive marker at the base of the now-steepened slope to the east of the road (on the right side of the car in plate 7.3B) might lead visitors to assume that Weir Point consisted only of that one hill on the east side of the pavement. In fact, at the time of the battle, Weir Point was not a single point at all, but rather a horseshoe-shaped series of elevations and swales, the open end of which faced to the north (see map 7.1). During their occupation of Weir

Point, Reno's men took up positions around the entire feature. Captain Benteen and Company H were on the far northwest elevation, seen behind the horses' heads in the second vintage photo, while Lieutenant Edgerly with Company D was at the north-

east end, with the other companies arrayed in between.[38] The view of Godfrey and Camp on the gentler original slopes gives a much more accurate picture of the battle-day appearance of Weir Point.

Despite the clues in the title of plate 7.4A, taken by L. A. Huffman in 1916 and later issued as a postcard, this picture of General Godfrey and Walter Camp proved difficult to match. They were clearly on a very high spot, in sight of DeWolf's marker, and with the Little Bighorn Valley just behind them. We scaled every bluff on the valley side of the road from the Reno-Benteen defense site to the two-humped saddle on the west side of Weir Point but could not find the spot. When the original camera position was finally located on the east side of Weir Point, it became clear why this photo fools the eye. At first glance, the high, rounded peak just behind Godfrey and Camp seems to be the top of the terrain feature they posed on. A closer look reveals that their section of the hill ends just behind the horses' hooves. The higher section behind is actually the peak of the southernmost of the two humps on the saddle-shaped *western* side of Weir Point, separated from the two men by Weir Point's central swale and the old wagon trail. This is more evident in the modern photo, which also shows the current road between the two sides of Weir Point emerging from the graded notch and skirting the bluff tops on the left side of the picture. Once found, the location is obvious. Even the faint trail through the grass on top of the point remains visible in the modern photo, as does one of the rocks beneath Godfrey's horse—good examples of the fine state of preservation of the Little Bighorn Battlefield.

From Godfrey and Camp's commanding viewpoint, they would, indeed, have seen DeWolf's marker standing alone. Also visible in the background is that sweeping loop of

Of greater historical significance, though, is the assertion in Huffman's title that Godfrey and Camp also viewed "the hill up which James Pym carried water." Perhaps the most heroic aspect of the Little Bighorn conflict was the danger-filled sorties to the river by volunteers from Reno's command to bring desperately needed water to the wounded men on the hill. Of the twenty-four Medals of Honor awarded at the Little Bighorn, nineteen went to soldiers who either dashed to the river or provided covering fire for those who did.[39] Private James Pym of Company B, cited for bringing "water to the wounded at great danger to life and under a great and most galling fire of the enemy," was one of the medal recipients. Wounded in the right ankle, Pym survived the battle.[40]

On the southern end of the Reno-Benteen defense site, near the position manned by Captain Benteen and his Company H, a steep and narrow gully down to the river has traditionally been known as Water Carrier's Ravine. According to accepted history, here heroic men descended to the river to complete their dangerous mission and obtain water. However, Water Carrier's Ravine would be nowhere in sight from the position Godfrey and Camp occupy in plate 7.4A. Huffman's title clearly implies that Pym's route to the river was near the hill on which DeWolf's marker rests. Most likely it was the same ravine used by Reno's men to ascend the heights after their chaotic river crossing, which brought them up to the northern end of the defense site, a good distance from Water Carrier's Ravine to the south. What are we to make of this discrepancy?

Many men took part in the attempts to obtain water. In addition to the nineteen Medal of Honor recipients, at least three others participated making a total of twenty-two or more.[41] Even an Indian account tells of a man being killed while going for water, although that has not been substantiated.[42] Given the number of soldiers involved, it is not unreasonable to assume that more than one ravine was used. Likely the largest and best-organized sorties did take place on the south side of the defense perimeter held by Benteen's Company H. Indeed, Godfrey said that "parties of volunteers were formed to get water under the protection of Benteen's lines."[43] This would be consistent with the presently marked Water Carrier's Ravine. But we must also assume that Godfrey told Camp and Huffman that James Pym used a different route, as reflected in the photographer's title. Indeed, Pym's Company B was positioned just above the ravine near the DeWolf marker during the hilltop siege, making his use of that route even more likely.[44]

Battle historian Edgar Stewart (whose 1955 book, *Custer's Luck*, remains highly regarded half a century after its publication) asserted, "Many unorganized efforts to reach the river were made by troopers grown reckless and desperate by the agony of an ever increasing thirst."[45] This 1916 L. A. Huffman photo is evidence that the heroic dashes to the river took place in more than one ravine.

When photographer Edward S. Curtis visited the Little Bighorn for the second time in 1907, he had three of the Crow Indians who had served as scouts for Custer show him around the battlefield.[46] Six Crow scouts had guided Custer to the Little Bighorn. Two (White Swan and Half Yellow Face) went into battle with Reno. The other four were with Custer's battalion until shortly before he engaged the Sioux and Cheyenne. One of them, Curley, had become well known just after the battle when word spread that he was the only survivor of Custer's ill-fated command, a claim he never actually made. Nonetheless, Curley was photographed and interviewed repeatedly. His three fellow Custer scouts—

White Man Runs Him, Goes Ahead, and Hairy Moccasin—had received scant attention until Curtis invited them to accompany him around the field and tell him about the battle.

Their narrative differed sharply from the accepted versions of the story, most markedly in their assertion that Custer had paused for forty-five minutes on a high point on the bluffs, where he watched Reno's defeat and declined to go to the major's aid.[47] Genuinely troubled, Curtis consulted with President Theodore Roosevelt, who advised him not to print this story.[48] Curtis agreed, publishing instead a vague description of the fight, which contained a confusingly marked map, used few photographs, and ultimately

attracted little attention.[49]

Throughout his life, Curtis quietly continued to believe that Custer had witnessed the rout of Reno's troops and had done nothing. His original manuscript describing this incident, put aside as Roosevelt had suggested, was entrusted to his son, Harold P. Curtis, with instructions to eventually donate it to a museum. The Smithsonian Institution received the Curtis papers in 1988.[50] A short time later, a group of previously unknown Curtis glass-plate negatives surfaced, showing the three Crow scouts at various points on the battlefield.[51] This fortunate coincidence has raised interest in Curtis among Little Bighorn students.

the Little Bighorn River that was skirted by Reno's retreating men. It is now dry, as can be seen in the modern photo.

THE CROW SCOUTS

This Curtis photo (7.5A) is one of the newly found group mentioned in the sidebar above. A study of the Curtis papers at the Smithsonian yields an approximate idea of where the three Crow scouts claimed that Custer watched Reno's defeat; but this photograph shows us exactly. Here White Man Runs Him, mounted in the central foreground, along with Goes Ahead standing and Hairy Moccasin mounted on the right, pose for Curtis—looking toward the Indian village and the site of Reno's valley fight. Matching the photo, we found that they were on the northern peak of the western side of Weir Point, a location that fits the written descriptions.[52] This is the same spot manned by Benteen and Company H during the Weir Point occupation (and visible behind the horses' heads in plate 7.3A). Few, if any, scholars of the battle accept the story of Custer's idle wait, but this photograph clearly is the historical document that most accurately tells us where the three Crow scouts said it took place.

In this picture (7.6A), from the left, the three Crow scouts Goes Ahead, Hairy Moccasin, and White Man Runs Him pose with Curtis and interpreter Alexander Upshaw. The scouts all hold envelopes, perhaps containing payment for guiding Curtis around the field and telling him about the battle. They are in the same spot as the previous photo pair but with the camera turned in the opposite direction, looking southeast, away from the valley. The crowd of men and horses in the vintage view make it difficult to see the background landmarks, which are more easily viewed in the modern comparison photo. The camera is on the northern hump of the western side of Weir Point. Looking along the right side of the image, one can see the terrain dip into the low point of the saddle-shaped feature and then rise up to the top of the southern peak. The road runs through the central middle ground. The car, facing south toward the Reno-Benteen defense site, is parked opposite the interpretive sign and the foot trail up to the top of the eastern side of Weir Point.

It is also clear in our modern comparison photo that this northern extension of Weir Point's western side is the highest part of the entire Weir Point feature. During the occupation of Weir Point by Reno's command, Captain Benteen stated that he had "planted a guidon on the highest point that overlooked that country," and battle theorist Charles Kuhlman would later assert that Benteen and his Company H had taken up this position.[53] Custer most likely did not spend forty-five minutes here watching Reno's defeat, as the Crow scouts maintained, but Benteen apparently did position his company on or near this peak during the tentative move to Weir Point on June 25, 1876.

OPPOSITE TOP: *7.5A. White Man Runs Him, Goes Ahead, and Hairy Moccasin on the bluffs along the Little Bighorn River overlooking the village site, photo by Edward S. Curtis, 1907. Courtesy of Museum of New Mexico, Neg. No. 160453.*

OPPOSITE BOTTOM: *7.5B. 1997.*

ABOVE TOP: *7.6A. Edward S. Curtis with three Custer scouts and interpreter, photo by Edward S. Curtis, 1907. Courtesy of National Anthropological Archives, Smithsonian Institution, #95-9804.*

ABOVE BOTTOM: *7.6B. Sandy Barnard (l.) and Brian Pohanka (r.), 1999.*

8

CUSTER'S APPROACH ∽

ONE OF THE more baffling and disputed phases of the battle at Little Bighorn encompasses the movements of Custer's column from the time his five companies left Reno Creek until their initial engagement in the vicinity of Medicine Tail Coulee, some three-and-a-half miles to the north. Ten individuals who started out with the column left before Custer arrived at the site of the Last Stand, and seven of them recounted their experiences in official testimony, written memoirs, or interviews by journalists and historians. But the often-conflicting details of those stories—evolving and elaborated over time as they were presented to subsequent generations of Little Bighorn enthusiasts—leave modern researchers with a complex and daunting tangle of contradictory evidence and possibilities.

Sergeant Daniel Kanipe of Company C and trumpeter John Martin of Company H (serving as an orderly with Custer's headquarters) were dispatched as couriers with instructions to hasten the pack train and Benteen's battalion to the scene of the impending battle. Kanipe believed that Custer's fateful decision to turn northward rather than follow Reno's force across the river was due to the presence of at least fifty and possibly as many as a hundred Indians spotted on the bluffs north of what is now called Reno Creek.[1] The sergeant recalled that Custer's column moved at a "trot and gallop all the way," up the slope and over the rolling crest that would later be the site of the Reno-Benteen siege.[2] The rapid pace of Custer's advance was confirmed by Martin, who informed the 1879 Reno Court of Inquiry, "we went on a jump all the way."[3]

From the bluff top Custer was finally able to see the extent of the Indian village in the valley below. It was immense, and contrary to his expectations, the lodges were still standing. Far from being intimidated or apprehensive, Custer seems to have welcomed the sight. Martin remembered his commander exclaiming, "Courage, boys, we have got them. The Indians are asleep in their tepees."[4] Kanipe noted that the troopers shared their commander's enthusiasm, "cheering and eager for the fight, . . . yelling and urging their horses ahead at break neck speed."

"Hold your horses, boys," Custer shouted. "There are Indians enough down there for all of us." At this point, the sergeant related, Custer's five companies were riding parallel to one another, in columns of twos, and Reno's battalion was visible advancing toward the village.[5]

In the vicinity of Sharpshooter Ridge—the elevation just north of what was destined to be the Reno-Benteen defense site—Kanipe was dispatched with verbal orders for Captain McDougall to hurry up the pack train. McDougall was to come straight across country, to cut off any packs that slipped loose on the mules, not pause and tighten them—unless they were ammunition packs. If the sergeant encountered Captain Benteen, he was to tell him to "come on quick" with his three companies because a big Indian camp had been discovered.[6]

The fortunate Kanipe did encounter Benteen's command and delivered Custer's message.[7] Lieutenant Edgerly remembered that as Kanipe rode along Benteen's column, he shouted, "We've got 'em boys," while Lieutenant Godfrey heard the sergeant exclaim, "They are licking the stuffing out of them."[8] In Godfrey's view, and likely Benteen's as well, Kanipe's enthusiasm implied that they had captured the village.[9] John Mahoney, a trooper with the pack train escort, informed researcher Walter Camp that the sergeant "said to the boys after he had delivered his message to McDougall, 'They're fighting to beat hell up there.'"[10]

Some ten to fifteen minutes after Kanipe rode off, Martin was sent back with a similar message—Custer's famous "last order." Hastily scrawled by regimental adjutant W. W. Cooke, it read: "Benteen—Come on. Big village. Be quick. Bring packs. P.S. Bring pacs [sic]." Most students of the battle place Custer's battalions at the time of Martin's departure somewhere in the depression now known as Cedar Coulee, a defile that led northward to the broader valley of Medicine Tail Coulee, which, in turn, provided a natural avenue of approach westward to the Little Bighorn and the village beyond.[11]

Retracing the column's route, the trumpeter gained the crest of the bluffs and briefly surveyed the valley below. Martin gave differing versions of his story in the years to come, and whether he witnessed the retirement of Reno's skirmish line to the timber or Indians galloping to confront Custer in Medicine Tail Coulee continues to be debated by students of the battle. But in his earliest account, testifying at the 1879 Reno Court of Inquiry, Martin said simply, "I saw Major Reno's battalion was engaged. I paid no further attention to it."[12] As he continued on the back-trail, Martin encountered Boston Custer, riding overland to join his elder brothers in the fray. Boston pointed out that Martin's horse had been wounded, which we may interpret as clear indication of some hostile Indian presence east of the river.[13]

When Martin reached Benteen, the captain inquired about Custer's situation. "I said I supposed that by that time he had made a charge through the village," the trumpeter testified, "and that was all I said." Benteen stated that Martin "said the Indians were all skedaddling."[14] Edgerly, who was nearby, recalled that the trumpeter "was laughing and seemed very much elated, said it was the biggest village he ever saw, that they had found the Indians all asleep in their tepees, that Major Reno was charging it and killing everything, men, women, and children."[15] Benteen seems to have come to the unfortunate conclusion that by the time he reached the scene of action with his battalion and the slow-moving pack train, the fighting would be all but over. The tragic fallacy of that assumption would haunt Benteen and immerse his name and reputation in a bitter controversy that continues to this day.

Accompanying the Custer battalions when they turned north from the valley of Reno Creek and ascended the bluffs east of the Little Bighorn were five scouts, the eldest and acknowledged leader of whom was the half Santee Sioux, half French-Canadian interpreter, Mitch Boyer. With him rode a quartet of young Crows: White Man Runs Him, Hairy Moccasin, Goes Ahead, and Curley. Boyer perished with Custer, but the other four survived and recounted their experiences in interviews that continue to confound historians with a daunting amalgam of contradictions, insights, and impossibilities. The most prolific of the group in his verbal recollections was Curley, who early on achieved a measure of celebrity in military and journalistic circles as a "survivor" of Custer's Last Stand and whose notoriety clearly irritated his fellow Crow scouts. As is so often the case with Little Bighorn, an element of personal acrimony must be factored into the sifting of evidence and the striving for objective analysis.

During a 1907 visit to the battlefield, photographer Edward S. Curtis recorded a number of images included in this volume, emphasizing the role of the veteran scouts White Man Runs Him, Hairy Moccasin, and Goes Ahead. The three accompanied Curtis over the field and shared their recollections, conveyed principally by White Man Runs Him via interpreter Alexander Upshaw. The controversial nature of the scouts' revelations clearly impressed Curtis, who realized that the implication of gross mismanagement on Custer's part challenged the general's heroic image.

As compiled by Curtis, the Crow narrative describes Custer halting his northward advance in the vicinity of Weir Point while the scouts rode ahead to the northern extension of the bluff overlooking the ford at the mouth of Medicine Tail Coulee. After pausing to fire into the village, the Crows rode back to Custer, who proceeded to observe the stalemate, defeat, and demoralized retreat of Reno's battalion in the valley below without taking any action on Reno's behalf. White Man Runs Him said that six of Reno's survivors were brought to Custer, who despite the dire state of affairs ultimately chose to continue north with his five companies. Custer's

force entered Medicine Tail Coulee, advanced on the ford, and was repulsed by the Sioux and Cheyenne. At this point Mitch Boyer told the three young scouts—minus Curley, who all agreed had left prior to this point—that they could seek safety. Boyer rode on with Custer's command.[16]

In later accounts given to Walter Camp and General Hugh Scott, White Man Runs Him similarly describes watching the Reno fight, then accompanying Custer into action at Medicine Tail Coulee before being released by Boyer. At this point the Sioux were charging across the ford and in the process of surrounding Custer's companies.[17] In 1919, White Man Runs Him gave a somewhat different version of events in which Custer's column moved down Cedar Coulee while the scouts rode along the river bluffs and then watched while Custer was repulsed at the ford. Boyer then released them, and rode down from the bluff to join Custer in Medicine Tail Coulee.[18]

Hairy Moccasin offered a generally parallel view of events as to observing Reno's defeat, firing into the village, and continuing north with Custer. In one account he describes taking part in the fighting on the level ground near the ford, but in another he says that Custer sent them back from a dry gulch out of sight of the village.[19]

According to the account of Goes Ahead, however, the scouts saw considerably less of Custer's actions than his comrades alleged. The account he provided Walter Camp is for the most part consistent with his story as recorded in Orin G. Libby's 1920 anthology, *The Arikara Narrative*. Left behind when Custer's column turned down Cedar Coulee, the Crows observed Reno's valley fight from Weir Point and then continued north to the bluff overlooking the ford at the mouth of Medicine Tail Coulee. There they dismounted and fired into the village before backtracking southward. Goes Ahead implied that Curley had left them early on and that Boyer rejoined Custer from the vicinity of Weir Point, rather than from the crest above the ford. In his 1909 account, interpreted for Camp by Russell White Bear, Goes Ahead stated, "We three Crows did not see Custer after he turned down the coulee to [the] right. Did not see Custer fight. Did not see [the]

Map 8.1. Custer's Approach

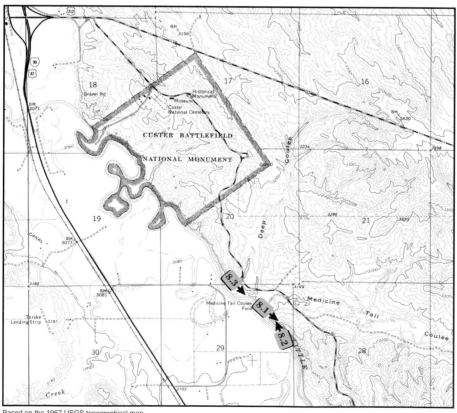

Based on the 1967 USGS topographical map

beginning or any part of it. Do not know whether Custer went north of Dry Coulee [Medicine Tail Coulee]."[20] Three years later, in the account eventually published in Libby's volume, Goes Ahead added an intriguing observation—that before leaving their northernmost position the Crows "heard two volleys fired and saw the soldiers' horses standing back of the line in groups."[21] He does not state where this line was, and it is possible that the engagement Goes Ahead saw or heard occurred not at the ford but on the rising ground north of Medicine Tail Coulee.

In neither of these accounts does Goes Ahead claim to have joined Custer at the ford or to have participated in a fight in Medicine Tail Coulee. In Camp's view, this lent credence to Goes Ahead's version of events, for had the scouts lingered with Custer's force, "they would have met Benteen's and Reno's commands together when they went back south along the bluffs, instead of Benteen's only, as they certainly did."[22] Two later students of the battle, Wayne Wells and Joseph Sills Jr., suggested that the three Crows had turned south some ten minutes prior to the commencement of Reno's retreat from the timber and fifteen to twenty minutes before the remnants of the major's command reached the crest of the bluffs.[23]

Three decades before his fellow scouts told their stories to Curtis, the handsome young Crow called Curley entered the historical record of Little Bighorn when his account was published in the *Helena Herald* on July 15, 1876. He was interviewed many times in the following years, the last version of his story given shortly before his death in 1923. Some accepted Curley as a trustworthy eyewitness (indeed, a participant and survivor of Custer's last battle), while others rejected his recollections as elaborate fabrications. He remains one of the most controversial and intriguing figures in the saga of Little Bighorn.[24]

In most of his accounts Curley claimed to have stuck by Boyer when the other Crows turned back—having witnessed Reno's defeat in the valley—and to have accompanied Boyer in the initial stages of Custer's fight. Several times Curley described an attempt by Custer's forces to charge across the ford at the mouth of Medicine Tail Coulee, the repulse of which precipitated a beleaguered withdrawal to the final battlefield. Sometimes he described the advance of several companies toward the river, and at other times he implied that the Gray Horse Troop (Company E) had been detached for that purpose while Custer led the other companies northward. Occasionally, he made no mention of a charge at the ford and implied that the heavy fighting had commenced on the high ground farther

north, at Finley-Finckle Ridge or Calhoun Hill. At this point, according to several of Curley's interviews, Boyer urged him to make his escape from Custer's doomed command. Heading east, he watched the final stages of the battle from a high ridge and ultimately made his way to the mouth of the Little Bighorn, where he brought word of the disaster to the steamboat *Far West*.

It is worth noting that in 1919, when Curley told his story to General Hugh Scott in the presence of another scout (White Man Runs Him), his account varied little from those of the other Crows. In this version the scouts remained on the ridge overlooking the valley when Custer turned down a ravine to the right, rode farther north and fired into the village, then turned back when Boyer rode off to rejoin the soldiers. As he rode south, Curley witnessed Reno's retreat from the timber, encountered a group of Arikara running off some horses from the valley onto the bluffs east of the river, and saw "two groups of soldiers" on the ridge north of where Reno later made his stand. At this point Curley left the other Crows in search of water and eventually made his way to the mouth of the Little Bighorn.[25] The presence of both Arikara and soldiers can, in fact, be documented in the vicinity where Curley said he observed them.

At the beginning of Reno's valley fight, prior to the halt and deployment of the skirmish line, about a half-dozen Arikara (or Ree) auxiliaries accompanying the major's battalion went in pursuit of a group of women and children on the east bank of the Little Bighorn. They abandoned that quarry in favor of a substantial herd of Sioux horses, nearly thirty of which they stampeded across the level ground and up the bluffs beyond, followed by a group of Sioux intent on recapturing their animals. The Arikara Strikes Two noted that as he gained the crest, "some soldiers passed by and fired on us by mistake," while Little Sioux described "a few straggling shots" from "the rear of a body of soldiers going downstream."[26] While it is possible that these troopers were the rearguard of one of Custer's battalions, more likely they had fallen behind the rapidly moving column. Another group of Rees, following Custer's trail, encountered two cavalrymen whose horses had given out. The Arikara named Soldier remem-

bered that one trooper was "trying to get his horse up, . . . cursing and swearing, pounding his horse's head with his fists and kicking him under the belly."[27]

The troopers were a "set of fours"—the traditional cavalry squad—consisting of Privates John Brennan, John Fitzgerald, Peter Thompson, and James Watson, members of Company C. Thompson, the only one of the four to leave an account of his experience, noted that Brennan and Fitzgerald had dropped out of the Custer column two miles beyond the lone tepee. Brennan had turned his horse to the rear rather than assist Thompson, whose mount was staggering with exhaustion.[28] Seventh Cavalryman John McGuire later told Walter Camp that it was the general opinion that Brennan and Fitzgerald had turned back "out of cowardice."[29]

Private Watson's horse was also giving out, and Thompson recalled that Sergeant August Finckle of Company C had briefly assessed their predicament before spurring on to catch up with Custer's rapidly moving force. Custer's first courier, Sergeant Kanipe, believed that Watson and Thompson must have fallen behind sometime after he departed with his message and claimed that Thompson's horse was later recovered near the head of Cedar Coulee. Walter Camp, who accepted some but not all of Thompson's story, placed the event somewhere north of Reno's defense site and about two miles south of Custer's final battlefield.[30] Thompson continued on foot for some distance before turning back and eventually joining Reno's and Benteen's companies. Though his published narrative may have been embroidered, Thompson's claim to have encountered a group of Indian scouts herding horses, and a band of hostile Sioux, coincides with the movements of the Rees and their pursuers over the bluff top in the vicinity of Weir Point–Sharpshooter Ridge. In any event the quartet of Company C stragglers were spared the fate of their comrades on Custer's field.

It can be reasonably assumed that once Custer reached Medicine Tail Coulee, at or near the mouth of Cedar Coulee, he turned his column westward toward the river and the village beyond. If his column had crossed the river at Medicine Tail Coulee Ford (also known as Minneconjou Ford and Ford B), the soldiers would have struck the northern end of the encampment, near the Cheyenne circle. Why Custer either was not able to or did not choose to strike there remains one of Little Bighorn's mysteries. It may be, as archaeologist and historian Richard Fox postulates, that the flight of hundreds of noncombatants—by this point thoroughly alarmed by Reno's attack—drew Custer northward in an attempt to cut off their escape.[31] Some students of the battle believe that some soldiers were repulsed in a fight at the ford and that Custer himself may have been fatally wounded there.[32] A more likely scenario is that the column was engaged prior to reaching the ford, causing Custer to deploy all or part of his force onto the heights north of Medicine Tail Coulee.

In their testimony before the Reno Court of Inquiry, military witnesses expressed doubt that any sort of sustained action had occurred at Medicine Tail Coulee Ford. In part, this was because the nearest dead soldier was found a good distance from the riverbank. Lieutenant Godfrey "saw no evidence of fighting" at the ford and said that the first body was "a half or three-quarters of a mile" from that point.[33] Lieutenant DeRudio saw a few tracks of shod horses by the river but no signs of a struggle there. He stated that the nearest soldier corpse was probably "500 yards from the ford" and noted that "the marks on his pants showed he was a trumpeter."[34] The dead man in question may have been Company G trumpeter Henry Dose, who, like Martin, had been attached to Custer's headquarters detail. Henry Petring of Company G informed Walter Camp that Dose "was found half way between Custer and Reno with arrows in his back and sides," and James Boyle, also of Company G, noted that Dose was "found on [the] flat near Ford B between two coulees."[35] The bodies of Corporal John Foley of Company C and First Sergeant James Butler of Company L were also discovered in this sector of the battlefield, although the precise location of their remains and the circumstances of their deaths remain conjectural.

Most Indian accounts imply that little if any fighting occurred at the ford proper and that the combat in Medicine Tail Coulee was brief. Several recalled that Custer's approaching column had initially been discovered by noncombatants fleeing Reno's attack and seeking safety in the hills east of the Little Bighorn.[36] Shave Elk, later known as Thomas Disputed, was among a small group of warriors heading up Medicine Tail Coulee when he encountered Custer's force. "The soldiers came down this coulee toward the river and stopped just a little while, but not long," he remembered, "and the Indians crossed over and attacked them."[37] While several Indian veterans of the battle noted that Custer's men had gotten close enough to the river to fire into the village, a close reading of their stories indicates that this was generally something they assumed rather than witnessed.[38] The majority of warriors had engaged Reno, and by the time they hastened to confront the new soldier threat, Custer was on the ridges east of the Little Bighorn. Those who recalled a brief clash in Medicine Tail placed the event no closer than one-quarter to half a mile from the ford.[39] Many of these warriors would ultimately engage Custer near the river, but at a point some one and a half miles northwest of Medicine Tail, in the vicinity of Deep Ravine and other crossing points beyond Custer Hill.

Because Custer's column was apparently subdivided into two battalions—one commanded by Captain Yates and the other by Captain Keogh—this early phase of the battle may have encompassed two separate engagements. Some Indian accounts support this scenario. Flying By stated that as Custer's force approached the village, "the command divided into two parts."[40] Two Eagles recalled that some of Custer's men approached the river, were engaged prior to reaching the ford, and withdrew to Finley-Finckle Ridge; another group moved across the high ground east of the river to a position on Calhoun Hill.[41] Most students of the battle have come to believe that Yates's battalion (generally assumed to comprise Companies E and F) advanced toward the ford, while Keogh moved over the high ground to the east with his battalion (Companies C, I, and L). Numerous .45-55 shell cases discovered on the ridge a mile northeast of the ford provide clear evidence that soldiers opened fire from that location.

In 1943, about 150 expended shells were located by Edward Luce on a ridge just over half a mile north of Medicine Tail Coulee.

Luce reported that the cases were three to four yards apart and along a line 100 to 150 feet long. Luce interpreted his findings as indicating a brief dismounted action by a portion of Custer's command; "Luce Ridge" may in fact be the site of the first significant firing by Custer's troopers.

In the 1920s, local rancher Joseph Blummer had discovered a similar indication of an action by Custer's command within half a mile of Luce Ridge where the crest that overlooks Medicine Tail Coulee Ford angles northwest toward Custer's final battlefield. Subsequent exploration of the site by Colonel Elwood Nye and R. G. Cartwright yielded more than a hundred expended shells fired by the soldiers, and this position has come to be known as "Nye-Cartwright Ridge."[42] More recently, rancher Henry Weibert found still more shells. Although a precise figure is impossible to determine, the total number of cases recovered on Nye-Cartwright Ridge would seem to be at least three hundred to four hundred and possibly more. The greatest concentration of cases lay in groups along a line about 150 yards long at the point where the ridge begins to slope down to the valley of North Medicine Tail or Deep Coulee.[43] Calhoun Hill is half a mile northwest, and one might reasonably assume that elements of Custer's force—probably Keogh's battalion—engaged warriors harassing the column as the troopers moved northward to the decisive battleground.

A substantial clue to the identity of these Indians is found in the recollections of Cheyenne tribal historian John Stands in Timber, whose grandfathers, Lame White Man and Wolf Tooth, played notable roles in the battle at Little Bighorn. According to Cheyenne oral history, Wolf Tooth, another warrior named Big Foot, and a band of fifty or more Cheyennes first engaged Custer's column—threatening the soldiers from the north while they were "still going down" (presumably down Medicine Tail Coulee). "It was the first skirmish of the battle," Stands in Timber said, "and it did not last very long."[44] Stands in Timber clearly placed this action in the Luce and Nye-Cartwright Ridge sector, where he accompanied historian J. W. Vaughn on a metal-detecting foray that located still more of the soldiers' shells. After this initial clash

the warriors disengaged, and the soldiers continued northward, although the Wolf Tooth–Big Foot band would eventually strike again.

Another Cheyenne, the young warrior Wooden Leg, recalled that three Cheyennes and four Sioux were the first to cross the river and engage Custer's force on a high ridge "about two miles east from the Cheyenne camp." The band was soon joined by other Indians, who "exchanged shots" with the soldiers "at long distance, without anybody being hurt."[45] Wooden Leg was not an eyewitness to this skirmish, but the details are further indication of warriors dogging Custer's movements east of the Little Bighorn River. Though more nuisance than threat at this point in the engagement, the harrying warriors compelled the soldiers to respond with carbine fire, thus buying time for the noncombatants to make their escape from the threatened village. The continued flight of the women and children downriver served to draw Custer northward, as he attempted to maintain his offensive and achieve the victory that he believed lay within his grasp.

MEDICINE TAIL COULEE

The vintage image on the facing page (8.1A) is another Curtis photo of the three Crow scouts, who told him that while Custer watched Reno's fight, they advanced farther north along the bluffs and fired into the village. From left to right, Hairy Moccasin, Goes Ahead, and White Man Runs Him dramatically recreated the moment. They were on the high bluffs just to the south of Medicine Tail Coulee Ford. The view is to the south. Weir Point, mostly obscured in the vintage photo by the horse closest to the men, is clearly visible in the left distance in the modern comparison photo. Erosion has occurred at the edge of the steep bluff; otherwise, the scene is little changed. How long the scouts stayed with Custer's command before turning back has been much debated, and the scene they created here may never have happened.[46] One thing is certain, though: Curtis created a photograph that is more than a thrilling image by a great artist. It is also a historical document of what the three scouts related to him, more accurate than any written word or map.

TOP: *8.2A. White Man Runs Him on the bluffs near Medicine Tail Coulee Ford, photo by Edward S. Curtis, 1907. Courtesy of Museum of New Mexico, Neg. No. 160460.*

BOTTOM: *8.2B. 1997.*

This photograph (8.2A) was taken just to the north of the previous one, with the camera facing in the opposite direction, toward the north. The location again is the high bluffs south of Medicine Tail Coulee Ford, with White Man Runs Him posed as if firing into the village. Just beyond White Man Runs Him, the terrain falls off steeply, down to the mouth of Medicine Tail Coulee and the ford. The horizon line is a bit out of focus in the vintage photo, and the scout blocks part of the view, but the background landmarks are clear in the modern comparison photo. The auto road curves through the left middle distance. The stand of trees in the center background marks the cemetery, the Stone House, and at its far right the visitors center. To the right of the trees, Custer Hill (in shadow) slopes up to its high point and the monument. Once again Curtis has created a visually striking image and a historical record of what White Man Runs Him related, all with one click of the shutter.

Most early theories of the battle focused on Medicine Tail Coulee Ford as the spot where Custer wanted or tried to cross the Little Bighorn River and attack the village. But such a battle at the ford would have caused significant casualties, and historical accounts place only one soldier body anywhere in the general vicinity. Even that fallen trooper was at least a few hundred yards from the crossing. Overall, evidence for a pitched battle at Medicine Tail Coulee Ford is scant.[47]

In recent years, Richard Fox has suggested that while some element of Custer's command did approach the ford and likely drew Indian fire, the withdrawal was not forced but chosen. Facing a rapidly emptying village, Custer may have decided to swing north to cross the river farther downstream and cut off the fleeing noncombatants. To the warriors confronting him, this maneuver may have appeared to be a retreat. But Custer's command was still on the offense

and not under heavy Indian pressure as they headed north, and this action at Medicine Tail Coulee Ford was likely a minor skirmish.

Another explanation can be offered for the ongoing perception that Custer attacked at Medicine Tail Coulee Ford. Quite simply, with its low banks and shallow water, it was an excellent place to cross the river and gain access to the village as these photographs show.

In this 1909 view (8.3A) from the epic work *The Vanishing Race*,[48] a group of Crow chiefs guide their mounts effortlessly across the river. In the modern photo, nothing has changed. Even if the water level had been a bit higher in June 1876, when the battle was fought, Medicine Tail Coulee Ford remains the easiest crossing place on the Little Bighorn River between the Reno-Benteen defense site and Custer Hill. Another psychological factor is the long-held but incorrect belief that the village stretched from the point of Reno's initial attack to the area below Custer Hill, which would place this ford at the village's midpoint. In fact, the Cheyenne circle that marked the northern end of the encampment was actually opposite Medicine Tail Coulee Ford on the day of the battle, but the village moved north that night. Observers shortly after the battle mistook the two adjacent camps for one huge village.[49] Knowing Custer's temperament, most believed that he would have found a spot to charge into the heart of the village, so it is easy to make the assumption that Medicine Tail Coulee Ford *must* have been the place.

TOP RIGHT: *8.3A. "Chiefs Fording the Little Big Horn," by Joseph Dixon, 1909. Courtesy of James Brust.*

BOTTOM RIGHT: *8.3B. 1997.*

THE BUTLER MARKER AND DEEP COULEE ⌒

A SPECIAL INTRIGUE surrounds First Sergeant James Butler of Company L, whose body was found distant from the others amid signs of a desperate struggle. General Godfrey, whose remembrances of the battle have been influential, stated that as the surviving members of the Seventh Cavalry made their way toward Custer's field on the morning of June 28 to face the shock of burying their comrades, "the first dead body we came upon was the body of Sergeant Butler. . . . He had several wounds and he was scalped and otherwise mutilated. . . . When we lifted his body to place it in the shallow grave, we found underneath it a large number of empty cartridge shells. This fact and his several wounds gave evidence that he had sold his life dearly."[1]

Butler's body lay in an isolated location, between Custer Hill and the Reno-Benteen defense site, in or near lower Deep Coulee or the adjacent rise, not far from Medicine Tail Coulee Ford. Was he the first one killed as Custer's command moved northward? Was he the last to fall, racing to get help for his beleaguered comrades? And exactly where had this soldier made his brave and lonely stand? Debate over Butler's death would eventually lead to the moving of his marker, a rare event in the history of the Little Bighorn Battlefield.

The most precise description of Butler's death site was given by Sergeant Stanislas Roy of Company A, a Medal of Honor recipient as a water carrier. Walking a route similar to Godfrey's, he said that the first body found was that of Corporal John Foley of Company C, whose remains were on "the little rise between the two coulees." Roy referred to the elevation between the mouths of Medicine Tail Coulee and Deep Coulee (also known as North Medicine Tail Coulee), a few hundred yards from where the former meets the river at the ford. Foley, he said, lay on the side of the rise toward the "coulee running up to the battlefield," which would be Deep Coulee. Roy continued, "Butler lay 200 or 300 yds. beyond and across the ravine," toward the first group of Company C troopers lying dead on the main battlefield, a location that would place Butler's body off the rise and down into Deep Coulee.[2]

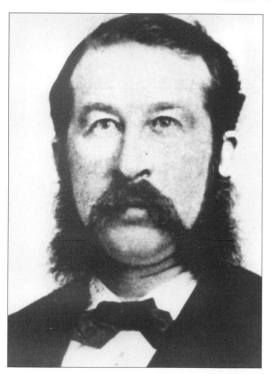

First Sergeant James Butler. Courtesy of Little Bighorn Battlefield National Monument, National Park Service

Roy's distances and description can be confusing. Deep Coulee is far wider than three hundred yards, but its floor is not flat. In fact, just to the north of the rise on which Roy said he saw Foley's body on the way to the main battlefield is a narrow ravine too small to merit a separate name. Roy's route would next have taken him up onto a small hummock, still very much in Deep Coulee, but across that little ravine. A marker for Butler would later sit on that hummock.

Reports also state that other bodies were found in the general vicinity of lower Medicine Tail Coulee, lower Deep Coulee, the rise between them, and the ford nearby, though no widespread engagement apparently took place in that area. A number of witnesses described "the body closest to the river," usually focusing on Medicine Tail Coulee Ford, a place widely theorized to be the site of Custer's initial attack on the village. The man who fell closest to the ford may have been Trumpeter Dose, but "first body" accounts range from two hundred or three hundred yards from the river to a half-mile or more.[3] The latter distance would stretch up into Deep Coulee or onto the adjacent rise, reaching both the sites designated by Godfrey and Roy as having been where Butler's body lay. Different observers traveling different routes would have encountered different first bodies, of course, so great care must be used in attempting to relate these reports to Butler.

In addition, human remains have been found in Deep Coulee over the years. One such find, described in a 1905 newspaper clipping, has been interpreted by former battlefield historian Don Rickey and others as the discovery of Butler's body in Deep Coulee.[4] But in fact, the news piece mentions neither Butler nor Deep Coulee, and no persuasive case can be made for the identification of the body as Butler's.[5] A 1928 find of a human skeleton by Crow tribal member Frank Bethune higher up in Deep Coulee has likewise fueled speculation about Butler, but here, too, no real case can be made that this was the first sergeant's body.[6] Other remains have been discovered in the vicinity as well, all without a definite connection to Sergeant Butler.[7]

Godfrey and Roy were both specific in their identification of Sergeant Butler, though. God-frey said that Butler was the first body encountered; Roy said Foley was first and Butler second. Perhaps God-frey overlooked Foley, making Butler the first body he saw, but the map in his well-known *Century Magazine* article put Butler up on that rise where Roy said he saw Foley.[8]

How are we to reconcile this discrepancy? In the legend accompanying Godfrey's map, he notes that Butler "belonged to Captain Custer's troop, and may have been carrying a message to Reno." Captain Tom Custer served on his brother's staff on the day of the battle but ordinarily commanded Company C— Butler was in Company L. Did Godfrey misidentify the body found on the rise? Interestingly, Foley, the man Roy said was found at that spot, was from Company C. Also, Foley was a corporal, a far more likely candidate to be chosen as a messenger, as Godfrey theorized this man had been, than a first sergeant, such as Butler. Did Godfrey mix up Butler and Foley?

ABOVE: *First Lieutenant Edward S. Godfrey. Courtesy of Brian Pohanka*

BELOW: *Map 9.1. Butler Marker and Deep Coulee*

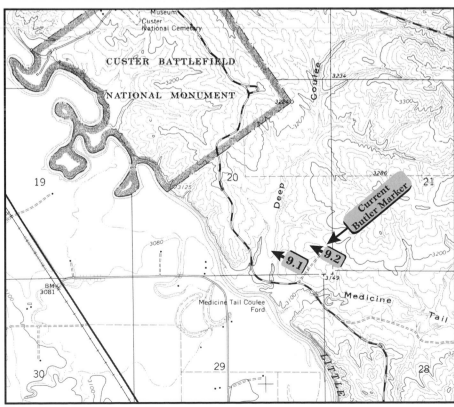

Based on the 1967 USGS topographical map

Finally, one other consideration must be factored in: A number of Indian accounts tell of a soldier who rode off from the main group in an attempt to escape, then shot himself.[9] Could the body on the rise be that trooper? As in so many aspects of the Little Bighorn, the answer eludes us. But the image that endures is of the beleaguered Sergeant Butler, wounded but fighting to the last.

Among the prime sources of information on where Custer's men fell are the individual marble markers that dot the field. Although subject to inaccuracies, the stones are our most reliable witnesses. Captain Sweet apparently never set a marble marker for Sergeant Butler in 1890, though; his report makes no mention of one.[10] The only reference to a marker for Butler prior to the World War I era is a vague mention by early superintendent Eugene Wessinger that an uninscribed stone and wooden stake had once been in place where Sergeant Butler fell, but as of 1916, they could no longer be found.[11]

In 1891, R. B. Marshall mapped the Custer Battlefield for the United States Geological Survey (his map was not published until 1908). He placed Butler on the rise between Medicine Tail Coulee and Deep Coulee, but we have no record of what guided him to that spot. Godfrey's map in *Century Magazine* (published in January 1892) showed Butler's body on the same rise. One might speculate that Marshall and Godfrey had a common source or that Godfrey influenced Marshall, but no real evidence exists for either possibility.

In June 1916, on the occasion of the fortieth anniversary of the battle, General Godfrey visited the battlefield accompanied by Walter Camp, L. A. Huffman, and others. Godfrey placed a wooden stake at the spot where he said Butler had fallen. However, the location of this stake, too, was soon lost, as Wessinger noted: "General Godfrey knows the exact spot where Sergeant Butler fell, he told Mrs. Wessinger this summer, that he put a new stake there but left no information as to the location of the new stake."[12]

Godfrey and Camp wanted to see Butler's death site marked with a stone matching the others on the field. Godfrey asked Wessinger to see to a marker placement and may have contacted officials in Washington, D.C., as well.[13] In the summer of 1917, Camp revis-

ited the battlefield, but no Butler stone had been placed. He again urged Wessinger to obtain one.[14] That autumn, Wessinger wrote to his superiors, "I have located the spot where Sergeant James Butler fell, General Godfrey marked the place with a small wooden stake in June 1916 painted white on one side and written in lead pencil Sergeant Butler, and if it is still desired to put a permanent marker on the spot, I shall be pleased to do so."[15]

Here Wessinger implied that he had located Godfrey's white wooden stake, and given Camp's visit a couple of months earlier, he certainly should have. About two weeks later, in reply to inquiries from Washington, D.C., Wessinger sent a description of how a marble marker for Butler should look but erroneously gave the date June 26, 1876, for the sergeant's death.[16] Evidently, such a stone was furnished, and it was probably placed in Deep Coulee some four hundred yards from the river. However, in late 1919, Camp wrote to Godfrey suggesting that a request be made to Washington for a Butler stone.[17] At that point, Camp seemed unaware that a stone for Butler was on the field, albeit with the wrong date. Perhaps it was never actually placed or was in a spot (i.e., Deep Coulee) where Camp would not have looked for it or expected it to be.

Shortly after, in January 1920, likely at Godfrey's urging, the quartermaster general told Wessinger that a new marker would be furnished for Butler with the correct death date of June 25, 1876.[18] That new, properly dated stone was dispatched the following month, February 1920, with instructions that it replace the misdated one on the field.[19] Wessinger put it on a small hummock in Deep Coulee, presumably at the spot of the earlier wrong-date marker.

This photo pair (9.1A and B) shows the Butler marker in its original location, and the modern comparison photo confirms that it was on a low rise in Deep Coulee. This is a spot consistent with Roy's description of where Butler perished but does not match Godfrey's. The vintage photograph was taken by L. A. Huffman, and the original negative is now at the Montana Historical Society. The society's cataloguing information tentatively dates it as 1916, grouping it with the many other images made by Huffman while at the battlefield with Godfrey and Camp that year.

TOP LEFT: *9.1A. Sergeant Butler marker, photo by L. A. Huffman, circa 1926. Courtesy of Montana Historical Society, #981-195.*

BOTTOM LEFT: *9.1B. 1995.*

But at the time of Huffman's trip to the Little Bighorn in June 1916, no inscribed marble marker for Butler had yet been placed, so this photo must have been made later, perhaps in 1926.[20] Unfortunately, a small clump of grass blocks our view of the date cut into the marble, so we cannot tell if this is the earlier version marked "June 26, 1876," or the later one with Butler's correct day of death.

The Butler marker remained in Deep Coulee until the tenure of Superintendent Luce, who took up his post in 1941. By that time, new artifact finds were reshaping theo-

ries of the battle. Starting with Joseph A. Blummer in 1928 and expanded on by Colonel Elwood Nye and R. G. Cartwright a decade later, investigators found a series of several hundred expended cartridges on a ridge (which now bears the names of the latter two men) southeast of Calhoun Hill.[21] These finds on Nye-Cartwright Ridge indicated that Custer's men had engaged the Indians from this previously unknown battle site. Luce took up the hunt, and in 1943 he found another ridge even farther south and east that contained another one hundred to two hundred empty army cartridge cases grouped at skirmish distance. In a spate of correspondence with other battle researchers in the autumn of 1943, the superintendent excitedly discussed his discovery that summer on what was to become known as Luce Ridge.[22] As he theorized about the significance of his find, he began to question the location of the Butler marker, still in Deep Coulee where Wessinger had placed it more than twenty years earlier. "This Sergeant Butler monument is the sticker," he wrote to fellow researcher William A. Graham. "What I think is, that the marker is placed on the wrong ridge and should be about 600 yards north and east of where it is today."[23]

In 1947, Luce explained his theory to Aubrey Haines, who later became Yellowstone National Park's historian but at that time was its assistant engineer. "Captain Luce . . . told me," Haines said, "that a 1st Sgt. brought up the rear of the troop, and that he thought Butler, in his 'tail-end Charley' role, was shot off his horse while following L-Troop as they moved up the broad ridge between Medicine Tail Coulee and the rough draws that descend from Custer Hill, after Custer's men were turned back from the ford at the mouth of Medicine Tail Creek. In support of that contention, he showed me a line of firing positions farther up that same ridge, which he called 'the Custer find.' . . . The stakes were still in place where Luce had found cartridge cases of a brief delaying fire-fight."[24]

"The Custer find" was what we now call Luce Ridge. In the ensuing years, some confusion has developed about its exact location, but the best evidence shows it to be east and north of the rise on which the Butler marker currently sits.[25] A straight line drawn from Medicine Tail Coulee Ford to Luce Ridge would go right up and over that small elevation near the confluence of Medicine Tail Coulee and Deep Coulee, east of the ford.

In early 1947, while Luce and Yellowstone's chief naturalist, Dave Condon, were working on an interpretive trail sign for Butler, Condon noticed that the marker (then still in Deep Coulee) was 1,200 feet away from the spot designated for it on the 1891 USGS topographical map. They scouted toward the 1891 map location and discovered one live cartridge shell, an expended one, and a specially made horseshoe that they thought had come from an officer's horse (not Butler's). These three finds were made along the way to, but not at, the 1891 USGS Butler site.

Luce said, "We will probably move the marker to where it is shown on the 1891 Geological Map." Referring to Wessinger's uncertainty about the proper site, Luce added, "I also have letters written by former superintendents who said they didn't know where to place the Butler marker, and that [one said] he placed it 'where I think it should be.'"[26]

Having realized that the Butler marker was not in the spot marked for it on the 1891 map, and aware that it had been placed in Deep Coulee by a prior superintendent (Wessinger), who wasn't sure where it belonged, Luce convened a conference to discuss the matter. On June 24 and 25, 1947, he was joined by Casey Barthelmess, George Osten, Charles Kuhlman, and Maurice Frink. They agreed that Butler's marker was not where it was shown on the 1891 map, a fact they confirmed by surveying a line from Weir Point to the Custer monument. The 1891 Butler location was on that line, but the Butler marker in Deep Coulee was not. The conferees rejected the idea that Butler had been used as a messenger, believing he would have been stationed in the rear of his troop and should have fallen closer to where they were known to have operated. No mention was made in the 1947 conference report of any artifacts or of an existing marker, pipe, or stake at the 1891 site. They unanimously recommended that the Butler marker "be moved from its present location to the spot in which it is shown on the U.S.G.S. map."[27]

Luce turned to Haines, who in his role as assistant engineer at Yellowstone helped with projects at Custer's battlefield. "In the last week of August, 1947—Captain Luce showed me a topographic map . . . and asked me if I could locate on the ground the place shown as the grave of 1st Sgt. Butler," Haines said. "The next day I got out my transit and steel tape . . . and I staked out the site shown on the map."[28] The details of Haines's survey, performed on August 27, 1947, are confirmed in a detailed memorandum written by Edmund B. Rogers, Yellowstone National Park superintendent. Distances between the existing Butler marker, Medicine Tail Coulee Ford, and the newly surveyed Butler gravesite on the 1908 edition of the 1891 USGS map were documented. The small scale of the map led Rogers to believe that the stake placed by Haines at the surveyed spot was accurate within thirty feet of the location designated in 1891.[29]

Within weeks, Luce sought permission to relocate the Butler marker. On September 16, 1947, he submitted a report of the June conference, along with other historical evidence, to his superiors at the National Park Service. His request was granted on October 6, 1947.[30] It would be two years, however, before the task was accomplished. On July 21, 1949, a group of interested battle students moved the Butler marker from the spot it had occupied in lower Deep Coulee to the 1891 map site, on the rise separating that drainage from Medicine Tail Coulee. Their report, prepared by Major George H. Zacherle on August 3, stated their reason: "According to old maps showing the locations of those killed during the Battle, the marker was misplaced."[31]

A story soon took hold that Captain Luce moved the Butler marker because he had discovered an iron pipe stuck in the ground at the new spot. In his classic work, *Legend into History,* published in 1951, Charles Kuhlman speaks of "the iron stake discovered by Captain Luce in 1948."[32] In a 1974 review article on the Butler marker, R. L. "Pinky" Nelson elaborated on this story. In his version, Luce had located an iron stake "some distance away from the Butler marker" in the early 1940s. Convinced that this pipe represented Butler's original gravesite, Luce reputedly had Haines plot its location and found: "Eureka! The iron stake was in exactly the place indicated as Sgt. Butler's grave on the map."[33] Nelson created a dramatic story but got the events out of order, as the surveying had occurred before any stake marked the spot. Even Major Zacherle, who wrote the official report of the 1949 marker-moving team, expanded on this erroneous story in 1977: "While digging the hole for relocating the marker several empty cartridge cases were discovered, showing that Luce's deductions were correct and that Butler had defended himself to the last."[34] But Zacherle's 1949 report had made no mention of artifacts at the new Butler site. It did, however, reveal the possible source of Zacherle's later

confusion. After the group had replaced Butler's marker, they proceeded to Luce Ridge and found some cartridges there.[35] Twenty-eight years later, Zacherle had telescoped events and mistakenly recalled that the cartridge case discoveries were at the Butler site when they were actually at Luce Ridge.

Is there any basis for the notion that Luce and his colleagues were guided to their new Butler spot by any vintage artifact, be it an iron pipe, a stake, or a cartridge? Luce never made such an assertion. In addition, Luce kept a series of artifact maps, which remain in the archives of Little Bighorn Battlefield National Monument. Those maps show no relic finds at the Butler marker site.[36] Haines said that Luce simply asked him to survey the 1891 Butler location on the ground, without mentioning any iron pipe or artifact find. Indeed, when Haines identified the spot, nothing was there—no pipe, stake, or cartridges on or in the barren ground. He simply placed his own wooden stake to mark the location for Luce.[37] Furthermore, historian Ken Hammer later asked Luce what the basis for the relocation had been. The superintendent replied that triangulation or some other surveying technique had been used; he made no mention of artifact finds.[38]

How, then, did the iron pipe story arise? One clue is contained in a 1948 letter from George Osten to Earl Brininstool. Osten, who was present at the 1947 battlefield conference and knew the events well, said, "The National Park Service had a couple of surveyors who made a survey in accordance with the Marshall [1891 USGS] map . . . thus locating the site of the Butler marker. . . . We drove out to the spot, which had been indicated by an iron stake in the ground, and Luce intends to have this marker rest there."[39] Here the iron pipe makes its first appearance, presented in its proper context, as a marker of the 1891 map–derived Butler site *after* it was surveyed. Haines had placed a wooden stake at the surveyed spot in 1947. Perhaps Luce replaced it with a more permanent metal pipe when he realized that he was not going to move the marker that season. For others who joined the story after that point, it would be easy to misunderstand that the pipe was a recent place marker and not a historic artifact. The evidence is overwhelming, though, that the Butler

marker was moved to its present location by Superintendent Luce in 1949 solely on the basis of the 1891 USGS topographical map and not because of any artifact finds at the site (see map 9.1).

So—after all this confusion over his burial marker—where did First Sergeant James Butler die? Whatever the truth, the Butler marker would remain in Deep Coulee for more than thirty years, until Luce brought things full circle by moving it to the location marked on the 1891 map.

One piece of evidence, though, has not previously been studied—a historical photograph. When Godfrey placed a stake at the Butler site in 1916, photographer L. A. Huffman was there to capture the scene. This photo shows Godfrey, Camp, and a soldier holding a small hatchet; the trio are looking at a white wooden stake they seem to have just placed in the ground. Camp was present when Godfrey placed the stake in 1916,[40] and Huffman was at the battlefield with the two men only in that year, so we can safely assume that this image records the historic event.

This photo has received little attention, but more than any other document, it can tell us where Godfrey marked Butler's gravesite in 1916. The picture shows the men at a high elevation; when we took it onto the field, we quickly ascertained that it had not been taken anywhere in Deep Coulee. Ascending the rise between Deep Coulee and Medicine Tail Coulee, we went to the current Butler marker. We were then at the proper elevation, but this was not the right spot either. In the 1916 photo the men seem to be at the edge of an elevation, with a steep drop-off behind them. Remaining up on the rise, we walked toward the side that overlooks Deep Coulee and soon found the spot where the 1916 photo had been taken, about 125 yards west of the current Butler marker.

The 1916 photo confirms that Godfrey, indeed, identified that rise between Deep Coulee and Medicine Tail Coulee as the site of Sergeant Butler's death, just as he had on his 1892 map. The small scale of that map made precise location impossible—it simply confirmed that Godfrey had placed Butler's body somewhere on that rise. The photo, however, gives us a clearer picture. Even though memories might dim over the forty years that had passed between the time of the battle and the 1916 visit, the landscape at the edge of the rise overlooking Deep Coulee is different from that at the current Butler site in the middle of that elevation. Even if he could not recall the precise spot, Godfrey would likely have remembered that the body he found was along the edge and not in the center. So the 1891 map site where the Butler marker has been since 1949, located in the middle of the rise, is not the spot identified by Godfrey.

Interestingly, Sergeant Roy's description of finding a body on the side of the rise toward "the coulee running up to the battle-field" (which would be Deep Coulee), closely matches Godfrey's spot, but Roy said it was Corporal John Foley that he had found there.[41] Since Godfrey said it was Butler, and Roy said it was Foley, we are uncertain who the man was. But in all likelihood, someone died at or near that spot.

The mysteries that arose along the Little Bighorn River on those desperate days in late June of 1876 are not solved easily, and we still know neither the site nor the circumstances of Sergeant Butler's death with any certainty. Initially unmarked, his gravestone sat first in Deep Coulee and now sits on the adjacent rise, but the evidence for either location is weak, and a 1994 survey of both the old and the new site by Douglas Scott and Douglas McChristian revealed nothing.[42] No archaeological research has been conducted on the rise overlooking Deep Coulee where Huffman's camera captured Godfrey placing his white wooden stake for Butler in 1916. Would a survey of that spot finally yield up Butler's remains? It would be foolhardy to make such a prediction, but certainly the effort should be made. In the meantime, First Sergeant James Butler and his moving marker, like all mysteries involving brave men at the Little Bighorn, will continue to intrigue us.

10

FINLEY-FINCKLE RIDGE ~

THE SOUTHERNMOST of the marble markers dotting Custer's final battlefield stand on either side of the modern park road leading to the Reno-Benteen Defense Site. Twenty-two stones are placed along a ridge running south-southwest from Calhoun Hill, fifteen of them positioned on the lower end of the elevation not far from where the park road passes through the boundary fence. Variously designated Calhoun Ridge or Finley-Finckle Ridge, this is clearly a place where soldiers fought and fell. Another eight markers, not readily visible unless one leaves

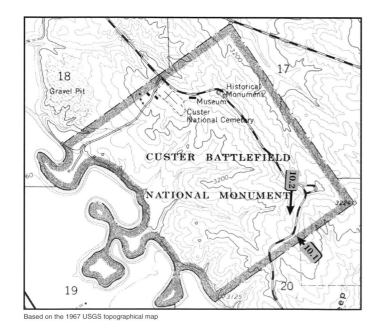

Based on the 1967 USGS topographical map

Map 10.1. Finley-Finckle Ridge

the road, are scattered west-northwest along a swale leading from the flank of the ridge toward Deep Ravine. Archaeological evidence confirms that an engagement occurred in the upper reaches of Calhoun Coulee, as this feature has come to be known.

The slain soldiers interred in this sector were possibly those referred to by Captain Godfrey in his testimony at the 1879 Reno Court of Inquiry. "There were some 15 or 20 bodies buried in one place by my company," Godfrey recalled. "All the troops I found there appeared to have made a stand." The captain thought that these dead men belonged "to different companies" but conceded that "all were not recognizable." Godfrey supposed that "they had been dismounted there and been fighting," as he noted "a good many cartridge shells."[1]

A significant clue to the identity of these men was provided by Little Bighorn veteran Daniel Kanipe, the sergeant whose dispatch with a message to the pack train spared him the fate of his comrades in Custer's command. Corresponding with Walter Camp, Kanipe described how he had identified the bodies of fellow Company C Sergeants Jeremiah Finley and August Finckle on the ridge below Calhoun Hill and the remains of First Sergeant Edwin Bobo among the dead of Captain Keogh's company. During a 1909 visit to the battlefield, Kanipe pointed out to Camp the markers that he believed designated where his friends had perished. Finley and Finckle lay near their slain horses, Finley at the southern end of the ridge and Finckle between that point and Calhoun Hill. Both were mutilated and "stuck full of arrows." Additional insight into Finley's fate appears in letters from Company M survivors Jean Baptiste Gallenne and John Dolan. Gallenne noted Finley "with his head cut off, after having been scalped," while Dolan "saw a man named Finley, whose head was crushed in, and by whom were lying some twenty of his own cartridge shells."[2]

Given the nature of the 1870s cavalry tactics, the presence of two of the three Company C sergeants implies that the company was deployed on Finley-Finckle Ridge. If the nominal commander of Company C, Captain Thomas Custer, was attached to his brother's staff—as a strong body of evidence suggests—command of the company on June 25 would have devolved to Second Lieutenant Henry M. Harrington.[3] Harrington's body was never identified, but one might reasonably suppose that he perished with his troopers on or near the ridge. In a traditional company formation, First Sergeant Edwin Bobo would have been on the right of the line and the acting second sergeant (likely Finley) on the left. If Harrington had chosen to deploy his company in platoons, the officer would have had two options: to supervise two platoons, one under Bobo and the other under Finley, or to take personal command of one platoon, giving command of the other to Bobo. The fact that Bobo was able to extricate himself from the slaughter on Finley-Finckle Ridge may indicate that a portion of the command, possibly a mounted platoon, did likewise.

Further evidence for this scenario comes from Theodore Goldin of Company G, who recalled seeing the hoofprints of "shod horses in broken order" leading from the Finley-Finckle position back toward the high ground of Calhoun Hill. Goldin also noted a "faint trail" of cavalry horses leading from Finley-Finckle Ridge toward Deep Ravine. The latter may have been made by mounted soldiers cut off amid the debacle or by the stampeded animals of troopers who had dismounted to fight on foot.[4]

In the last two decades a number of Little Bighorn scholars have come to believe that the soldiers who fell in the Finley-Finckle Ridge area were not killed in a pressured retreat from Medicine Tail Coulee Ford but rather were members of Company C who were deployed there from an earlier position on or near Calhoun Hill. While any reconstruction of Custer's last fight is by nature speculative, a significant body of evidence can be presented to support this hypothesis. The recollections of Indian veterans of the battle in particular lend credence to this view.

According to this theory, the southern portion of the battlefield, centered on Calhoun Hill, was occupied by the battalion commanded by Captain Keogh, comprising Companies C, I, and L. The locations of the dead soldiers, Indian recollections, and archaeological findings suggest that Captain Yates's battalion—Companies E and F—operated some distance from Keogh's command, at least as far north as the present-day national cemetery and probably beyond that point. Custer likely accompanied Yates and may have been seeking a ford that would enable his command to strike and capture noncombatants fleeing downriver in reaction to Reno's attack on the village's southern end.

With many warriors having initially engaged Reno's battalion on the skirmish line, in the timber, and in the chaotic pursuit back across the Little Bighorn, Indian pressure took some time to build against Custer's five companies. Keogh probably enjoyed half an hour to forty-five minutes of relative tactical stability, and the deployment of Company C must have been a controlled and seemingly logical reaction to the situation as he saw it. Most likely the move was intended to check the growing number of Indians gathering on Greasy Grass Ridge, an elevation that parallels the river some four-tenths of a mile southwest of Calhoun Hill. Battle artifacts indicate that Greasy Grass Ridge was a substantial warrior firing position, while the basinlike depression behind it could easily have concealed a force several hundred strong. Typically eschewing head-on mounted charges in favor of stealthy infiltration, the Sioux and Cheyenne used the topography to their advantage. From Greasy Grass Ridge they could work their way north toward Deep Ravine as well as eastward into the tributary of the ravine now known as Calhoun Coulee.

The stone at the southern end of Finley-Finckle Ridge that marks where Sergeant Finley died is some 350 yards from Greasy Grass Ridge, a distance well within range of the troopers' Springfield carbines, while the upper portion of Calhoun Coulee is even closer. Unfortunately for the men of Company C, their sally prompted a determined and ultimately decisive reaction from their defiant foe. Urged on by the Cheyenne war leader Lame White Man and other stalwarts, the Indians lashed out at the troopers in a counterattack that inspired simultaneous forays by warriors elsewhere on the field who caught sight of the impetuous onslaught.[5]

A number of Camp's Indian informants recalled how the charge drove the troopers from Finley's position back toward Calhoun Hill, and Camp incorporated the event in his evolving theory of the Custer fight. Two Eagles noted that as the embattled troopers retreated, "some of the soldiers were mounted and some were dismounted. The most of those dismounted had lost their horses." In other words, the led horses of the dismounted men were stampeded. At close quarters and in a pursuit the intrepid warriors were in their element. Yellow Nose, a Cheyenne who gained renown for capturing a cavalry guidon in the victory over Custer, likely performed the deed in this phase of the battle. His friend Brave Bear remembered that "Yellow Nose and 4 others rode right in among the first company that dismounted, and scattered the company in every direction."[6]

This sudden and dramatic turn of events had dire consequences for Custer's entire command, most immediately for the men of Company L, positioned atop Calhoun Hill.

Seen in this photo pair (10.1A and B) is the first cluster of marble markers found on the Custer field when approaching from the south, an area now known as Finley-Finckle Ridge. The view is to the northwest, with the monument on Custer Hill seen in the center distance. In this area Kanipe identified the bodies of Jeremiah Finley and August Finckle. Kanipe told Camp, "The first dead soldier [on the main battlefield] was Sergeant Finley of my own company. . . . His body was stuck full of arrows."[7] Kanipe pointed out Finley's stone to Camp, who, in turn, marked it on one of his maps of the battlefield.[8] Camp's

map shows the middle marker of the group of three in the left foreground (arrow) to be Finley's death site although the marker is inscribed as an unknown. The perspective in the photo is confusing—that middle marker is the most southerly and thus the site that would have been encountered first as the men of Reno's command made their way toward the main field. Also identified by Kanipe and mapped by Camp was the gravesite of Sergeant Finckle. His stone, too, is marked as an un-known. It can also be seen in the 1894 photo. That view shows two groups of three markers each in the foreground. Beyond the grouping on the right are three more stones in the middle distance, the rightmost of which is Finckle's (double arrow).

The modern photo, taken in 1995, provides some interesting comparisons. The monument on Custer Hill is visible in the same spot, but to its left are many changes along the horizon. In the 1894 view, the background landscape is bare except for some of the early grave markers in the national cemetery. Not even the Stone House, completed in November of 1894,[9] can yet be seen. The modern photo shows the visitors center, the Stone House, and a much-expanded national cemetery, all surrounded by trees. Closer to the camera position, the modern park road bisects the group of markers. The location of the three markers in the left foreground, with Finley's in the middle, is unchanged. The Finckle marker is likewise in its original position but is obscured by a bush in the 1995 view.

Dramatically changed, though, is the group of three markers in the right foreground, the middle one of which was missing in 1995. The authors reported this discovery to officials at the Little Bighorn Battlefield National Monument. Subsequent research by seasonal park ranger Michael Donahue revealed the original marker base still present below the ground, and Superintendent Neil Mangum had the marker replaced in 2000, restoring this group of stones on Finley-Fickle Ridge to its original configuration.[10]

In pair (10.2A and B) the same grouping of markers on Finley-Finckle Ridge is viewed from the opposite side. The view is to the south, toward the Reno-Benteen defense area, and away from Custer Hill and the cemetery. The marker for Sergeant August Finckle is

TOP: *10.2A. "Markers west of Calhoun Hill," photograph by Walter Camp, circa 1908. Courtesy of Little Bighorn Battlefield National Monument, National Park Service, #11262.*

BOTTOM: *10.2B. 2000.*

now the closest to the camera, leftmost of the group of three in the left foreground (double arrow). Highest on the little knoll in the left background is the group of three that includes Sergeant Jeremiah Finley's stone, visible in the middle of that small grouping (arrow).

In the modern photo the Finckle marker is in the same spot that it was in the vintage view, but it is now partly obscured by a bush. Vegetation has increased in general, almost totally blocking our view of the far right marker in that group of three containing the Finckle stone. Some grading has taken place to create the modern automobile road, and a culvert now drains water beneath the road-bed. Just above the culvert is the small grouping from which a marker was missing. Three are visible in that location in the vintage photo, but only two in the modern one. Shortly after our comparison photo was taken in September 2000, that missing marker was replaced.

I I

CALHOUN HILL ~

A S THE BURIAL parties made their way across Custer's field on June 28, 1876, those whose course took them over the elevation at the southern end of Custer Ridge known today as Calhoun Hill were impressed that the soldiers who perished there had apparently put up a considerable fight. The amount of expended ammunition, evidenced by the shell cases of Springfield carbines, the patterns of those cases on the ground, and the location of the bodies indicated a degree of tactical cohesion not apparent elsewhere on the battlefield. At this point, most of the dead were men of Company L, commanded by First Lieutenant James Calhoun, the husband of Custer's sister, Margaret. Calhoun's body was found at the northern edge of his company's position, and nearby lay the corpse of his junior officer, Second Lieutenant John J. Crittenden.

In his testimony before the Reno Court of Inquiry, Lieutenant Edgerly stated, "We found Lieutenant Calhoun who was in the rear of the first platoon of his company. About 20 or 30 feet from there was Lieutenant Crittenden lying in the rear of the second platoon, both about 15 or 20 feet in [the] rear of their platoons." This would seem to indicate not only that the officers of

Company L had died in their proper place, but also that the two platoons had been fighting back to back, in a defensive perimeter. Lieutenant Edward Maguire, General Terry's engineer officer, provided further evidence of this, reporting, "The men and their empty cartridge shells were found in a semi-circle around the crest."[1]

At the Reno Court of Inquiry, Captain Moylan, Calhoun's brother-in-law, related his impression that Company L had been "killed in regular position of skirmishers." Moylan testified that he had counted twenty-eight shells around one body and that other shells were scattered between the intervals of the slain skirmishers. In a letter to Lieutenant Calhoun's brother, Moylan noted that he had counted forty shell cases by one of the corpses. If fired by a single individual,

LEFT: *First Lieutenant James Calhoun. Courtesy of Little Bighorn Battlefield National Monument, National Park Service*

RIGHT: *Second Lieutenant John J Crittenden. Courtesy of Little Bighorn Battlefield National Monument, National Park Service*

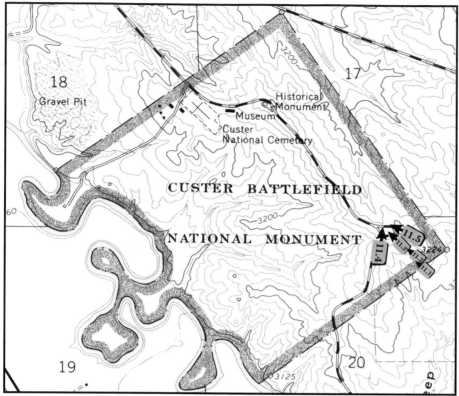

Based on the 1967 USGS topographical map

Map 11.1. Calhoun Hill

place to do so. In some respects the hill is a smaller version of the Reno-Benteen defense site. While any hypothesis is theoretical at best, one might speculate that had Custer established all five of his companies on Calhoun Hill, their concentrated firepower might well have held his numerically superior foe at bay. That he did not do this seems further confirmation of the theory that Yates's battalion continued northward in an offensive posture while Keogh's three companies assumed a holding position on and near Calhoun Hill, ready to deal with any developing warrior threat and to coordinate with Benteen's battalion after their anticipated arrival.

Assuming that Custer's command operated in two battalions in the earlier action at Medicine Tail Coulee—Yates moving toward the ford and Keogh onto Nye-Cartwright Ridge—all five companies may have subsequently united for a time on Calhoun Hill before Yates pulled off to the north. Conversely, the two battalions may never have reunited prior to the last, decisive stages of the battle. Several of Walter Camp's Indian informants indicate just such a division of Custer's force. Flying By noted that the soldiers divided into "two parts," while Two Eagles described one group retiring from the vicinity of the ford to Finley-Finckle Ridge, with another group moving from the Nye-Cartwright position to Calhoun Hill.[3]

Both battalions of Custer's command appear to have arrived on what was destined to be their final battleground with military cohesion intact, an indication that the number of warriors had yet to reach alarming proportions. Following the battle, Lieutenant E. J. McClernand, Second Cavalry, noted shod hoofprints signifying that "a double column of fours"—possibly the two companies under Yates—had moved from South Medicine Tail Coulee, across a rise to North Medicine Tail Coulee (or Deep Coulee) and from there onto the Calhoun-Finley elevation. Lights, a Minneconjou veteran of the fight, remembered that the troopers were "in company formation and apparently in good order" and stated that although "shooting was indulged in by both soldiers and warriors," the action "was not very vigorous."[4]

Following what may have been a long-

that number of ejected shells would indicate that the trooper in question had exhausted the available rounds in his cartridge belt. Clearly Company L had done a good deal of firing before the Lakota and Cheyenne took their position.[2]

Visitors to the Little Bighorn Battlefield who examine its terrain and its military potential cannot help but be struck by how natural a defensive position Calhoun Hill is. Nearly as high in elevation as Custer Hill—the site of the Last Stand half a mile to the northwest—the crest of Calhoun Hill is slightly bowl shaped, and thus would have provided a modicum of cover to the troopers deployed there. The rear of the hill descends to a depression that runs northwest some three hundred yards to the point where the dead of Keogh's Company I were found. Horse Holders' Ravine, as this feature is known, was most likely just that: a place where Company L's led horses were concealed under the supervision of the "number four" trooper of each set of fours.

If Custer had intended to assume a defensive posture following the initial clashes near Medicine Tail Coulee Ford and on Luce and Nye-Cartwright ridges, Calhoun Hill and its environs would seem to have provided a good range firefight with the Wolf Tooth–Big Foot band—those fifty to seventy-five Cheyennes east of the river who had been harassing Custer's northward advance—Keogh's battalion pulled off of Nye-Cartwright Ridge and headed for Calhoun Hill, half a mile to the northwest. Archaeological findings reveal that a portion of Keogh's command was initially posted on the southeastern flank of Calhoun Hill, as shell cases and bullets of both soldiers and Indians were intermingled there.[5] The occupation of this position made sound military sense, as the elevation commanded the northern portion of Deep Coulee, denying the warriors that natural avenue of infiltration. Company C may have been dispatched down Finley-Finckle Ridge at this point in the action to check those warriors who were moving from the southern reaches of Deep Coulee to the cover of Greasy Grass Ridge. With Company I held in reserve, Keogh's battalion had assumed an almost textbook deployment reflective of tactical cohesion rather than desperation.

The situation changed dramatically with the sudden assault on Company C sparked by Lame White Man and other warrior leaders. Young Two Moon remembered how this "first charge" drove the soldiers "to the top" of Calhoun Hill.[6] But that formidable position did not immediately fall to the inspirited Sioux and Cheyenne. Calhoun's troopers clearly maintained a steady rate of fire that may well have accounted for the "volleys" heard by Reno's and Benteen's men. Pulling back to the crest of the hill, Company L adjusted its platoon lines to face the growing threat to the west, covering the retreat of the surviving Company C men; in so doing they yielded their earlier position on the southeastern slope to a growing number of warrior foes. Archaeological surveys have revealed that many of those warriors were well armed with rapid-fire Henry rifles, blazing away at Calhoun's skirmishers some two hundred yards distant. This strategic Indian strong point has become known as "Henryville."[7]

Numbers and firepower soon began to tell in the Indians' favor. Maintaining the initiative, warriors used the cover of ridgelines and ravines east of Custer Ridge to infiltrate behind Calhoun's position, taking Keogh's

Two Moon. Courtesy of Little Bighorn Battlefield National Monument, National Park Service

Company I under fire and threatening the led horses of both companies. When the vulnerable mounts were stampeded, as many were in this phase of the battle, they took with them the troopers' reserve ammunition, a factor that both General Godfrey and the Hunkpapa war leader Gall believed to be the decisive factor in the fight for Calhoun Hill. As the warriors swept through Calhoun's collapsing perimeter, Gall saw the soldiers "shot down in line where they stood."[8]

Their officers dead, the remnants of Companies C and L scattered northward through the defile of Horse Holders' Ravine, men and animals falling to bullet and arrow, or struck down by club and lance, as the tide of disaster rolled down upon the embattled troopers of Company I.

TOP: *11.1A. View of Calhoun Hill, photo by Christian Barthelmess, circa 1896. Courtesy of Montana Historical Society, #PAc 95-68, C-422.*

BOTTOM: *11.1B. 1996.*

OPPOSITE TOP: *11.2A. "Custer Battlefield, Montana," photo by F. Jay Haynes, 1894. Courtesy of Montana Historical Society, #H-3150..*

OPPOSITE BOTTOM: *11.2B. 1995*

The vintage photo of this pair (11.1A) was taken by Christian Barthelmess on Calhoun Hill in the mid-1890s, looking north toward Custer Hill, which can be seen in the center distance. Four marble markers are prominent in the foreground, with another small grouping to the left of those and a bit farther back. An additional marker is on the far right of the picture, although it is difficult to see because of the lightness of the image. In the distance beyond these markers arrayed across Calhoun Hill, many additional stones are seen in the area defended by Keogh, trailing toward Custer Hill. In the left background, the Stone House and cemetery are visible. A careful look at that section of the photograph reveals an obelisk to the right of the Stone House: This is the Fort C. F. Smith marker (see chapter 15).

Calhoun Hill was a fine defensive position,

with a commanding view of the lower elevations to the southeast and southwest, and evidence for organized skirmish-line fighting is stronger here than in other parts of the field. The first skirmish line was oriented in an east-west alignment, and those troopers, firing to the south, would have been facing the camera in these photos as they defended themselves against warriors in the Henryville area. The skirmish line later reformed in a north-south orientation, the soldiers firing toward the west, or left in the photos. This change in position was likely necessitated by the upsurge in combat in the Greasy Grass Ridge and Calhoun Coulee sectors.[9]

Despite the heavy fighting, the photos show surprisingly few markers on Calhoun Hill. Although both Company L officers perished on the hill, many of the men apparently extricated themselves and made their way to the Keogh area.

In the modern comparison photo, the auto road runs horizontally through the foreground of the picture. The four prominent markers closest to the camera are in the same positions, though the one on the right of the group is partly obscured by an interpretive sign. The isolated marker on the far right edge of the Barthelmess view is clearly seen, still in the same spot. The markers behind and to the left of the four prominent ones are present, but the ground was raised to create the roadbed, putting those stones almost completely out of sight in the modern photo. Custer Hill and the monument are visible just where they were in the center background. On the far left, trees fill the cemetery area, obscuring the Stone House, but the visitors center, opened in 1952, is readily seen.

In this 1894 photograph by F. J. Haynes (11.2A), taken several years earlier than the preceding vintage photo, the view is in the same direction but the camera is closer to the prominent group of four markers in the foreground. Visible over the leftmost of that group of four are two stones, close to each other, that are the markers for Lieutenants Calhoun and Crittenden. The close positioning of the bodies of these two officers of Company L and the fact that each was behind a different platoon of the company provide further evidence of tactical stability on Calhoun Hill.

The modern comparison photo (11.2B) gives a good view of the sweep of the auto road through the Calhoun Hill loop. Again we see the interpretive marker, which has since been removed. Much less prominent, both because vegetation has increased and because the present generation of markers is shorter, the two stones for Calhoun and Crittenden can still be seen above the leftmost of the foreground group. They sit just to the northwest of the auto road. The background landscape shows the visitors center, cemetery, Stone House, and surrounding trees.

Locke's 1895 view (11.3A) was taken in the same direction as the previous two historical photos but closer yet to the group of four markers that fill the foreground. The paired markers in the middle distance are those for Calhoun and Crittenden. To the left of that pair and the two behind them, the terrain enters into a depression that is relatively well hidden from view. This is Horse Holders' Ravine, the naturally sheltered area where Captain Keogh's Company I may have waited in reserve during the early fighting on Calhoun Hill and where the horses likely were hidden.

Crittenden's marker, accompanied by a footstone, is seen on the left of this 1912 photograph by Elsa Spear (11.4A). Spear captioned this marker "Lieut. Crittenden's grave," while written beneath Calhoun's stone on the right is "Lieut. Calhoun marker." The words below this image are correct. Calhoun's body had been recovered in 1877 and moved to Fort Leavenworth, Kansas, so the marble memorial simply noted the spot where he had fallen. But in 1912, Crittenden's body still lay beneath his marker and this was truly his grave until his remains, along with the headstone

The body of Lieutenant Calhoun was found after the battle surrounded by shell casings from his revolver, which indicated close-range fighting.[10] Nearby lay the body of Lieutenant Crittenden of the Twentieth Infantry, who had been assigned to the Seventh Cavalry for the summer campaign against the Sioux and Cheyenne. Crittenden had a glass left eye—the aftermath of an injury suffered when a cartridge exploded in his face while he was hunting at Fort Abercrombie, Dakota Territory, on October 25, 1875. Eight months later, that glass eye, shattered by an arrow, would aid in the identification of the young lieutenant's body.[11]

The bodies of all the soldiers killed in the battle received a hasty burial after the fighting had ceased. A year later, in the spring of 1877, the army sent an expedition to the Little Bighorn to recover the remains of the officers. General Crittenden wrote to General Sheridan: "I respectfully request that the body of my son . . . be left in the grave in which he was buried, and on the field where he fell. I will be very grateful if the party removing the bodies will pile up stones or in any simple way make my son's grave so that the spot can be identified, as I hope at some future time to place a headstone over my boy."[12] Thus, Crittenden was left as the only officer buried on the battlefield.

that had honored him, were moved to the battlefield cemetery and reburied with full military honors on September 11, 1931.[13]

A story would later surface that Crittenden's body was moved to the national cemetery to make way for construction of the auto road loop through the Calhoun Hill sector of the battlefield. When family members questioned the propriety of the removal of the body, they were reassured that the superintendent had moved Lieutenant Crittenden's grave to the cemetery so that it might be better cared for and that it had not impeded the roadway.[14] The modern comparison photo bears out this explanation. The auto road is behind the camera position, and the current Crittenden marker, placed in 1938 at the site of his original headstone after his reburial in the cemetery, is well away from the roadbed.[15]

Photo 11.5A shows that at one time, a barbed-wire enclosure surrounded Crittenden's grave. Probably meant to protect the gravesite, it had instead fallen into disrepair, creating a haunting image. This picture clearly shows that the headstone, privately supplied by the Crittenden family, was beveled and thinner than the standard markers used on the field, and a smaller marble stone was in place at the foot of the grave. The view is to the north, with Custer Hill and the monument visible on the horizon just above the footstone. In the modern photo, the current marker is in the same spot as the original headstone; the footstone and fencing are gone. More vegetation is present, but the scene is equally desolate.

TOP: *11.4A. "Lieut. Crittenden's grave, Lieut. Calhoun marker," photo by Elsa Spear, 1912. Courtesy of Paul and Teresa Harbaugh Collection.*

CENTER: *11.4B. 1998.*

BOTTOM LEFT: *11.5A. Crittenden's grave, photographer and date unknown. Courtesy of Glen Swanson.*

BOTTOM RIGHT: *11.5B. 1995.*

12

THE KEOGH SECTOR ⌒

WITH THE EXCEPTION of Custer Hill, the largest collection of marble stones on the Little Bighorn Battlefield marks the point where Captain Myles W. Keogh of Company I perished among troopers of his command on the eastern face of Battle Ridge. More than forty markers are clustered in several distinct groups on the gradual slope that rises above the northern end of Horse Holders' Ravine, eighteen of them around the stone bearing Keogh's name. About thirty others are scattered northwestward in the direction of Custer Hill, with nine stones on the western or river face of Battle Ridge. Today, as was true in 1876, the pattern evokes the image of a defensive stand, followed by a beleaguered retreat and the near-annihilation of Keogh's soldiers as the survivors attempted to reach the site of the "Last Stand."

After identifying the bodies of his fellow sergeants Finley and Finckle, Daniel Kanipe came upon the horse of Company C's First Sergeant Edwin Bobo in the ravine between Calhoun and Keogh's position.

Survivors of Companies C and L seemingly had fallen back toward Keogh's Company I, taking casualties along the way. As Sergeant Kanipe identified the fallen, he observed a "pile of men lying around Captain Keogh," First Sergeant Edwin Bobo of Company C among them. John Fox of Company D told Camp that he recognized men from three companies in the Keogh group, further evidence that troopers of Companies C and L may have joined Company I in their desperate rally before being shot down and overrun. Seventh Cavalryman Theodore Goldin thought that the disposition of the dead where the Irish-born officer was found resembled "a hollow square with Keogh and one or two others in the center."[1]

Captain Myles W. Keogh. Courtesy of James Brust and Glen Swanson

Testifying at the Reno Court of Inquiry, Lieutenant Edgerly stated, "Captain Keogh had evidently been wounded as we found that his leg had been broken and the sergeants of his company had got around him and were killed with him." Edgerly later remarked that Keogh's horse, Comanche, who survived the slaughter, "had a wound just where Keogh's left leg would have been." Like most of the bodies on the field, Keogh's had been stripped, but unlike many others, he was spared mutilation, perhaps because of the Catholic emblem, an Agnus Dei, that he wore on a chain about his neck. It had not been removed. In addition to First Sergeant Frank Varden and Sergeant James Bustard, the dead of Company I identified near their slain commander included Keogh's orderly, Edward Lloyd, Corporal John Wild, and trumpeter John Patton, whose corpse lay across Keogh's chest. The company guidon bearer had apparently perished nearby, for when Keogh's gauntlets were discovered in a captured Indian village less than three months later, they were wrapped in the swallow-tailed flag.[2]

Despite his best efforts Edgerly was unable to identify the body of Keogh's second-in-command, First Lieutenant James E. Porter, among the mangled dead in the Company I sector. The officer's fate was ascertained when Doctor Holmes O. Paulding came upon the canvas lining of Porter's buckskin jacket amid the detritus of the abandoned Indian village, "a bullet hole through the right breast and deeply stained with blood." A month after the battle Lieutenant Simon Snyder, Fifth Infantry, confided in a letter to his mother that "Porter's head could not be found though it is thought beyond a doubt that the trunk of his body was identified." In the early twentieth century, a marble marker inscribed with Porter's name was erected amid a group of stones northwest of the Keogh group. Though spurious, its placement reflects the views of Captain Sweet, who decided not to set the stone provided for Porter at the time of his 1890 expedition to the field. "I am morally certain Porter fell with his troop," Sweet informed Walter Camp, "and his remains mutilated beyond human recognition."[3]

The bodies at Keogh's position and those scattered between that point and Custer Hill did not appear to reflect the same level of tactical cohesion that had been apparent at Calhoun Hill. In their testimony before the Reno Court of Inquiry, officers of the Seventh chose their words carefully, but the implication was apparent. Lieutenant George Wallace noted, "They appeared to me to have been killed running in file. . . . They were killed at intervals." Edgerly thought that "some

retreated faster than others. . . . There were no regular lines, but still evidence that there had been a line." Visiting the field in 1877, Lieutenant John Bourke confided to his diary his belief that the soldier line "broke" at Calhoun Hill and "stampeded" to where Keogh was found. "It looked to me as if Keogh must have attempted to make a stand on foot to enable Custer to get away," Bourke wrote, "because he and his company died in one compact mass whereas from here on the graves are scattered in irregular clumps and at intervals like that in a slaughter of buffaloes." Bourke's interpretation seems to be confirmed by the results of the 1980s archaeological surveys, for while a number of Indian-fired bullets were located in the Keogh sector, evidence of protracted resistance by the soldiers was markedly absent.[4]

Indian narratives of the combat echo the views of Lieutenant Bourke and other military observers. Runs The Enemy described a group of soldiers who made a stand "all in a bunch" before giving way and retreating along the ridge "like a stampede of buffalo," while Little Hawk told of chasing the soldiers "like buffalo." Flying Hawk noted that some "made a stand" at Keogh's position, "and when the most of them were killed the others fell back toward Custer Hill, fighting and falling."

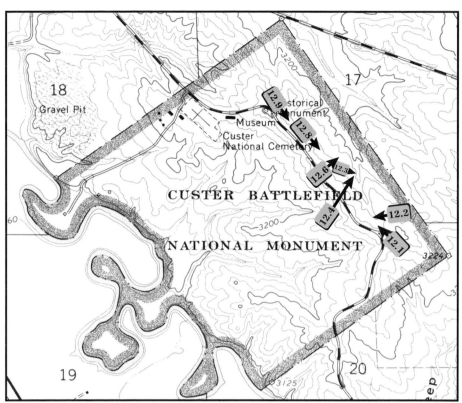

Based on the 1967 USGS topographical map

Map 12.1. The Keogh Sector

First Lieutenant James E. Porter. Courtesy of Little Bighorn Battlefield National Monument, National Park Service

TOP: *12.1A. "No. 7, Custer's battle-field on Crow Agency, Montana, along the B. & M.R.R. Battle fought June 25th, 1876. Custer and all of his men were killed. Photographed and copyrighted by H. R. Locke in 1895, Deadwood, S.D." Courtesy of Montana Historical Society, #946-605.*

BOTTOM: *12.1B. 1995.*

Warrior accounts imply that many of the led horses of Keogh's company were stampeded. Troopers who retained their animals hastened northward without offering much resistance, while the more numerous dismounted men attempted to fight their way out on foot, "shooting as they passed along," as Foolish Elk recalled.[5]

At this stage of the battle the great Oglala warrior Crazy Horse galloped through the collapsing soldier position in a series of "bravery runs" that inspired others to emulate his daring. Indians who had been firing on Keogh's company from the ridges to the east, and those who had pushed onto Calhoun Hill when the men of Company L began to fall

back, rushed their blue-clad foe and engaged the solders in close-range and even hand-to-hand combat. He Dog noted the troopers were split "into two bunches" by Crazy Horse's charge, the led horses stampeding over the ridge toward the river, while White Bull described leading a foray into the midst of the retreating enemy. "We rode among them," he said, "and pulled them off their horses." Lone Bear told of cutting through the soldiers at a point halfway between Keogh's stand and Custer Hill and expressed his belief that "the fighting was the hardest" in the Keogh sector. In fact, Indian losses were not excessive, although one of the fatalities was the Cheyenne leader Lame White Man, who fell on the western slope of Battle Ridge.[6]

The virtual destruction of Keogh's battalion left the Seventh's commander with only the two companies of Captain Yates's battalion, and one of those, Company E, was involved in an increasingly desperate struggle in the environs of Deep Ravine.

The depression that runs from left to right through this 1895 photo by H. R. Locke (12.1A) is called Horse Holders' Ravine. The naturally sheltered nature of this ravine is easily seen, and horses and men within would have been protected from view.

Locke's photo was taken on the eastern slope of Horse Holders' Ravine, looking north through the main Keogh battleground toward Custer Hill and the monument, which can be seen on the horizon in the middle of the picture. Marble markers are visible along the entire length of the ravine, as men of Companies C and L were cut down along their retreat route. In the right middle ground of the photo, on the far side of Horse Holders' Ravine, about twenty stones mark the site where Captain Keogh and a number of men fighting around him died. From that point on the trail of markers straggles toward Custer Hill to the north, marking the route taken by the survivors of Companies C, I, and L toward their comrades fighting there.

In the modern comparison photo, little has changed except for the cars on the auto road along the ridge to the left. Marker concordance is excellent in this section of Horse Holders' Ravine, with nearly all the stones in the 1895 photo still in the same spots one hundred years later.

No. 7, Custer's battlefield on Crow Agency, Montana, along the B. & M. R. R. Battle fought June 25th, 1876. Custer and all his men were killed. Photographed and copyrighted by H. R. Locke in 1895 Deadwood, S. D.

In 1909, on one of Daniel Kanipe's visits to the battlefield with Walter Camp, the sergeant brought his wife along.[7] Her presence had special significance, for in addition to being the wife of one battle veteran, she was the widow of another. Born in North Carolina, Missouri Ann Wycoff was eighteen when she married Edwin Bobo in 1872. She served as a laundress for her husband's Company C, and the couple had two children before Sergeant Bobo's death at the Little Bighorn. Less than ten months later, on April 12, 1877, she married Kanipe. Their marriage would produce eight more children.[8]

LEFT: *12.2A. Missouri Ann Bobo Kanipe standing among the Keogh markers, photo by Walter Camp, 1909. Courtesy of Little Bighorn Battlefield National Monument, National Park Service, #11265.*

BELOW: *12.2B. 2000.*

This photograph (12.2A) was taken in the same direction as the preceding one, looking north toward Custer Hill and the monument. The northeast end of Horse Holders' Ravine is seen in the foreground. Mrs. Kanipe stands amid the group of markers for Keogh and the men who perished near him, including her first husband, Edwin Bobo. North of that group, an irregular trail of markers meanders toward Custer Hill, showing where men fell as they retreated. The modern comparison photo is striking in its similarity to Camp's 1909 image, with excellent marker concordance and almost no change in the landscape.

TOP: *12.3A. "Grave of Col. Keogh," photo by Stanley J. Morrow, 1879. Printed from the original glass-plate negative as modified and retitled by L. A. Huffman, variant of Morrow #189, "Decorating the graves on Custers Battle field. Col. Keogh and thirty eight men massacred" (also issued as #38, "Decorating the graves on Custer's Battle field"). Courtesy of Montana Historical Society, #981-367.*

BOTTOM: *12.3B. Brian Pohanka, 1994.*

This well-known image (12.3A) is among the earliest photographs ever made of the Custer battlefield. It is part of Stanley J. Morrow's 1879 set of views (see appendix). Captain George K. Sanderson of the Eleventh U.S. Infantry, who led the reburial detail that Morrow accompanied from nearby Fort Custer, appears prominently in this photo, looking at a large wooden memorial erected in honor of Captain Keogh and the men who perished fighting beside him. The wooden cross, topped by a wreath and propped up by a stick and stones, is inscribed "Col. Keogh and 38 soldiers of Company I, 7 Cav killed here June 25 1876." Several soldiers are at work in the background, one of whom is lettering a smaller wooden marker for Corporal John Wild. The view is to the southeast, the opposite direction from the preceding two photographs in this section. These men were working in the area that contained the largest cluster of dead soldiers in the Keogh sector, near the spot where Mrs. Kanipe posed in the preceding vintage view. The large wooden cross was not the grave marker for Keogh or any other individual, but rather a memorial to the entire group of Company I men killed in this area.

In the modern comparison photo, author Brian Pohanka stands just down the slope of a hill where the soldier behind the one painting Wild's marker had stood. Behind the next hill, Horse Holders' Ravine angles through the photo. The large wooden cross is now gone, and no monument is present to honor the whole group. Seven marble markers for individual soldiers now fill this area. Keogh's stone is the middle one of the three in the row closest to the camera.

Plate 12.4A, a mid-1890s photograph by Christian Barthelmess,[10] shows the markers for Captain Keogh and those who died near him. It is the same marker grouping seen in the preceding vintage picture, but with the camera facing due east rather than southeast, bringing into view one additional stone in the left background. A large wooden cross again commemorated the entire group of Company I dead, but it is a replacement for the one seen in the 1879 photo. The lettering read, "Here fell Captain Keogh and 38 men of his Company I, 7 Cavalry. June 25, 1876."

In the other vintage photo (plate 12.5), of unknown date but likely later than the

The marker on the far right of Keogh's group is inscribed only as "U.S. soldier." It is in the same spot as the wooden headboard lettered for Wild in the 1879 view (12.3A). This marker site underwent archaeological excavation in 1984. At the periphery of the two-meter-square excavation were bones of an individual about seventeen years of age—too young to be Wild.[9] This creates a puzzle in identification.

This still could be Wild's initial grave on the battlefield, with the bones of the younger person belonging to an adjacent burial. Or perhaps someone other than Wild was buried here. However, Captain Sanderson and his men, on the field to tend graves less than three years after the battle, had reason to think that Corporal John Wild perished at this spot. That information, known to us only through a photograph, should not be lost or forgotten. If Wild were not killed at this exact spot, he likely was nearby. With identified markers for enlisted men all too rare, an association between Wild and a particular stone should be maintained.

preceding Barthelmess image, the same cross seems to have been in place, but shortened in height and with the lettering worn off. The ultimate fate of these two generations of wooden cross memorials is not known, though a 1984 archaeological excavation around Keogh's marker yielded small fragments of deteriorated wood that may have been their remnants.[11] By the time Mrs. Kanipe posed in this area in 1909, the crosses were gone.

Keogh's marker is the one in the center of the front row of three, while the unidentified stone at the site of the headboard lettered for Wild is just to the right of the captain's.

In the modern comparison photo (plate 12.4B), we see excellent marker concordance (the stone on the far right of the vintage photo is outside the field of view of the recent picture.) Interestingly, that was not always the case. At some point, for reasons and by hands unknown, Keogh's marble marker was moved to a more isolated spot about eighty yards north. Author Brian Pohanka, using primary source research that included descriptions of

TOP LEFT: *12.6A. "Peter Thompson, Mr. and Mrs. Kanipe, and Curly," photo by Walter Camp, 1909. Courtesy of Little Bighorn Battlefield National Monument, National Park Service, #11193.*

TOP RIGHT: *12.6B. Sandy Barnard (l.) and Brian Pohanka (r.), 1998.*

CENTER: *First Sergeant Edwin Bobo. Courtesy of Little Bighorn Battlefield National Monument, National Park Service*

BOTTOM: *12.7. Cluster of markers around Keogh's, 1998.*

Keogh's body being found among many others, Walter Camp's map of the battlefield, and photograph 12.4A, realized the error. In 1982, he and then–battlefield historian Neil Mangum investigated the spot where historical sources indicated that the Keogh marker should be, and they found its original brick base still in the ground. The Keogh marker was then moved back to its proper location.[12] Our modern comparison photo shows that Keogh's marker is back in the spot where it stood in the 1890s.

"When I came to the pile of men lying around Captain Keogh I recognized Serg. Edward [*sic*] Bobo," Kanipe told Camp.[13] Walter Camp took this photograph of the Kanipes flanked by battle veteran Peter

Thompson on the left and Crow scout Curley on the right. Daniel and Missouri Ann Bobo Kanipe each rest a hand on a marker inscribed only "U.S. Soldier." Although no caption or inscription appears on Camp's photo, the Kanipes logically would have struck such a pose next to the marker of her former husband and his friend, First Sergeant Edwin Bobo. Bobo, a member of Company C, died fighting among men of Company I.

Matching this photo proved surprisingly difficult. The key terrain feature is the hump in the mid-background between Sergeant and Mrs. Kanipe, but in direct sunlight, it can be difficult to distinguish that ridgeline from the one behind it. Fortunately, as authors Sandy Barnard and Brian Pohanka posed where the Kanipes had stood, shadows created by a passing cloud separated that small hump from the more distant background. Once located, the marker touched by the Kanipes in 1909 turned out to be in the group of nineteen that are close to the spot where Keogh fell.

Photograph 12.7 shows the entire cluster of markers around Keogh. The fifth from the right, next to the plastic traffic cone, is Keogh's marker, while the one the Kanipes flanked in 1909 is on the far left (north) of the group, just in front of Sandy Barnard. We assume that this unidentified stone, touched by both his friend and his widow in front of Camp's

camera in 1909, marks the death site of First Sergeant Edwin Bobo.[14]

Walter Camp took photograph 12.8A from a spot farther north than the preceding images in this section, closer to Custer Hill, which was behind him as he faced in a southeasterly direction. More markers are now visible. Those for the men who died in the cluster around Keogh can be seen in the middle distance, just before the terrain fall-off into Horse Holders' Ravine, which angles through the middle of the view. The landscape seems to show the effects of a grass fire, so we date this photograph to 1908, the year of the first recorded fire at the battlefield.[15]

In the modern comparison photo, the current footpath follows the old wagon road. As usual, marker concordance is good, with two important exceptions. The two markers on the far left of the foreground grouping are present in their historical locations but are now obscured from view by a bush. Continuing right along the line of stones, an extra marker (arrow) appears in the modern photo between the group of three and the tightly bunched cluster of four. This is the spurious marker for Lieutenant Porter, Keogh's junior officer.

The canvas lining of Porter's buckskin jacket was found in the village, but his body could not be identified on the field and the site of his death was not marked.[16] Hence, no marble marker was placed for him in 1890. In 1910, Superintendent Oscar Wright set a stone to commemorate Porter. Wright told his superiors that he had put the marker in its proper spot "as near as was possible to ascertain," but his evidence for this location is unknown, and we believe that he simply chose a location among others of the dead lieutenant's company.[17] Though Porter's body was not identified, it was probably buried as an unknown and subsequently marked with a stone inscribed "U.S. Soldier." This photo pair proves that there had never been a body at the spot where Superintendent Wright put the Porter marker, and the location is spurious.

On the far right side of Camp's 1908 photo (12.8A), an isolated marker (double arrow) that appears on the steep eastern bank of Horse Holders' Ravine is not present in the modern view. After our comparison photo revealed this marker to be missing, John Doerner (chief historian at Little Bighorn

Battlefield) investigated further. Doerner identified another historical photo made in 1901 that also showed the marker in place in Horse Holders' Ravine.[18] On August 8, 2001, Doerner and seasonal ranger-researcher Michael Donahue explored the area with an iron probe and metal detector. Although no brick marker base could be located, a .50 caliber, 450-grain bullet impacted from long-range firing was located one inch below the ground near the site of the now-missing marker. Based on the photographic evidence and the artifact find, historical accuracy was restored when the marker was replaced in Horse Holders' Ravine on October 11, 2001, at the spot where it stood in 1908.[19]

TOP: *12.8A. View of the Keogh sector, photo by Walter Camp, 1908. Courtesy of Little Bighorn Battlefield National Monument, National Park Service, #11271.*

BOTTOM: *12.8B. 2000.*

Frontier reporter Mark Kellogg of the *Bismarck Tribune*, who also served as a correspondent for the *New York Herald*, was the only newspaperman to ride with the Seventh Cavalry to the Little Bighorn. Like the others who went into action with Custer's immediate command, he was killed in the battle, but the exact site of his death has remained a mystery.

The strongest historical accounts suggest that Kellogg perished some distance northwest of Custer Hill, near the Little Bighorn River. But a wooden stake with Kellogg's name, its origin obscure, eventually appeared a good distance from the river on the east slope of Custer Hill, a short way past the Seventh Cavalry monument and in view of the marker-strewn area where Keogh died. When Captain Sweet's expedition set the original marble markers in 1890, they noted this stake, but because Kellogg was a civilian, no stone had been provided for them to place at the site. Instead, Sweet replaced the Kellogg stake with a wooden headboard supplied by the quartermaster at Fort Custer.[20] In 1896, Kellogg finally received a marble marker, paid for by the *New York Herald* and erected at the spot where his earlier wooden memorials had been.[21]

TOP RIGHT: *Mark Kellogg. Courtesy of Sandy Barnard.*

BOTTOM RIGHT: *12.9A. View of the Kellogg marker, photographer unknown, late 1890s, printed from the original glass-plate negative. Courtesy of Sandy Barnard.*

BOTTOM LEFT: *12.9B. 1997.*

Vintage photo 12.9A shows the marble marker placed for Mark Kellogg in 1896. To our knowledge, this is the only known image of the first Kellogg stone. No vintage print has ever been located, but the original glass-plate negative, owned by author Sandy Barnard, was used to print this picture. Befitting the fact that the newspaper had paid for the stone, the inscription read: "Sacred to the memory of Mark Kellogg, Correspondent of the New York Herald who fell here with Gen'l. Custer, June 25, 1876." Though darkened somewhat on the lower portion, the stone is barely chipped and not cracked, and we believe that this photo was taken within a few years of the marker's placement. The camera was facing to the southeast, toward the main group of markers in the Keogh sector and Calhoun Hill beyond, but little of the background is visible because the Kellogg marker fills the frame.

Kellogg's original marble marker eventually fell victim to wear and vandalism. Battlefield superintendent Edward Luce prevailed upon both the *New York Herald-Tribune* and the *Bismarck Tribune* to fund a replacement, which was erected on July 18, 1942.[22] That new Kellogg marker is seen in our modern comparison photo. It is in the same spot as the first one, and the wording is similar, but because two newspapers rather than one had provided funding, the words "and reporter for the Bismarck Tribune" were added. Unfortunately, this photo pair cannot resolve the mystery as to where on the field Kellogg actually fell, and this location east of Battle Ridge may not be accurate. But these pictures show that the current Kellogg marker is in the same spot marked for him since the nineteenth century.

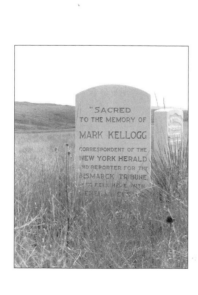

BELOW CUSTER HILL

OOKING TOWARD THE river valley from the crest of Custer Hill, site of the legendary Last
Stand, visitors to the Little Bighorn Battlefield can see marble stones, scattered in an irregular line, leading toward the winding gulch called Deep Ravine. Many will hike down the
trail that leads to the ravine, interpretive brochure in hand,
as they attempt to conjure in their mind's eye something of
the drama, bravery, and violence of that bloody Sunday in
1876. In the historiography of a battle markedly characterized by disputed theories and contradictory evidence, few
aspects are as subject to varying interpretation as the events
that transpired on the so-called South Skirmish Line and in
Deep Ravine.

The narrow upper portion of the ravine is some seven
hundred yards southwest of Custer Hill, and the intermit-
tent drainage covers another seven hundred yards to its gradually broadening mouth at the bank of the Little Bighorn.
Standing at the end of the Deep Ravine trail, one is struck
by the isolation of the place. Custer Hill with its memorial
and cluster of stones is out of sight, blocked by the rising
ground. The ravine itself, a precipitous gash in the rolling
landscape, seems somehow both mysterious and sinister. The
burial parties who made their somber round of the battlefield found it to be a place of horror. Soldiers vomited at the
sight and stench as they tossed earth down on the decomposing remains.

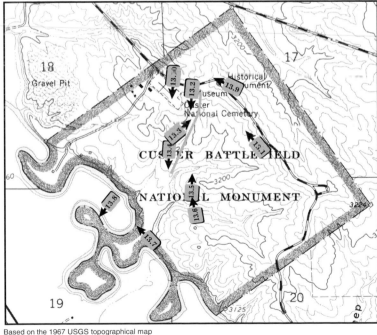

Map 13.1. Below Custer Hill.
South Skirmish Line, Deep Ravine,
Cemetery Ridge, and Captain
Sanderson's Camp

Based on the 1967 USGS topographical map

According to witnesses' recollections, the number of slain troopers discovered in the confines
of Deep Ravine ranges from twenty-two to thirty-four, though the figure most often given is
twenty-eight. Other bodies lay in the swale above the northern lip of the depression, and a few

isolated individuals were found farther south. Many of the dead in the ravine appeared to be men of Company E, the Gray Horse Troop, and of those whose identities could be determined, eight were recognized as members of that company.[1] Two of Company E's three sergeants were there, along with two of the four company corporals who accompanied the Custer command. The presence of First Sergeant Frederick Hohmeyer and the other three noncommissioned officers implies that the Gray Horse Troop fought in this sector as a unit.

Captain McDougall, former commander of Company E, stated, "In the ravine I found most of the troop, who had used the upper sides of the ravine for a kind of breastwork, falling to the bottom as they were shot down."[2] At the Reno Court of Inquiry McDougall testified, "About half were in the ravine and the other half on a line outside," and he speculated that they had been "attacked on both sides."[3] Captain Moylan thought that the troopers had been "fighting and retreating." He said, "I could see where they had passed down the edge and attempted to scramble up the other side, which was almost perpendicular." Moylan added, "The marks were plain where they used their hands to get up, but the marks only extended halfway up the bank."[4]

Just why these cavalrymen entered what proved to be a veritable deathtrap was a question that elicited a variety of speculation. "Their position was lower than that of the Indians and they had to defend themselves from the enemy in front and rear," Lieutenant DeRudio observed. "It looked like they were separated from the main body and made a stand for themselves."[5] In his characteristically forthright and ironical manner, Captain Benteen testified, "They could not shoot out of the ravine and they certainly did not go into it to shoot out of it." He theorized that these were wounded men who had sought

shelter there, "possibly to hide."[6] In later years, General Godfrey asserted, "I firmly believe that these men belonged to Lieutenant [James G.] Sturgis' Platoon and had been ordered to locate a ford for crossing the river."[7]

Adding to the mystery of the deployment at Deep Ravine is the fact that the body of Company E's commander, First Lieutenant Algernon E. Smith, was found on Custer Hill. Because no other member of the Gray Horse Troop was identified at the site of the Last Stand, Smith may have been wounded or killed earlier in the fighting.

In that case, command of the company would have devolved upon Second Lieutenant James G. Sturgis, son of the Seventh Cavalry's senior officer, Colonel Samuel Sturgis. The lieutenant's bloodstained shirt and underdrawers were found in the abandoned Indian encampment, at a point not far from the mouth of Deep Ravine. Godfrey claimed to have discovered "several headless bodies" in the same area, while others recalled finding the severed and fire-blackened heads of two of Reno's men.[8] Seventh Cavalry veteran George Glenn claimed, "Another head looked to me [to be] that of Lieutenant Sturgis."[9] That young Sturgis was officially listed as missing or unidentified may well have been an effort to spare his family the grim reality, and by 1878 a spurious "grave" and headboard had been erected for the fallen officer in the basin below Custer Hill (see plate 13.2A).

Today not a single marker stands in Deep Ravine, where so many witnesses recalled finding twenty-eight dead, for the simple fact that Captain Sweet's detail erected none there in 1890. However, between the edge of the ravine and the basin at the foot of Custer Hill, visitors to the battlefield can count more than fifty of the ubiquitous soldier stones—a fact that has led some Little Bighorn historians to conclude that if the markers truly indicated where troopers fell, then they must represent a structured defensive deployment on Custer's part. The concept of a "South Skirmish Line" is prominently featured in many battle reconstructions, including Charles Kuhlman's *Legend into History*. However, several problems with this interpretation are obvious. Not only is the supposed line dominated by higher ground, but if troopers were positioned at standard five-yard intervals, the expanse would have necessitated the deployment of virtually the entire Custer command.

In the course of his extensive research on the Custer fight, Walter Camp came to believe that many of the markers between Custer Hill and Deep Ravine were spurious, erected "to give the appearance of men fighting in line."[10] Camp seems to have reached that conclusion partly on the basis of Captain McDougall's recollection of "less than a dozen" bodies being discovered there and Lieutenant Richard Thompson's similar statement of finding "only 9 or 10 men" between the hill and the ravine.[11]

Other witnesses disagreed. While McDougall recalled "few or no dead cavalry horses between [the] top of [the] ridge and [the] deep ravine," Sergeant Roy remembered seeing "a number of dead cavalry horses" there.[12] General E. J. McClernand, who had gone over the field as a lieutenant of the Second Cavalry, saw no horses but stated that "there were more than ten men" between the ridge and the ravine.[13] Sergeant Kanipe remembered riding "along the line of dead bodies toward the river," and as early as 1879, Lieutenant Godfrey wrote of "many" dead on "the line" between Deep Ravine and Custer Hill.[14]

The 1980s archaeological surveys have confirmed that elements of Custer's force fought and fell along the South Skirmish Line, although their deployment may well have involved a movement to or from Custer Hill, rather than a defensive line per se. Discovery of numerous bullets fired by the attacking warriors and some by the soldiers, together with the partial remains of at least five individuals (one of them Custer's scout Mitch Boyer), provide irrefutable evidence of an action there.[15]

Some of the dead soldiers located between Custer Hill and Deep Ravine were undoubtedly men who rushed off the hill in the latter stages of the fight. Numerous Indian veterans described this event, most of whom took it to be a desperate attempt at escape rather than a tactical deployment. "Those who broke from the end of the ridge and tried to get away by running toward the river were dismounted," Good Voiced Elk recalled. "I saw many jump over the steep bank into this gully [Deep Ravine] in their effort to escape, but these were all killed."[16] One Bull and White Bull both remarked on the fact these troopers "had thrown away their carbines and had only six-shooters," while Tall Bull thought they were "firing their guns at random."[17] Respects Nothing said, "The Indians followed them and killed them with war clubs."[18] Just how many of the fleeing soldiers managed to reach Deep Ravine is open to question. "There were a few who tried to get away," Lone Bear remembered, but he did not see them gain the ravine proper.[19] Lights "saw a few of the soldiers jump over the banks" of the ravine, while Flying By stated, "Only four soldiers got into [the] gully toward [the] river."[20]

Because many troopers of Company E fought and died in the vicinity of Deep Ravine, perhaps their action preceded those final, chaotic rushes off Last Stand Hill. It may have been the result of a deliberate deployment by Captain Yates's battalion of Custer's command, which some students of the battle believe was attempting to cut off the northward flight of the village noncombatants. In addition to the ford at the mouth of Deep Ravine, at least two other potential crossing points on the Little Bighorn were within a mile-and-a-half radius of Custer Hill. These were almost certainly used by warriors seeking to protect their fleeing women and children, and some Indian narratives imply that fighting occurred north and west of the ridge on which the national cemetery is now located.

In 1907, Moses Flying Hawk drew a map for researcher Eli Ricker on which he noted "Indian Women Congregated" across the river northwest of Custer Hill. "Some of the Indians crossed from the place the women fled to," Flying Hawk said, "and went across at the lower crossing west of Custer Hill."[21] White Bull sketched a similar map for author Stanley Vestal, showing women and children gathered on the west side of the river in an area extending northward from a point opposite the mouth of Deep Ravine. White Bull told Vestal that the warriors "stayed between the troops and the women" and described a fight with two groups of soldiers below Custer Hill, one group having "white horses." White Bull's account indicates that this fight took place prior to soldiers "running down the hill" near the end of the battle.[22] Writing to cavalry veteran William O. Taylor in 1910, Charles

Captain George W. M. Yates. Courtesy of Little Bighorn Battlefield National Monument, National Park Service

Corn claimed that he had been the first to kill one of Custer's soldiers "while they were fighting the women folks move on the other side of the Little Big Horn."[23] Respects Nothing recalled that when he first arrived on the field in the Calhoun and Keogh sectors, he met other warriors "who had crossed the river at the lower crossing, just below the corner of the cemetery." He further remarked that some Indians "crossed the river above this lower crossing."[24] Cheyenne warrior Big Beaver "went north along the river thence to the right or east and came up towards Custer from the North side," entering the fray "just north and a little to the east of where the present monument is."[25]

Perhaps because their encampment was located at the northern end of the village, the Cheyenne seem to have constituted a majority of the Indian combatants in this stage of the battle. In the mid twentieth century, Cheyenne Tribal Historian John Stands In Timber illuminated some details of the fight on the northern flank. Stands In Timber said that the band of Cheyenne under Wolf Tooth and Big Foot, who had earlier engaged Custer on the ridges east of Medicine Tail Coulee Ford, continued to harass the soldiers as they passed over Custer Hill and "followed the ridge down to the present cemetery site." Undeterred, the troopers continued on, nearing the river at a point north and west of Cemetery Ridge, where they came under fire from warriors concealed in the brush. Several troopers were killed in this engagement and a number of their horses captured; Custer waited "twenty minutes or more" before abandoning his foray toward this northern crossing point.[26] In another account Stands In Timber locates Custer's pause on the flats, "below where the superintendent's house [Stone House] is now located," and notes that the soldiers remained there "for half an hour" before the fighting escalated.[27] If Keogh's battalion had been positioned on and in the environs of Calhoun Hill, the Cheyenne accounts seem to imply that Yates's battalion continued northward in an offensive posture before pulling back to Cemetery Ridge, perhaps as a reaction to the escalating fight in the Keogh sector.

As warrior pressure mounted, "the soldiers of the gray horse company" dismounted in the "big basin" below Custer Hill. At this point the Cheyenne Suicide Boys—a band of young warriors who had vowed to gain honors or die in the fight—launched a charge that inspired others to join them. "They galloped up to the level ground near where the museum now is," Stands In Timber said, "and stampeded the gray horses of the soldiers."[28] Company E may have been moving toward Deep Ravine—possibly in an attempt to contain the Indians infiltrating there—when they fell victim to this unexpected onslaught. As the Cheyenne historian related, "Indians coming from the north and from the south forced these gray horse soldiers into the big ravine," whereupon, "All the soldiers except the gray horse men retreated afoot up the slope of Custer ridge, driving the Indians east of the ridge."[29] Cheyenne oral history implies that these events were taking place at the same time as the collapse of Calhoun's and Keogh's companies. Lame White Man and Yellow Nose both figure prominently in the tribal narrative, and the general sense is one of a pitched battle in all sectors of the field.

Confronted with simultaneous crises on both flanks, Custer found himself with only one intact unit at his disposal—Yates's Company F—and some of that command may already have fallen, while others may have lost their horses, in the fight below the ridge. It was with those troopers, and individual survivors of the other companies, that Custer would wage his Last Stand.

SEVENTH CAVALRY ON PARADE

This stirring, artistic image (13.1A) of a column of the Seventh U.S. Cavalry marching on the Custer battlefield was made by photographer L. A. Huffman at the fiftieth anniversary of the battle in 1926.[30] The view is to the north, with the Stone House, cemetery, and flagpole readily visible. Custer Ridge, lined with spectators, rises up to the right of the Stone House toward Custer Hill and the monument, which were just out of the field of view on the right side of the image. The Seventh Cavalry contingent camped at the Crow Agency fairgrounds, to the north of the battlefield, and they are approaching from that direction.

The high point of the day was a cere-

mony at the Custer monument in which the Seventh Cavalry, led by General Godfrey, met a group of Indians led by White Bull, nephew of Sitting Bull. Godfrey and White Bull exchanged gifts and an emotional handshake of peace. The Indian group came up to the monument from the north, while the cavalry column marched to meet them from the southeast along Custer Ridge.[31] The 1926 Seventh Cavalry participants likely followed the route shown in this photo between the Little Bighorn River and Custer Hill, as they got into position for their approach to the monument from the southeast along Battle Ridge.

In the modern comparison photo, the two markers visible in the right foreground of Huffman's image are in the same spots, as are all other markers in the view, but because the 1995 picture was taken on an overcast day, they do not stand out as prominently. The visitors center now stands at the foot of Custer Ridge, near the right side of the stand of trees that have grown up around the cemetery area and obscure the view of the Stone House. The stillness of this scene provides an interesting counterpoint to the seemingly endless line of cavalry troopers who snaked through the landscape in 1926.

SPURIOUS STURGIS GRAVE AND MARKER

In 1876, Lieutenant Colonel George A. Custer was actually the second-ranking officer of the Seventh U.S. Cavalry; command of the regiment belonged to Colonel Samuel D. Sturgis. However, the fifty-four-year-old Sturgis was on detached service as commander of the Cavalry Depot in St. Louis

for almost two years prior to the Battle of the Little Bighorn, which placed Custer in field command of the regiment.[32] But another Sturgis fought and died with the Seventh Cavalry, the colonel's son, Second Lieutenant James G. Sturgis of Company M, who was serving with Company E on the day of the battle.

As was the case with Lieutenant Porter, Lieutenant Sturgis's body was never identified, but his bloody clothing and perhaps even his decapitated head were found in the Indian village.[33] Troubled that her son's body had not been located, a grieving Mrs. Jerusha Sturgis (no doubt aided by the fact that she was the wife of an high-ranking officer) was allowed to visit the battlefield in June 1878 to learn what she could of her son's fate. Escorted to the Little Bighorn by Colonel Nelson A. Miles and a contingent of Fifth U.S. Infantry soldiers from Fort Keogh, Mrs. Sturgis found a well-marked grave for her son, relieving her at least of the anguish of thinking that he had been buried as an unknown. The grave, though, was spurious, set up by unknown compassionate hands to ease Mrs. Sturgis's grief.[34]

This early fictitious grave for Lieutenant Sturgis was placed southwest of Custer Hill, in an area that would come to be known as the South Skirmish Line. A string of markers would eventually angle from a point about 350 yards below the monument on Custer Hill to the steep headwall of Deep Ravine. Some of these were Company E dead, found along this line near and in Deep Ravine. Because Sturgis fought with Company E on the day of the battle, this area was a plausible location to place the spurious grave, although a spot farther from Custer Hill and closer

ABOVE LEFT: *13.1A. Cavalry parade at the Custer Battlefield, photo by L. A. Huffman, 1926. Courtesy of Montana Historical Society, #981-197.*

ABOVE RIGHT: *13.1B. 1995.*

to Deep Ravine might have been a better approximation.

When photographer Stanley J. Morrow traveled to the battlefield in the spring of 1879, the spurious Sturgis grave was still in place. As can be clearly seen in plate 13.2A, it consisted of a mound of stones and earth, with a crude wooden cross lettered "Lt. Sturgis 7th Cav June 25, 76." Beyond, the landscape falls away toward the Little Bighorn River, a loop of which is seen in the distance. Morrow's title, "Supposed grave of Lieut. Sturgis," indicates that he knew this was not really Sturgis's grave, but rather a fictitious memorial set up for the young lieutenant. Morrow's original negative was eventually acquired by L. A. Huffman, who retitled this image "Grave of Lieut. Sturgis." That negative, now at the Montana Historical Society, was used to print the image for this book. Huffman may not have realized this was not a true grave, given his title on this photo. The historical record, however, leaves no doubt that Sturgis's body was never identified, so no accurate death site for him could ever be marked.

This fictitious grave would eventually disappear, leaving Lieutenant Sturgis again unmarked on the field. In 1910, at the same time Superintendent Oscar Wright set the previously mentioned stones for Lieutenants Hodgson and Porter, he set one for Sturgis as well. Our modern comparison photo shows former battlefield chief historian Douglas McChristian posed where the crude wooden cross for Sturgis stood in 1879. The modern Sturgis stone is seen a couple of yards to the left. Because Wright set the 1910 markers "at their proper places, as near as was possible to ascertain,"[35] he may have used the Morrow photograph as his guide.

Photograph 13.3A was taken below Custer Hill, looking northeast toward the monument, with the Little Bighorn River behind the camera position. The visible markers form a somewhat irregular line from the left middle ground to the right foreground along the so-called South Skirmish Line. The Sturgis marker seen in the previous pair would be just out of the field of vision where the path angles toward the left in the middle distance of the image.

Between the vintage photo and the modern, a number of changes can be seen in the landscape. On Custer Hill, a ten-foot-high fence, thirty feet on a side, surrounds the monument in the early picture. The fence was built in 1883, two years after the granite shaft was erected, and remained in place until 1963. Hence, it is seen in the vintage image and not in the recent one. In 1930, a four-foot-high fence, seen in the modern photo but not the early one, was placed around the grouping of fifty-two markers on the southwestern slope of Custer Hill.[36]

For years, visitors had worn a trail through the grass along the South Skirmish Line markers to Deep Ravine. In the early 1990s, a change in policy closed the Deep Ravine walking trail, and the vegetation returned. The trail was reopened in the late 1990s, and in 2000, a path of wood and gravel was constructed to accommodate visitors and protect the natural environment. That path is absent, of course, in the vintage photo but is obvious in the modern view.

The horse blocks some of the markers in the old photo. At first glance, two of those visible in the modern picture seem to be lacking in the historic view, but these may be optical illusions. Looking across the modern foreground marker grouping, just to the left of the one third from the right, a small stone appears that is not seen in the older photo. However, the camera seems to have been held at a slightly lower height in the vintage picture, which may have been enough to hide that marker behind the little foreground elevation. Likewise, just to the right of the fourth foreground marker from the left, there seems to be a pair of smaller stones where only one can be seen in the older photo. Careful scrutiny under magnification reveals that two markers can be seen in the early picture, only they are lined up so that the one in front almost obscures the one

RIGHT: *13.4A. "Smith's Command, Looking West,"* photographer unknown, undated photo, probably 1920s. Courtesy of Edward S. Godfrey Collection, U.S. Army Military History Institute, RG48-S, box 2.25.

BELOW: *13.4B. 1998.*

behind. Thus, once again marker concordance proves to be good.

The "Smith" of the title of photo 13.4A refers to First Lieutenant Algernon E. Smith, who commanded Company E on the day of the battle. The light-colored mounts of Company E, known as the Gray Horse Troop, made them noticeable from around the field during the battle. This photo, taken toward the southwest, shows the lower end of the South Skirmish Line, Deep Ravine, and the Little Bighorn River and valley beyond. Company E is thought to have operated in this area because a number of its troopers were killed here or in Deep Ravine. Godfrey's title on this photo lends credence to the presence of Company E in this sector. Lieutenant Smith's body, however, was found on Custer Hill, making it likely that he had been an early casualty and had been carried to the rel-

ative safety of the hill as his company fought below.

The vintage and modern photos both show the markers on the southern end of the South Skirmish Line as they trail down to the headwall of Deep Ravine, whose dramatically steep sides are evident in both views. Marker concordance is excellent, although a bush in the modern photo hides one of the stones on the left side of the distant marker group in the vintage view. Just beyond that distant group of eleven markers, erosion is evident and a section of the lip of Deep Ravine has slid into the chasm, a phenomenon that is apparent in the next photo pair also.

View 13.5A is the opposite of the last, taken on the far (southwest) side of Deep Ravine, looking back up the South Skirmish Line toward Custer Hill and the monument. The camera position for the preceding photo pair was up the trail beyond the dark bush that is seen in the center just below the horizon line in the more recent picture. (That same bush appears in the right foreground of the modern comparison photo in the preceding pair, 13.4A and B.) In Roahen's 1940s picture in this pair, the horizon line is bare except for the monument on Custer Hill, while in the modern comparison photo the visitors center and trees near the cemetery appear. Marker concordance is excellent between the early image and the recent one.

What is strikingly different is the appearance of the northeast wall of Deep Ravine in the foreground of the photographs. In the 1940s view, the walls were nearly perpendicular and resembled a cliff. In the recent image,

Deep Ravine has always been the most striking terrain feature on the battlefield, both for its imposing physical characteristics and for its reputation as a place of dreadful death. Numerous post-battle descriptions related that some twenty-eight soldiers either deployed in the ravine or were driven there, only to be trapped by the steep walls and cut down by the Indians.[37] Hand marks that poignantly ended halfway up the precipitous embankment bore mute witness after the battle to the fate of the men who had been trapped and tried to escape.[38] The large number of decomposing bodies lying inaccessible in the steep walled ravine could be "buried" only by throwing dirt on them from above.[39]

No reliable report mentions those bodies ever being removed from Deep Ravine, yet no markers were ever placed there for them. Many scholars of the Custer battle believe that the fallen troopers remain buried beneath the surface of Deep Ravine to this day and that the markers that should have stood at the death sites of these men were placed on the South Skirmish Line instead. Despite a concerted effort to find the bodies during several of the archaeological projects, their location remains a mystery. Archaeological studies of Deep Ravine began in 1984 and continued in 1985 and 1989. They concluded that the bodies may be buried more deeply than remains on other parts of the battlefield as a result of erosion, drainage, and sediment deposit. Comparison photos such as these showing slumping of the steep side walls onto the ravine floor were part of the evidence that led to this conclusion.[40]

TOP: *13.6A. "Custer Battlefield, Montana," photo by F. Jay Haynes, 1894. Courtesy of Montana Historical Society, #H-3145.*

BOTTOM: *13.6B. 1995.*

OPPOSITE TOP: *13.7A. #37 "Bluff on the Little Horn, where some of Custer's men were driven to a watery grave" (also issued as #188, "Bluff where some of Custer's men were driven into the Little Horn and drowned"), photo by Stanley J. Morrow, 1879. Courtesy of Montana Historical Society.*

OPPOSITE BOTTOM: *13.7B. 1994.*

significant erosion is evident and a large part of the clifflike section has collapsed, creating a much gentler slope into the ravine but also possibly burying artifacts that might have been on the floor of the chasm. This collapsed area corresponds to the section of fallen ravine lip in the previous modern photo (13.4B).

This 1894 view (13.6A) by F. Jay Haynes from the far side of Deep Ravine was taken along the same line of sight as the Roahen photo in the previous pair but from a camera position farther away from the monument. Deep Ravine angles through the photo from left foreground to right middle ground. The

three observers are standing on the southwest lip of the ravine. Because the camera was farther from the edge of the ravine, we cannot see all the way to its floor. The horizon of the vintage view shows only the monument in the center, surrounded by the 1883 ten-foot fence. The monument stands in the same spot in the modern photo, with the high fence removed and the shorter one around the markers on the slope just barely visible under high magnification. To the left in the recent picture, the roof of the visitors center and the trees near the cemetery can be seen.

Haynes's 1894 photograph, printed for this book from the original glass-plate negative at the Montana Historical Society, is remarkably sharp and clear. The South Skirmish Line markers are distinctly seen where they stood just four years after they were placed. Because the modern photo was taken on an overcast day, with a smaller-format negative, and at a time when the grass was lighter and provided less contrast, the markers are not as visible. But examination under high magnification reveals that the markers have remained essentially in the same spots in the 101 years between 1894 and 1995.

From Custer Hill, the terrain slopes in a southwesterly direction toward the river. Nearest the monument, where fifty-two marble markers are contained within a fence, the incline is steeper. It then flattens out until it meets the Little Bighorn River in a series of steep bluffs, a portion of which can be seen in Morrow's dramatic photo of 1879 (13.7A). Morrow's title clearly stated his belief that some of Custer's men were driven off these cliffs and drowned in the Little Bighorn River. The source of his information is not known, and no other historical account verifies this information. Although one or more soldiers may have fled to these bluffs only to be killed there, such a scenario is not part of the usually accepted story of the battle.

The modern comparison photo shows that erosion has taken place, which is not surprising given the precipitously steep yet porous nature of the bluffs. Overall, though, the scene is quite similar, and little has changed on this section of the battlefield.

In early April of 1879, Captain Sanderson was given the task of tidying up the ap-

195

TOP: *13.8A. "Capt. Sanderson camp at the ford while gathering and burying bones" (also issued as #43, "Capt. Sanderson's camp at the ford, while gathering the bones and building the monument"), photo by Stanley J. Morrow, 1879. Courtesy of W. H. Over Museum, #305.*

BOTTOM: *13.8B. 1994.*

pearance of Custer's battlefield, remarking the graves, and burying all bones—human or animal—that were still in view. As seen here in an image by Stanley Morrow (13.8A), who accompanied them, Sanderson's men set up a camp alongside the Little Bighorn River. A variant of this photo shows one of the wagons and the men in different spots (see appendix). In addition, this four-tent camp appears in the distance in two views taken from Custer Hill (see plates 14.2 and 14.3). Despite Morrow's ample imagery, this photo and its title posed a pair of associated mysteries—where was the camp and what ford was it at?

Two factors made it difficult to pinpoint

the campsite: the meandering course of the Little Bighorn River below Custer Hill, and our presence on the field when full foliage in the trees shielded background details that had been visible when Morrow shot this view with the limbs bare in early April. Examination of the Morrow photos taken on Custer Hill seemed to indicate that the camp was on the far (west) side of the river. However, efforts to locate it by approaching the water from that direction proved fruitless. Returning to the east or battlefield side, we were able to maneuver along the winding river and reach the spot, which is around a bend just upstream (left) of the bluffs in the previous photo pair. The view in this Morrow photo is to the west, with the river just behind the camera set up on the bank.

Because the camp was set up on the east bank, Sanderson and his men did not have to cross the river to reach the main battlefield and do their work. Why, then, did Morrow make special mention of "the ford" in his title, and which crossing did he mean? The answer is not clear. Perhaps the river course was different in 1879 and a crossing was necessary to reach the battlefield from this campsite, but it seems unlikely that Sanderson would have chosen so inconvenient a spot. This site is also near what has been termed Ford D, a crossing place north of Custer Hill that has been proposed as Custer's destination in action beyond Last Stand Hill.[41] For now though, the "ford" of Morrow's title remains an uncertainty.

❧❦

A MAJOR commemoration was held on the tenth anniversary of the battle, bringing together veterans from both sides, local dignitaries, a military detail, and photographer D. F. Barry. Hunkpapa chief Gall, who had fought Custer a decade before, spent the evening of June 24, 1886, escorting guests around the field as he told them what he knew about the battle.[42] Gall's narrative, related that day to the likes of Captain Edward S. Godfrey, would heavily influence early battle histories.

Barry also heard Gall's remarks. He later wrote to battle historian William A. Graham: "On the 10th anniversary Gall showed us where Gen'l. Custer dismounted and fought in skirmish line on the east side of the Little Bighorn. That he never crossed the river, or got into the valley on the west side. Gen'l. Frank Baldwin—good soldier—and a fighter—got his Lieut. Bowen and Co. out at 6 A.M. and I made two photos—his company firing in skirmish line—showing just where General Custer dismounted and kept backing up untill [sic] he reached the high point where he fell."[43]

Barry's two photos of First Lieutenant William H. C. Bowen's Company K, Fifth U.S. Infantry, recreating Custer's skirmish lines are presented on the next two pages. Taken just after dawn on June 25, 1886, they are dramatic examples of Barry's skill as a photographer and have been reproduced many times but little studied. Barry clearly stated that Gall himself pointed out these locations where Custer's men dismounted and fought. Where on the field were these photos taken? We were able to match both, and our modern comparison photos give the answer.

In the first of the two (plate 13.9A), the soldiers are lined up in the shallow depression just across the road from the front door of the present visitors center. In the second (plate 13.10A), the line is formed in what is now the cemetery area, just west of the gravestones in Section A, on a ridge overlooking the valley and the Little Bighorn River. Until recently, almost all histories of the battle considered Custer Hill to be the far northern end of the field—the spot to which Custer's troops were driven or deployed and made their last stand. But recently gathered evidence suggests that one battalion of Custer's immediate command—Companies E and F under Captain Yates, accompanied by Custer and his headquarters staff—advanced beyond Custer Hill still on the offensive, into the current cemetery area and perhaps all the way down to the Little Bighorn River.[44]

It is difficult to know how literally to take Barry's photographic interpretation of Gall's story. In both photos the troopers are firing toward Custer Hill, yet Barry told Graham they were backing up in that direction, so they presumably would have been shooting the other way. This may merely have been artistic license on Barry's part, to enhance the dramatic impact of the photographs or to simply allow the men to face the morning sunlight. However, evidence indicates that some warriors occupied Battle Ridge while Yates's battalion maneuvered below, so the soldiers may have fired toward Custer Hill.[45] Can we believe that elements of this battalion skirmished in the exact spots shown in the Barry photos? Perhaps they did. But at the simplest level, these two photo pairs provide further evidence that Custer advanced and fought beyond the hill that now bears his name.

Hunkpapa chief Gall. Courtesy of Little Bighorn Battlefield National Monument, National Park Service

TOP: *13.9A. Skirmish line on Custer Battlefield, June 25, 1886, photo by D. F. Barry. Courtesy of Little Bighorn Battlefield National Monument, National Park Service, #670.*

BOTTOM: *13.9B. 1995.*

I 4

CUSTER HILL ∽

THE FIGHT THAT occurred on Custer Hill has been so often portrayed in art and film—from grandiose canvases to humorous caricatures, heroic epics to satirical burlesques—that even the most pragmatic researchers and historians find their quest for the truth obscured by the pervasive imagery of the Last Stand. The buckskin-clad figure of the Seventh's commander, standing amid the dwindling shambles of his two battalions and blazing away at hordes of assailants can be hero or fool, inspire veneration or contempt, but the image endures.

A visit to the site reinforces rather than diminishes the legend. That northern elevation of the windswept ridge with its mass grave and memorial; the thickly clustered markers for the fallen soldiers enclosed by an iron fence on the grassy slope; the crowds of visitors, curious, indifferent, or impassioned; the vastness of the landscape spanning the limits of the horizon beneath that magnificent big sky—all conspire to say, "Here it happened; this was Custer's Last Stand." The enduring sense of place was doubtless a compelling draw to the many photographers whose images provide a visual chronicle of Custer Hill through the decades.

As is invariably the case with the Battle of the Little Bighorn, many questions about the action on Last Stand Hill will never be fully answered: the names and company assignments of all those who perished on the hill, the duration of the combat there, the point in the action at which Custer fell, the identity of the warrior who slew him, if Custer's corpse was actually recognized by his foes, where and when the last soldier was slain. The recollections of those who stood on that carnage-strewn slope in the aftermath of the battle were understandably dominated by memories of the gruesome scene. "The horror of sight and feeling over the bodies of all these brave men after lying in the hot sun for three days I will not attempt to describe," interpreter Fred Girard told Walter Camp. "The stench of dead men was nauseating."[1] Similarly, First Sergeant John Ryan wrote, "I served through the Civil War and saw many hard sights on the battlefield, but never saw such a sight as I saw there."[2] At the time no one was particularly interested in making a tactical analysis of the engagement; the daunting ordeal of burying the dead was the grim and overriding preoccupation.

Estimates of the number of bodies located on Custer Hill vary from witness to witness.

Lieutenant Wallace put the figure at twenty or thirty, Thomas O'Neill of Company G said thirty-five, and Sergeant Ryan remembered forty-five in the group with Custer.[3] The most specific recollection came from Lieutenant Godfrey, who stated that forty-two dead soldiers and thirty-nine horses were found there.[4] Today, fifty-two markers stand within the iron fence that encloses the site of the last stand, their placement virtually unchanged from the time of their erection by Captain Sweet's detail in 1890. Clearly, some of these were among the surplus markers intended for Reno's battlefield. The most obvious example of a spurious stone is the one bearing the name of Lieutenant Harrington, whose body was never identified and who likely perished elsewhere.

Despite wounds, mutilation, and exposure to sun and heat, a fair number of the Custer Hill dead were recognized by their comrades—more so, in fact, than was the case elsewhere on the field. Near their commander lay other members of the headquarters staff: Captain Tom Custer, adjutant W. W. Cooke, chief trumpeter Henry Voss, and Sergeant John Vickory. The bodies of Custer's relatives Boston Custer and Harry Armstrong "Autie" Reed were interred on the hillside, as was a corpse believed to be that of assistant surgeon George E. Lord. One witness claimed that the body of Sergeant Major William Sharrow was located north of the main concentration of dead, although Sharrow is generally listed among the unidentified.[5]

A few men of Captain Keogh's battalion apparently managed to reach the site of the last stand, including two or possibly three troopers of Company L (Privates Charles McCarthy and Thomas Tweed and perhaps Francis Hughes) and two of Company I (Privates Edward Driscoll and John Parker).[6] Although several sorrel horses—the color of mount ridden by the soldiers of Company C—lay on the summit of the hill, the only enlisted man of that company recorded by name was Private Ignatz Stungewitz, who was recognized by Lieutenant Godfrey.[7] The commander of Company E, Lieutenant Algernon Smith, was likewise the only member of the Gray Horse Troop identified on the hill, indicating that he may have been wounded or killed prior to his unit's engagement at Deep Ravine.

Most of the troopers killed on the hill were men of Company F, known in the Seventh as the "Band Box Troop" for their habitually spruce and polished appearance. Both company officers—Captain Yates and Lieutenant Reily—were identified there, as were Corporal William Teeman and Privates Anton Dohman, Gustav Klein, William Lerock, and Werner Liemann. Private Dennis Lynch stated, "Fourteen F Troop enlisted men lay around Custer." Edward Pickard recalled, "It made me sick to see my fellow-troopers of F troop lying on the hillside, disemboweled, with stakes driven through their chests, with their heads crushed in, and many of them with their arms and legs chopped off."[8] Presumably other members of the company were among those on the hill who were unidentifiable, and it would seem that Yates's company was present at least in platoon and probably company strength for Custer's last stand.

The belief that Custer Hill was the site of last-ditch resistance by the five companies is evident in the observations of those who examined the ground on June 28, 1876. "It seemed to be a rallying point for all of them," Lieutenant Edgerly testified at the Reno Court of Inquiry; "It was the last point."[9]

The presence of almost as many dead horses as men on the hill fostered the widespread conclusion that the animals had been shot down to serve as breastworks for the beleaguered troopers. Lieutenant Wallace stated, "They had apparently tried to lead the horses in a circle on the point of the ridge and had killed them there and apparently made an effort for a final stand."[10] A few witnesses, Lieutenant Hare and Sergeant Kanipe among them, were less certain. Kanipe informed Walter Camp that he did not think the animals had been shot to form a "corral," as they were "scattered all over the hill."[11]

Conversely, Seventh Infantry captain

ABOVE: *Second Lieutenant Henry M. Harrington. Courtesy of Brian Pohanka*

BELOW: *Second Lieutenant William Van Wyck Reily. Courtesy of Little Bighorn Battlefield National Monument, National Park Service*

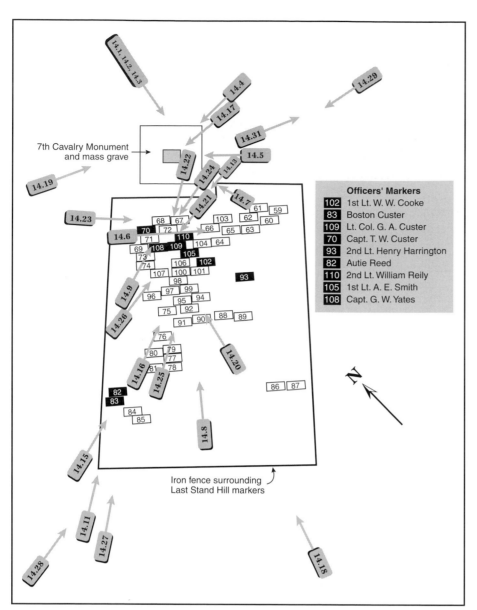

Officers' Markers
102	1st Lt. W. W. Cooke
83	Boston Custer
109	Lt. Col. G. A. Custer
70	Capt. T. W. Custer
93	2nd Lt. Henry Harrington
82	Autie Reed
110	2nd Lt. William Reily
105	1st Lt. A. E. Smith
108	Capt. G. W. Yates

7th Cavalry Monument and mass grave →

Iron fence surrounding Last Stand Hill markers

TOP: *Map 14.1. Custer Hill, Markers on Last Stand Hill*

BOTTOM: *Captain Thomas W. Custer. Courtesy of Little Bighorn Battlefield National Monument, National Park Service*

the ridge. Lieutenant Wallace saw four or five troopers "piled up in a heap beside a horse," with the general "lying rather across one of the men."[15] Stripped but neither scalped nor severely mutilated, the Seventh's commander had bullet wounds in the head and upper torso, either of which would have proved fatal. Private Jacob Adams later asserted, "I think the wound in the temple killed him, as it had bled and run down his face, and the other wounds had not bled any. . . . The blood was still oozing from the wound and running down his face and, his mustache being turned into his mouth, the blood coursed through the mouth and out at the lower side."[16] Opinions as to which round had first struck Custer and whether the bullets had entered the left or right side of his body vary from witness to witness, although the lack of powder burns on the head wound caused most to reject the notion that he had committed suicide.

Tom Custer was found some fifteen to twenty feet from his elder brother and somewhat higher on the ridge. He lay face down—pummeled, slashed, disemboweled, and filled with arrows. According to Sergeant Ryan's memoirs, the captain's head "was smashed as flat as the palm of one's hand," while Lieutenant Godfrey noted that "his features were so pressed out of shape as to be beyond recognition."[17] Indeed there was some doubt as to the identity of the mangled corpse until someone thought to look for a tattoo of the Goddess of Liberty and the initials TWC that Tom had on one of his arms. "Of course the flesh had turned black," Ryan noted, "but on close examination we found those letters, and that was conclusive evidence."[18]

Adjutant Cooke's body was discovered between two horses just below the crest of the hill; among other mutilations his thighs had been cut open and one of his long side whiskers skinned off as a unique scalp-lock, apparently by the young Cheyenne Wooden Leg. Nearby was a corpse clad only in a blue shirt and socks that several officers believed to be that of Doctor Lord, while Lieutenant Smith was positively identified behind a slain horse on the upper portion of the hill. DeRudio stated, "Lieut. Riley [*sic*] lay near Custer and his body was shot full of arrows," although Edgerly stated that Reily and

Walter Clifford saw "slain horses, placed head to tail."[12] The horses that Clifford described were most likely a group of animals found close together on the crest of the hill, near where Custer's body was discovered. Lieutenant DeRudio recalled, "Five or six horses lay as if they had been led there and shot down for a barricade. These horses were all sorrels from Company C."[13] The bones of those mounts were still in place a year later, when Captain Sheridan's expedition arrived to exhume the remains of the slain officers. Sheridan testified, "It was a rough point or narrow ridge not wide enough to drive a wagon on. Across that ridge were 5 or 6 horses apparently in line, and looked as if they had been killed for the purpose of resistance, but the remains were found in a confused mass."[14]

By most accounts, George Custer, his brother Tom, and Lieutenant Cooke were among the dead on or just below the crest of

Captain Yates were found in a group of dead somewhat farther down the slope.[19] Boston Custer and Autie Reed were still lower on the ridge: a hundred yards from the general's body, Edgerly reported, and two hundred yards distant by Godfrey's recollection. The young civilians may have been among those Godfrey described when he wrote, "A short distance below his [Custer's] position a number of bodies were found, indicating an attempt to escape."[20]

Although most of the burials on Custer's field were perfunctory and inadequate at best, as a rule the slain officers fared somewhat better, and of these George and Tom Custer received special attention. Several troopers subsequently claimed to have performed that solemn task. O'Neill told Walter Camp that he was digging a grave for his friend, Sergeant Vickory, when Lieutenant Wallace came up and said, "O'Neill, I think that will be a good grave to bury General Custer in."[21] Sergeant Ryan claimed that he and three comrades of Company M were the ones who interred the Custer brothers in a foot-and-a-half-deep excavation just below the "gravel knoll" on which the general's body had been discovered. Ryan recalled, "We wrapped the two bodies in canvas and blankets and laid them side by side in this shallow grave and then covered them with dirt. We took a basket from an Indian travois, turned it upside down, put it over the grave, and laid a row of stones around the edge to keep the wolves from digging them up. That was the best burial of any of the bodies on the field."[22]

In assessing the duration of the final stand, many of those who went over the ground on June 28 implied that the action on Custer Hill had been intense but likely not a protracted affair. As Wallace put it, "They had struggled but I do not think for any great length of time."[23] "I think there must have been very hard fighting," Lieutenant Hare testified. "Undoubtedly there was a very hard struggle."[24] Hare and DeRudio both spoke of finding "a few" expended cartridge shells on the hill, and Ryan recalled that he picked up "five or six shells" under Custer's body "but did not see others."[25] The piles of two dozen or more shells seen at Calhoun's position were apparently not in evidence on Custer Hill. However, the relative paucity of cartridge cases might be accounted for by the fact that the Indians habitually collected the cases after a fight.

Indian accounts of the last stages of organized resistance by the soldiers tend to support the impressions of the military witnesses after the battle. Dust, chaos, and ferocious combat apparently flared across the entire expanse of battlefield as the near-simultaneous collapse of Custer's tactical formations left only the headquarters contingent, Company F, and perhaps part of Company E to stem the warrior onslaught. He Dog stated that from the time Crazy Horse cut through Keogh's shattered units, "The fighting was going on everywhere." He Dog added, "The part of the line cut off fought their way up to others at the end of the ridge."[26] Pursuing the remnants of Keogh's battalion toward Custer Hill, some warriors rounded up riderless and stampeded cavalry horses, while others, as Iron Hawk later recalled, "followed along picking up arms and revolvers and ammunition and went to using these instead of clubs and bows and arrows."[27]

Archaeological evidence confirms that both captured military carbines and Indian firearms were brought to bear on Custer Hill. Some were fired from the northwestward extension of Battle Ridge, 500 yards distant, and some from Cemetery Ridge, 350 yards to the southwest. Other warriors were still closer. Exploiting folds in the terrain, they worked their way to a knoll just 150 yards east of the crest of Custer Hill. The barricade of slain cavalry mounts and expended shells discovered at the crest of the last stand position almost certainly indicate an effort by the soldiers to counter Indian fire both from the northwest—where more than forty Spring-field bullets were located—and from the nearby knoll.[28]

Indian recollections imply that while resistance at Custer Hill may not have lasted long, the fighting was particularly intense. Two Eagles asserted that "the only firm stand" took place on the hill and that "the soldiers fought the most stubborn" there.[29] Lone Bear characterized the troopers as "fighting hard," while He Dog, Flying By, and Hollow Horn Bear were among several Indian veterans who remarked that the soldiers seemed to have "plenty of ammunition."[30] Harrowing as their situation was, the cavalrymen managed to inflict some losses on their assailants.

Turtle Rib described the close-range combat with the encircled troopers in which his nephew had been felled by a cavalryman's bullet, and friends could be as dangerous as foes. "The Indians were all around," he said. "Some of them shot arrows and in the smoke and big dust hit their own men."[31] Big Beaver, a young Cheyenne who had joined the warriors concentrated on the slope of the knoll east of Custer Hill, observed the death of a feather-bonneted Lakota. "The Sioux would jump up and shoot towards the soldiers," he remembered, "then he would fall down and reload and crawl ahead again. He did this several times." Big Beaver was close behind the Lakota, who "jumped up to shoot again when a soldier bullet struck him in the forehead."[32]

Only when most of the troopers had been killed or disabled by the hail of bullets and arrows fired into their compressed perimeter did the Indians make their final attack. As the Arapahoe Waterman put it, "We rushed to the top of the hill and finished off all that were still alive."[33] Joining the charge over the crest and onto the western slope of Custer Ridge, Big Beaver noted, "No soldiers were standing up, but some were still firing that

were on the ground, or sitting up." While these were being killed, he saw "about 15" troopers running down the hill.[34] Flying By observed soldiers "running through Indian lines trying to get away."[35] The soldiers who died between Custer Hill and the Little Bighorn, perhaps in a desperate effort to reach Deep Ravine or the wooded riverbanks, were likely the last troopers to perish on Custer's field.

The fear and flight of the village noncombatants ended with the annihilation of the five companies, and those who had witnessed the fight hastened to gather the trophies of victory. "The women swarmed up the hill and began stripping the soldiers," Iron Hawk said. "They were yelling and laughing and singing now."[36]

This haunting view (14.1A), taken barely one year after the battle, is the earliest photograph of the Little Bighorn Battlefield. Both the photograph and the man who made it, John H. Fouch, were mysteries for more than a century, and the image itself did not surface until 1990.[37] Fouch's trip to the battlefield, related earlier, was a dangerous adventure in its own right. It was likely on the morning of July 7, 1877, one year and twelve days after the

battle and two days shy of his twenty-eighth birthday, that John H. Fouch became the first man to set up a camera on Custer Hill.[38]

Fouch's view was taken from the top of Custer Hill, where the large granite monument now stands, looking west toward the Little Bighorn River, a loop of which can be seen amid the trees that outline its course. Although grainy and later marred by spotting, this photograph, taken under the most difficult of circumstances, provides the clearest picture we have of the top of Last Stand Hill after the battle. Horse bones fill the immediate foreground, most prominently two skulls, one with the mane still attached—bespeaking the early date of this image. A boot top can be seen as well.

Just beyond this first grouping of bones is another, marked by a wooden stake and clustered around what appears to be a shallow pit. Some of the bones appear human, but in fact, all are from animals. Behind and just to the right of the wooden stake, a thinner one lies on the ground. Beyond all that, stretched in a horizontal line across the picture, are five

more of the thinner wooden stakes stuck into the ground. All the stakes appear to be of natural shape, with none four-sided or squared off.

Just beyond the row of five stakes, the vegetation suddenly seems less distinct as the terrain falls off down the steep slope of the hill. The view then continues through the relatively flat drainage below Custer Hill. On the right the landscape slopes up toward the present cemetery area, and on the left border of the picture, Deep Ravine can just barely be seen. The tree-lined river horizontally crosses the landscape, with the distant horizon beyond.

In the modern comparison photo, the granite monument (in place since 1881) fills the right side of the frame. It is surrounded by a grassy area, thirty feet on a side, which is the mass grave for all the bones gathered from individual burials around the field when the shaft was erected. The concrete footing that forms the border of the grass once held the ten-foot iron fence that stood from 1883 until 1963. The four-foot fence around the mark-

Postbattle eyewitnesses described the top of Custer Hill as a small knoll, some thirty feet in diameter, an area roughly equivalent to the grass around the granite memorial shaft today. About ten bodies were found there, including that of General Custer near the southwestern rim of the elevation. Six horses lay in a convex perimeter on the east side. Fouch's photograph matches these descriptions. The horse bones in the foreground were the eastern convex perimeter. The wooden burial stakes had been reset only days before by Sheridan's men, and seven in a field of view that does not cover the entire knoll top correlates well with the reported total of ten.

Evidence is strong that Custer perished atop the hill—not only in the testimony of witnesses just after the battle, but also in statements by Captain Sanderson and Lieutenant Roe, who led subsequent expeditions to the battlefield in 1879 and

1881 respectively.[39] Roe, whose men erected the granite monument that stands on Custer Hill to this day, said, "Its center is within six feet of the spot upon which were found General Custer's remains."[40] No individual markers stand on the knoll atop Custer Hill today, as is evident in our modern comparison photo, yet history tells us that some ten soldiers, including Custer, died there. A marble marker for Custer, stating that he "fell here," sits on the western slope of the hill, more than fifty feet from the granite monument. This may be explained, at least in part, by reports of Custer's body having been found atop the hill but then moved down the knoll to be buried.[41]

John Fouch's photograph is further evidence that Custer died on top of the hill. Fouch titled this photo, "The place where Custer Fell." The central point of the picture is the bone-strewn shallow pit with the thicker wooden stake, which is

on the southwestern side of the elevation, where Custer's body was said to have been found. It seems entirely likely that the stake was placed to mark the site of Custer's death. The shallow pit may have been an initial attempt to dig a grave for him, later abandoned for a spot farther down the hill. That burial location would later be mistaken for the actual site of his death.

No individual markers stand on the hilltop today, although the interpretive signage was recently changed to note that Custer did die there. Correlating Fouch's photo to the modern scene, that central wooden stake would be just a few feet from the granite shaft toward its southwest side, on the grass, behind the small flag and near the far corner of the monument visible in the modern photo. That is truly the place where Custer fell, not the marble marker site down the hill, and John Fouch's photograph gives the clearest view we have of it.

THE SUPPOSED LOCATION OF Gen. CUSTERS FALL/85   185

ers on the hillside can be seen in this image, though the stones are not visible because our view is blocked by the crest of the knoll. The background terrain features are similar, though thicker vegetation along the river blocks any view of the water.

In early April 1879, twenty-one months after John Fouch first stood on Custer Hill, photographer Stanley J. Morrow set up his camera very near the same spot. Unlike Fouch, who went to the battlefield on his own, Morrow had traveled to the Little Bighorn with Captain Sanderson's reburial detail. Morrow and his camera were to record their efforts at restoring the battlefield to a respectable condition.[42]

The first of Morrow's views from Custer Hill (plate 14.2) was taken from almost the same vantage point as Fouch's photograph, only a little to the left and closer to the wooden stakes. Our modern comparison of Fouch's photo (plate 14.1B) serves for Morrow's two hilltop views as well (plates 14.2 and 14.3). Once again, the camera was facing west on Custer Hill. The background landscape is nearly identical, showing the same prominent river loop, but no leaves were yet on the trees along the Little Bighorn, as it was early spring. Also visible just above a steep bank in

the middle of that loop are the four tents of Sanderson's camp (arrow, see plate 13.8A). On the left margin of the picture, Deep Ravine can be seen, this time with what may be a group of men, barely perceptible, working where the South Skirmish Line meets the edge of the chasm. A variant of this view shows two other clearly discernible groups of men working along the South Skirmish Line (see appendix).

The most important differences from Fouch's image are visible on the knoll atop Custer Hill. The bones and other items scattered about the hilltop in the 1877 view by Fouch have been gathered up in the center of the knoll in this photo. But the thicker wooden stake at the central bone pile in Fouch's photo, which we think marked the site of Custer's death, is still visible above the gathered relics, though they hide most of it. It is capped by an upside-down topless boot remnant. Also still visible are three of the five thinner burial stakes seen in the earlier view by Fouch. The third, though, is visible only in the right image of Morrow's stereograph, just to the right of the thicker stake with the boot top, which hides it in the slightly different perspective of the left stereo image.

Thus, little had changed between 1877 and

14.2. #185, "Bones on Custer's Battlefield showing spot where Custer made his last stand" (also issued as #34, "Gen'l. Custer's last stand, looking in direction of ford and Indian village"), photo by Stanley J. Morrow, 1879. Courtesy of W. H. Over Museum, #316.

BELOW: *14.3. "Where Custer Fell," photo by Stanley J. Morrow, 1879. Printed from the original glass-plate negative as modified and retitled by L. A. Huffman, originally Morrow #191, "Bones gathered on Custer hill before bur[y]ing them" (also issued as #40, "Bones gathered on Custer's hill previous to placing them in the monument"). Courtesy of Montana Historical Society, #981-368.*

1879 except for the gathering of bones on the hilltop by Sanderson's men—a first step toward getting them out of sight. But Morrow's photo does more than document the work of the reburial party. Both his title, "spot where Custer made his last stand," and the handwritten inscription on the vintage stereo card illustrated here, "The supposed location of Gen. Custer's fall," are evidence that Morrow understood this position atop Custer Hill to be the actual site where George Armstrong Custer died.

The next of Morrow's Custer Hill views (plate 14.3) was made from the identical camera position. The background is the same, with Deep Ravine seen on the left border of the left side of the stereo view. The river loop and Sanderson's four-tent camp are also evident. On top of Custer Hill, the pile is much larger, as bones had been gathered from all around the field. They block the view of almost everything on the knoll, but that central thicker wooden stake can still be seen, peeking over the bones with the boot still in place.

The bone pile in the Morrow views was on the area corresponding to the southwestern section of the grassy mass grave that surrounds the monument on Custer Hill today. The boot-decorated thicker stake was on the western edge of the pile, corresponding to the spot just off the southwest corner of the granite monument where we believe Custer's body lay after the battle.

Having gathered bones from around the field into the large pile on top of Custer Hill, Sanderson's men were ready for the next step. Burials in the sandy soil had been problematic, and rocks that might be used to cover gravesites were scarce.[43] But the trees along the river provided an alternative. With Morrow's camera there to document their actions, Sanderson's men began to place large pieces of cordwood in a perimeter around the bone pile, as seen in plate 14.4A.

The modern comparison photo shows that Morrow had shifted his camera position slightly to make this photo. He was still on the knoll atop Custer Hill, but with the camera facing more in a northwesterly direction. The granite monument and grass-covered mass grave, set up two years after Morrow's visit, fill the foreground. The 1879 landscape was starkly empty—the modern vista is much more full. Vegetation seems to be increased throughout the valley. Just past the monument is the four-foot fence that surrounds the markers on the western slope of the hill. Beyond that we see the visitors center, the tree-filled cemetery area, and the flagpole. Behind the far right iron fencepost, the entrance gate and ranger booth sit on a little rise that was bare in 1879.

TOP: *14.4A. "First Monument Custer Hill," photo by Stanley J. Morrow, 1879. Printed from the original glass-plate negative as modified and retitled by L. A. Huffman, originally Morrow #192, "Building the Monument on Custers Battle field" (also issued as #41, "Building monument on Custer's hill"). Courtesy of Montana Historical Society, #981-369.*

BOTTOM: *14.4B. 1994.*

Plate 14.5A, the last of Morrow's four atop Custer Hill, shows the final results of the work done there by Captain Sanderson's men. The large wooden pyramid, reinforced with dirt at its base and topped by a flag, is complete. Standing eleven feet high,[44] this structure, which became known as the "Cordwood Monument," served two important purposes. First, as one of Morrow's titles points out, "all the bones found on the field" were enclosed and protected from further scattering. But of at least equal importance is the fact that a monument now stood to honor the men who had fallen on this often-neglected field. Interestingly, in the foreground of Morrow's photo, a wooden stake lies on the ground, similar in appearance to the one seen at the central bone pile in Fouch's view and topped by a boot in two of Morrow's. Is this the same piece of wood, and was it left in the picture for some special reason? We are tempted to speculate that its presence on the south side of the Cordwood Monument is further evidence that this wooden stake had marked the site of Custer's death.

The modern comparison photo shows that Morrow had again shifted his camera position a bit, this time facing due north. The town of Crow Agency can be seen amid the trees in the background. In front of the monument and grassy mass grave, an interpretive marker explains: "The remains of about 220 soldiers, scouts, and civilians are buried around the base of this memorial. The white marble headstones scattered over the battlefield denote where the slain troopers were found and originally buried. In 1881 they were reinterred in a single grave on this site. The officers' remains were removed in 1877 to various cemeteries throughout the country. General Custer was buried at West Point."

In addition to the four photographs he made on the knoll top to document the successive steps taken in the construction of the Cordwood Monument, Stanley J. Morrow took another on the western slope of Custer Hill in 1879 (14.6A). Though these were the bones of horses, not men, their presence amid the crude wooden burial markers created an unsightly appearance, and Morrow likely made this photo to document the condition of the field before the cleanup. We can assume that Captain Sanderson's men removed these bones from the slope and interred them within the Cordwood Monument. The camera position faced south across the slope. Battle Ridge, extending south from the top of Custer Hill, can be seen running horizontally from the middle of the image to its right border.

In the modern comparison photo, despite grading to create the auto road,[45] the topography is similar, with Battle Ridge running horizontally through the middle of the picture. The four-foot fence enclosing the hillside markers has been added. Most striking, though, is the poor concordance between the crude wooden burial stakes of 1879 and the marble markers (see plates 14.8A and B). Of special importance are the several wooden stakes just below the lip of the ridge in the background of Morrow's photo (which would

Even before the erection of the Cord-wood Monument, plans had been set in motion for a large granite memorial both to honor the dead who fell in Custer's last battle and to stand over a common grave holding their remains. Although the memorial was ordered in February 1879, difficulties in transporting the almost-twenty-ton monument over long distances and through severe weather to the remote reaches of Montana Territory delayed its installation until July 1881.

Troops under First Lieutenant Charles F. Roe erected the granite shaft atop Custer Hill after earlier details had removed the Cordwood Monument and laid a foundation of stone and mortar. Roe's men then disinterred the remains of all soldiers buried in graves around the field and placed them in a trench dug around all four sides of the new granite monument, creating a mass grave that they felt would be both dignified and secure.[46]

The monument was built and shipped in three parts, the top two forming a truncated granite obelisk and the third its base. The four sides of the shaft were engraved with the names of the soldiers and associated scouts and civilians killed in the battle. Roe and his men used a crane made from timber cut along the river to set the eleven-foot monument on a mound of flat stones, bound with iron rods and mounded with earth, the total height above ground level being fourteen feet.[47]

ABOVE: *14.7A. #1205 "Custer Monument—Scout Curley," photo by F. Jay Haynes, 1882. Printed from the original glass-plate negative. Courtesy of Montana Historical Society, #H-728.*

RIGHT: *14.7B. 1995.*

had already been chipped in a number of places, most noticeably at the right base of the pyramidal portion on the side Curley was leaning on. Two years after it was erected, the monument and mass grave had to be protected by an iron fence, ten feet high and thirty feet along each side.[48] Hence, any early photograph that shows the monument before the high fence was placed around it has to date between 1881 and 1883.

The modern comparison photo reveals that Haynes's view was taken toward the northeast and shows the south and west sides of the monument. The west side, to the left in the picture, faces the Little Bighorn River and valley. The monument is little changed, but the earth around the base has been replaced by concrete. The mass grave around the granite shaft is covered with grass and bounded by a low concrete embankment that once formed the base for the ten-foot fence. The fence footing angles through the foreground of the photo. That high fence was removed in 1963, but the four-foot fence that was placed around the hillside markers in 1930 is visible in the nearest section of the foreground.

Plate 14.8A, a dramatic photo by D. F. Barry, was taken on the western slope of Custer Hill looking up toward the monument. Although undated, it was made between 1881 and 1883, after the monument was erected but before the fence was placed. By that time the

be outside the fence), where no markers now stand.

Stereo photograph 14.7A by F. Jay Haynes shows the monument as it appeared a year after Roe's men completed construction in 1881. Haynes poses with Curley, the best known of Custer's Crow scouts. Both hold rifles, and Curley's hat sits on the ground near his feet. This crisp image, printed from Haynes's original glass-plate negative, gives us a clear view of the monument's appearance in the early years. Unfortunately, vandalism was a problem even then, and the granite shaft mass grave around the monument contained all the remains from the individual burial sites around the field, moved there by Lieutenant Roe's 1881 expedition. The wooden stakes that had marked the original graves had been left in place by Roe's men, and a number of them can be seen in Barry's view. Almost all were crude and unfinished, except for one that appears to have been a more rounded headboard (arrow).

The modern comparison photo—showing the hillside, monument, and four-foot fence around the markers—is important for two reasons. First, it shows that the present marble marker for Custer, draped with a black cloth in our photo, is in the same spot as the rounded wooden headboard in Barry's ca. 1882 view. That more finished headboard was likely set to mark the site believed to be General Custer's post-battle grave. Captain Sheridan said that his 1877 exhumation detail had recovered Custer's body, but other eyewitnesses revealed that they had encountered difficulties in identification, leading some to doubt that the partial remains Sheridan brought back were actually Custer's.[49] Nonetheless, this pair of photos provides strong evidence that today's marble marker, incorrectly inscribed as the spot where the general fell, actually marks the location believed to be his burial site at the time of the 1877 exhumation.

Perhaps more important, though, is the number of marble markers seen in the modern view. These stones, which distinctly characterize the Little Bighorn Battlefield, were originally placed in 1890 by a military expedition led by Captain Sweet. He had been sent to the site of Custer's defeat with 249 of these stones and instructions to set one at the spot where each man had fallen.[50] That number of markers was a good approximation of the total killed on all parts of the field, including the sites of Reno's valley fight and blufftop defense. But 246 were placed by Sweet's detail on the sections of the field where Custer's immediate command had fought—far more than the 210 that has become generally accepted as the number killed with the general. Although historical accounts indicate that 42 is a more accurate estimate of the number of dead on Custer Hill, 56 markers were originally set there. Our modern comparison photo, covering the same field of view

ABOVE: *14.8A. View of graves and monument on Custer Hill, photo by D. F. Barry, circa 1882. Courtesy of Little Bighorn Battlefield National Monument, National Park Service, #418.*

LEFT: *14.8B. 1993.*

as Barry's image, shows 30 marble markers where wooden stakes or piles of stones indicate there had been only 12 graves. Hence, this photo pair provides proof that there are more marble markers than there were dead soldiers on Custer Hill.

At the tenth-anniversary observance in 1886, photographer D. F. Barry gathered a group of dignitaries at the Custer monument to make photo 14.9A. The camera was on the western slope of Custer Hill, facing east toward the monument, whose white granite is barely visible against the light sky. The guests stand in front of the ten-foot fence placed in 1883 to protect the monument and mass grave around it. On the slope below is evidence of a couple of gravesites marked by a wooden stake in one instance and stones in the other. Those posed in the picture are, from left, Corporal John Hall, Company D; Sergeant Ham (not a battle survivor); Captain Thomas M. McDougall; a Mrs. Mann; Captain Frederick Benteen; Captain Edward S. Godfrey; Mrs. Benteen; Doctor Henry R. Porter; a Mrs. Garity; Captain Winfield S. Edgerly; trumpeter George B. Penwell, Company K; and Crow scout White Swan, whose right hand shows evidence of wounds received in the battle.[51] In a similar photo, made by Barry at the same time and presented here as plate 14.10, he posed only the eight individuals who were battle survivors: from left, Hall, Porter, Godfrey, Benteen, Edgerly, McDougall, Penwell, and White Swan.

In the modern comparison photo (plate 14.9B), battlefield staff members Cliff Arbogast (left) and Guy Leonard stand where the dignitaries had posed. The high fence seen in the 1886 images was removed in 1963. Its concrete footing remains, and we used it to place poles where the old fenceposts had stood. The shorter fence seen in the modern picture is the one placed around the hillside markers in 1930.

As in the previous pair, more marble markers appear on Custer Hill than there were graves in the 1880s. In this modern photo, seven stones stand where only two burial sites were originally visible, and we cannot tell whether any of them match the early locations.

F. Jay Haynes made view 14.11A of Custer Hill in 1894 from a camera position below the main group of markers on the western hillside. The Little Bighorn River and valley were at his back. The granite memorial is seen atop the hill, surrounded by the ten-foot fence. The photograph documents the location of the marble markers just four years after they were set in place.

Careful examination of Haynes's view reveals forty-six marble markers, plus three memorials made of wood. Two are taller, narrower wooden headboards, which stand in the left foreground, each with an accompanying shorter footboard. The third is a large wooden cross, seen just below the lower right corner of the fence.

In the modern photo, a four-foot fence surrounds the hillside marker group. The monument sits in the same spot atop the hill, but the ten-foot fence around it has been removed. For the purpose of comparison, a National Park Service ranger stands on the old concrete footing of the original fence, where the right corner post used to be. A short way down the hill below his feet is Custer's marker, which we draped with a black cloth to distinguish it from the others. It is in the same spot where the large wooden cross stood in 1894.

The modern comparison photo also shows that the two taller, thinner wooden headboards and corresponding footboards in

the left foreground are no longer present. The footboards are gone altogether, and two marble markers, partly obscured by the fence, stand where the headboards had been. The stone on the left is for Boston Custer, the other for Harry Armstrong "Autie" Reed.[52] Eyewitness accounts after the battle leave some doubt as to where they perished and hint at difficulties locating Reed's remains. Their bodies may actually have been found farther from

OPPOSITE TOP: *14.9A. "Custer Monument, On Custer Battlefield, June 25th 1886," photo by D. F. Barry, 1886. Courtesy of Little Bighorn Battlefield National Monument, National Park Service, #421.*

OPPOSITE CENTER: *14.9B. Cliff Arbogast (l.) and Guy Leonard (r.), 1992.*

OPPOSITE BOTTOM: *14.10. "Reno Survivors at Custer Battlefield, June 25th 1886," photo by D. F. Barry, 1886. Courtesy of Little Bighorn Battlefield National Monument, National Park Service, #420.*

LEFT: *14.11A. "Custer Battlefield, Montana," photo by F. Jay Haynes, 1894. Courtesy of Montana Historical Society, #H-3144.*

ABOVE: *14.11B. 1995.*

CURLEY, ONE OF CUSTER'S TRUSTED CROW INDIAN SCOUTS.
CUSTER'S TRAGIC BATTLEFIELD WHERE ON JUNE 25TH, 1876 THE GALLANT MAJOR GENERAL AND HIS LITTLE BAND OF MEN WERE OVERWHELMED AND KILLED BY WARRIORS OF THE SIOUX AND CHEYENNE TRIBES—NEAR CROW AGENCY MONTANA ON THE BURLINGTON LINE VIA YELLOWSTONE AND GLACIER NATIONAL PARKS TO THE PACIFIC NORTHWEST.

the hilltop in the direction of the river than these markers indicate.[53]

Because Boston Custer and Autie Reed were civilians, no marble markers were supplied for them in the first group placed in 1890. But wooden headboards had been furnished for them at Fort Custer, and Captain Sweet erected those instead.[54]

The 1894 Haynes view shows forty-six marble markers, the Custer cross, and two wooden headboards, a total of forty-nine burials. The cross and headboards replaced, the modern photo shows fifty marble markers, not forty-nine. An isolated marker along the right fence line between pairs above and below it is not seen in the early view (arrow). This is the spurious marker placed in 1910 for Lieutenant Harrington.[55] Aside from that addition, the placement of markers on Custer Hill has changed little since 1894.

Haynes's 1894 image, without credit to him, would gain wide circulation on a postcard advertising railroad travel on the Burlington Route. We include a copy of that card as plate 14.12, a fitting tribute to the quality and importance of this Haynes photograph.

Sweet's men set a marble marker for Custer in 1890, but within a few short years it had been all but destroyed by souvenir hunters. No photograph of that original Custer stone is known to exist. Andrew Grover, first superintendent of Custer Battlefield National Cemetery, replaced Custer's badly chipped stone with a wooden cross in 1894.[56] That cross frequently appeared in early Custer Hill photos. The front of the cross was inscribed, "Here Fell Custer, June 25 1876."

The current Custer marker, inscribed as the place where he fell, stands on the same site as a rounded wooden headboard that was visible amid the crude burial stakes that predated the erection of the marble markers in 1890 (plate 14.8A). These linked comparison photos show that the early rounded headboard and the 1890s wooden cross both occupied the same spot as the current marble marker for Custer. The wording on the 1890s cross and the modern stone provides further evidence that the rounded wooden headboard originally at that location had special significance and was intended to indicate Custer's death place. As previously recounted, Custer actually fell on top of the hill but was likely buried some distance down the slope. It is quite possible, though, that by 1877, when Captain Sheridan recovered Custer's remains, he was unaware of the move downhill and assumed that Custer's body had been buried at the spot where the general was killed. Sheridan may have left the rounded headboard to mark that spot. The current Custer stone is thus at a site that has been specially marked since at least the early 1880s. Though probably not where Custer actually fell, it is likely where Sheridan's party exhumed the body they thought to be his in 1877.

This Haynes photograph (14.13A) of Custer Hill was taken in 1894, the same year as the view in the previous pair, but in the opposite direction, looking down toward the Little Bighorn River from the monument. The large wooden cross placed that year is prominently seen among the marble markers, its inscription ("Here Fell Custer, June 25 1876") clearly visible. As noted, Custer was likely killed on top of the hill, and this cross marks the site where he was believed to have been buried after the battle.

Haynes's photo is so sharp that we can read the inscriptions on a number of the marble markers. The one for the general's brother, Captain Tom Custer, is just in front and to the right of the large wooden cross. Historical accounts indicate that both were killed atop Custer Hill (but some distance apart), then buried beside one another in the same grave on the hillside after the battle.[57] The proximity of their respective markers points to a side-by-side burial at this downhill site.

The inscriptions on the markers of three other officers are also visible. To the right of Tom Custer's stone and almost level with it is the marker for Captain Yates, while to the left of the wooden cross and level with it sits the one for Lieutenant Reily. Directly behind Reily's marker, and partly obscured by it, is the stone for Lieutenant Smith. Evidence supports that Smith perished atop Custer Hill, along with George and Tom Custer and adjutant William Cooke. Smith and Cooke may have been moved downhill for burial as the Custers were. The marker for First Lieutenant William W. Cooke would be a bit downhill of Smith's but cannot be distinguished in this photo. Yates and Reily died on Custer Hill as well, although their actual death sites are less clear, and they may have been killed some distance below the knoll top.[58] We cannot know whether these markers are at the actual spots where these two officers fell, but Haynes's sharp photograph leaves no doubt as to the location of the stones just four years after their placement.

On the right side of the downhill edge of the main hillside marker group, the wooden footboards for Boston Custer and Autie Reed can be seen, their associated headboards just outside the field of view. Farther down the hill, the markers on the South Skirmish Line are

visible, winding toward Deep Ravine, which is in the left middle distance. The graves in the national cemetery can be seen on a rise in the right middle distance. In the more distant reaches of Haynes's view are the tree-lined Little Bighorn River and valley beyond.

Turning to the modern comparison photo, we see one marble marker, with part of its face darkened, that stands out from the others. This is the current stone for General

TOP: *14.13A. "Where Custer Fell, June 25, 1876—Custer Battlefield, Montana," photo by F. Jay Haynes, 1894. Courtesy of Montana Historical Society, #H-3152.*

BOTTOM: *14.13B. 1995.*

George A. Custer, inscribed as the place where he fell. It is in the same spot the large wooden cross was in 1894. The marker for Captain Tom Custer is in front and a bit to the right of his brother's, just as it is in the historical view. Likewise, the stones for Yates, Reily, and Smith are in the same spots where they were in 1894. The marker farthest to the left within the fenced group is the spurious stone for Lieutenant Harrington, placed in 1910. The footboards for Boston Custer and Autie Reed no longer exist and are not seen in the modern view. The current marble markers for the two young civilians, like the wooden headboards they replaced, are just outside the right edge of the image. The landscape beyond the fence is quite similar to that in Haynes's photo, although trees appear in the cemetery area and thicker foliage along the river blocks all view of the water.

A careful count in Haynes's 1894 photograph reveals forty marble markers and the wooden Custer cross, a total of forty-one burials (excluding the two footboards). Within the same field of view in the modern comparison photo also appear forty markers, including the dark-faced one for General Custer that replaced the cross, and the spurious stone for Lieutenant Harrington. However, since the latter marker was added in 1910, it is absent in Haynes' 1894 view. Hence the modern photo should show forty-two markers, including the "extra" one for Harrington. We cannot account for this discrepancy; the marker concordance seemed exact in the previous Custer Hill photograph (plate 14.11A) taken by the same photographer in the same year. But counting markers in photographs of Custer Hill can be a tricky endeavor. One stone might be hidden behind another when viewed from a certain angle, then be visible from a different direction. Possibly, too, a marker had fallen over, been hidden in the high grass when the photo was taken, then put back in the standing position later. Indeed, the early set of marble markers placed in 1890 fell easily and had to be reset frequently.[59] Even with minor count discrepancies, such as this one, the placement of markers on Custer Hill has changed little since 1894, despite the passage of more than a century, the ravages of weather, and the whims of thousands of visitors.

The preceding 1894 Haynes photograph may have had an impact in another area of Little Bighorn imagery. Nationwide interest in Custer's shocking defeat led to an outpouring of fanciful depictions of the battle. Most widely known is the lithograph "Custer's Last Fight," first issued by the Anheuser-Busch

14.14. "Custer's Last Fight," chromolithograph by Otto Becker, first issued by Anheuser-Busch Company in 1896. Courtesy of the Anheuser-Busch Companies.

Company in 1896 and circulated to this day. The image traces its roots to an oversized, mid-1880s painting of the same title by St. Louis artist Cassilly Adams. Exhibited around the country, it generated less profit than hoped for and ended up on the wall of a St. Louis saloon. When that establishment failed, brewery magnate Adolphus Busch, a major creditor, acquired "Custer's Last Fight." Busch engaged Milwaukee artist Otto Becker to rework Adams's painting prior to issuing it as a lithograph to promote his firm's products. When the print appeared in 1896, the image had been changed in a number of ways. The most prominent difference was in the background. Where Adams had shown a steep bluff behind the fighting in a scene that in no way resembled Custer Hill, Becker's rendition showed a fairly accurate depiction of the landscape, including the Little Bighorn River and valley.[60]

Becker acknowledged using photographs to create his version of "Custer's Last Fight."[61] Although he left no detail as to which specific photo or photos he had utilized, at least five different views of the Little Bighorn Valley taken from Custer Hill prior to 1895 are known to exist. Gerald Davidson and James Brust conducted a detailed comparison of the Becker lithograph and each of these five images. None of the five fits perfectly, although three are possibilities. The most convincing case can be made for this 1894 Haynes photograph as the likely source of Becker's background landscape in "Custer's Last Fight."[62]

View 14.15A by W. R. Cross, similar to plate 14.11A by Haynes, presents another sharp view of the markers on Custer Hill in about 1894. The monument and ten-foot fence are seen atop the hill, and marble markers dot the slope. In the left foreground the taller, thinner, wooden headboards and corresponding footboards for Boston Custer and Autie Reed are prominently seen. In the center of the view, below the right side of the fence, is the large wooden cross for General Custer. Erected in 1894 after his original marble marker had been destroyed by souvenir hunters, the cross is still in good condition in this photo. This photograph, like Haynes's, provides important documentation of the early marker placements.

In the modern comparison photo, the monument on top of the hill lacks the ten-foot fence. A four-foot fence surrounds the hillside marker group. In the left foreground, level with the spikes of the lower section of the fence, stand the marble markers for Boston Custer (left) and Autie Reed (right), in the same spots as the tall wooden headboards in the vintage view. The current stone for General Custer is again seen in the same place where the large wooden cross had been (arrow).

The Cross view shows forty-five marble markers, the Custer cross, and the two headboard-footboard pairs for Boston Custer and

TOP: *14.15A. "Custer Battlefield, Crow Agency Mont., General Geo. A. Custer and four Companies of the 7th Cavalry fell here, June 25th 1876. Views in the Black Hills and in Montana, On the B. & M. Railway, photo by W. R. Cross, Hot Springs, S. Dak.," circa 1894. Courtesy of James Brust.*

BOTTOM: *14.15B. 1999.*

Custer Battlefield, Crow Agency, Mont. — General Geo. A. Custer and four Companies of the 7th Cavalry fell here, June 25th 1876. Photo by W. R. Cross, Hot Springs, S. Dak.

Views in the Black Hills and in Montana. On the B. & M. Railway.

TOP: *14.16A. Visitors on Custer Hill, photographer unknown, circa 1894. Courtesy of Jerome Greene.*

BOTTOM: *14.16B. 1996.*

Autie Reed—a total of forty-eight burials. The modern comparison photo had to be made from a slightly different angle than Cross's original to keep the foreground markers readily visible through the lower section of the fence. This put the marker on the far right edge of the Cross photo out of the field of view in the modern one. The markers are harder to see in the recent photo because the grass is much higher. However, careful examination under magnification reveals forty-seven markers, the exact number seen in the

same field of view as Cross's early image. Thus, these two photos reinforce the conclusions drawn from the pair 14.11 A and B, that the current Custer stone is where his wooden cross was, the present markers for Boston Custer and Autie Reed stand where the early wooden headboards were, and the overall marker pattern has changed little in more than a century.

In view 14.16A, what appear to be several families, including a number of children, relax among the markers on Custer Hill. The image

is undated, but we estimate that it was taken in 1894 or soon thereafter, as the Custer cross, placed in that year and visible to the left of the tallest standing man, is still at its full height and in good condition. With the appointment of the first superintendent in 1893, the construction of the Stone House as the first permanent building on the site in 1894,[63] and the availability of rail transportation to nearby Crow Agency the same year,[64] Custer Battlefield had become a tourist destination by the mid-1890s, as these visitors demonstrate.

Modern visitors can no longer walk among the markers on Custer Hill, which are surrounded by the four-foot fence seen in the comparison photo. The current marble marker for Custer, marked with a black drape, is seen to be in the same spot that his large wooden cross occupied. The 1890s view shows twenty-seven marble markers plus the wooden cross for Custer, a total of twenty-eight burials. In the same field of view in the modern photo, we count twenty-nine. However, in the early image, one marker was likely hidden behind the woman standing, accounting for the different number. Some of the markers have been moved a bit, but the overall concordance is excellent. This is especially remarkable when we consider how easily the closely spaced markers could have been knocked over by visitors such as these, who not only moved among them but even leaned against them as the two young girls on the right did.

Plate 14.17A taken by H. R. Locke in 1894 to promote tourism on the Black Hills and Montana Railroad, gives a surprisingly unsightly view of damage to the base of the monument on Custer Hill. Perhaps railroad officials thought the public would not only accept this kind of deterioration as inevitable in such a harsh climate, they might think it was in keeping with the grim events that occurred on this site. Once a permanent superintendent arrived in 1893, problems such as this could be dealt with more readily. "[The] base of Custer Monument [is] to be repaired," Superintendent Grover noted in April 1896, "the frost having thrown the brick casing away from the stone foundation." The work was completed that June.[65]

The modern comparison photo shows the monument base in good repair and the mass grave area around it nicely planted with grass. The chipping of the section above the base, perhaps more the work of vandals than climate, has been partly repaired but can still be seen. The two top truncated sections engraved with the names of the soldiers are undamaged and unchanged in both photographs taken over a century apart.

Changes in the background are evident in the recent photograph. The ten-foot fence, inside which Locke set up his camera, is gone, and the four-foot fence around the hillside marker group is visible. Seen to the left of the

TOP: *14.17A. "No. 3. Custer's monument on Crow Agency, Montana, along the B. & M. R. R. Photographed by H. R. Locke, in 1894, Deadwood, So. Dak." Courtesy of Montana Historical Society, #946-601.*

BOTTOM: *14.17B. 1997.*

RIGHT: *14.18A. "Monument at Custer Battlefield," photo by Christian Barthelmess, circa 1896, printed from the original glass plate negative. Courtesy of Montana Historical Society, #PAc 95-70, Box 14.*

BOTTOM: *14.18B. 1996.*

Hill marker group. Once again, we see the monument atop the hill, enclosed by the ten-foot fence. Marble markers dot the hillside. Below the monument and a little to its left stands the wooden cross for Custer, still at its full height and in good condition, indicating that this photo was taken within a couple of years of the cross's 1894 placement. On the far left of Barthelmess's view are the wooden headboards and footboards for Boston Custer and Autie Reed. In the foreground, sitting next to a depression in the terrain, a dog adds a touch of softness to the stark scene.

In the modern comparison photo we see almost the entire confines of the four-foot fence, including all of the markers on Custer Hill. The current Custer stone, draped in black, is again seen in the same spot where his large wooden cross was. On the left, the modern marble markers for Boston Custer and Autie Reed stand where their respective wooden headboards were. Even the terrain depression in the right foreground is still visible, although partly obscured by increased vegetation.

Careful study of Barthelmess's view under magnification reveals forty-nine markers plus the Custer cross and the two headboard-footboard pairs for Boston Custer and Autie Reed, a total of fifty-two burials. That is the exact number of marble markers on Custer Hill

monument is a section of the cemetery that had not yet been set up in 1894. In the distance to the right is the transition road from Interstate 90 to Highway 212, leading to the entrance road to the national monument. Vegetation has increased along the river and around the cemetery. Then and now, however, the monument dominates the scene.

Plate 14.18A by Christian Barthelmess, taken from a camera position farther down the slope and at a different angle than plates 14.11A and 14.15A, shows the entire Custer

today. However, the current count includes the spurious marker placed in 1910 for Lieutenant Harrington, which would not have been seen in the Barthelmess photo, so we have a discrepancy of one. Counting the small-scale markers in a photo such as this can be a difficult endeavor. But this difference of one stone may be the first appearance of an extra marker seen in the historical view of a number of subsequent pairs. Even with this exception, the overall concordance is still good.

After taking the previous photo from a conventional vantage point, Christian Barthelmess with his dog walked around to the north side of the monument to make view 14.19A from an angle rarely used by 1890s photographers. He faced to the south, with the monument and ten-foot fence in the center of the picture and the upper portion of the western slope of Custer Hill and some of its marble markers visible on the right.

TOP: *14.19A. Untitled view of the Custer Monument, photo by Christian Barthelmess, circa 1896. Courtesy of Montana Historical Society, #PAc95-68, C-419.*

BOTTOM: *14.19B. 1996.*

It has been said that the top of Custer Hill was higher and more narrow at the time of the battle, and that grading over the years to place monuments and build roads and parking lots has lowered the hill significantly.[66] The three major projects on the hilltop prior to the date of this Barthelmess photograph (14.19A) were the building of the Cordwood Monument in 1879, the placement of the granite shaft in 1881, and the reburial of the dead from Fort Phil Kearny in 1888. Captain Sanderson, who supervised the construction of the monument in 1879, made no mention of grading the hilltop in his report.[67] When Lieutenant Roe's detail erected the granite monument in 1881, they did dig a hole eight feet on a side to create a foundation, then excavated the mass grave an additional ten feet in each direction. Hence, the total burial area, the monument in its center, would have been twenty-eight feet on each side. Roe likewise made no reference to grading the hilltop. It is not unlikely that he did so to some extent, but given the detailed descriptions in his report, if significant grading had been part of his activities, he probably would have mentioned it.[68]

Lieutenant George S. Young, who was in charge of the reburial of the Fetterman/ Fort Phil Kearny soldiers in 1888, told Walter Camp, "I buried these bodies near where the Custer monument now stands and I am sure no leveling was necessary, and none was done by me."[69] Young's testimony is of particular importance, for as a second lieutenant in the Seventh U.S. Infantry, he was part of the Terry-Gibbon column and was on Custer Hill immediately after the battle in 1876. Young thought that no marked grading had occurred atop Custer Hill, further stating to Camp, "As I recollect it, the ridge was amply wide for the purpose without doing any great amount of work. Being on the ground at the time of the Custer Massacre, and again in 1888, I am sure my statement is about correct."[70] Finally, Captain Owen Sweet, who placed the marble markers in 1890 and last visited the field in 1897, told Walter Camp that no grad-ing or change in the ground on Custer Hill had taken place between those years.[71]

Viewed from the angle at which Barthelmess took his photo, the contour of the Custer Hill knoll top has changed little since the mid-1890s. The earlier comparison photos likewise do not show major changes in the shape of the hilltop. To reshoot John Fouch's 1877 view (plates 14.1A and B), taken just a year after the battle, the camera and tripod had to be set up on the eastern edge of the flat area on top of the hill. There was no room to step farther back without going too far down the eastern slope to allow the image to be accurately recreated. This is strong evidence that the top of Custer Hill is not much wider now than it was at the time of the battle. Our comparisons of the 1879 Morrow hilltop views (plates 14.2–14.5) do not show striking changes either. Although grading had to be done to create the parking area and the roadbed east of the monument and south along Battle Ridge, study of early photographs does not support the notion of major reshaping of the top of Custer Hill.

In the modern comparison photo the monument is in the same place, of course. The ten-foot fence has been removed, but the concrete footing that held it remains. The northeast corner of the four-foot fence is visible on the right, and through it can be seen a few of the marble markers on the western hillside. The auto road slants through the foreground of the modern photo, before curving around the east side of the monument and heading south through the battlefield. The portion of the hill in front of the camera now appears steeper, indicating that the surface was graded to create the roadbed both in the foreground and on the far left edge of the image.

Plate 14.20A is a well-known double exposure made by Frank Purcell, a photographer from Billings, Montana, during the 1897 Decoration Day observance at the Custer battlefield. Purcell's photo, aside from the ghostly double exposure, is a typical 1890s Custer Hill view. Well-dressed visitors have gathered for the Decoration Day (Memorial Day) observance. A flag flies in front of Custer's wooden cross. Atop the marker-strewn hill sit the monument and surrounding ten-foot fence. In our modern comparison photo, the scene is as empty as Purcell's is full. The monument is in the same spot but now lacks the ten-foot fence. The shorter fence surrounds the hillside markers. Custer's stone, draped with a black cloth, is in the same spot as the earlier wooden cross. The 1897 view has a wider field of vision than our recent photo, but within the area covered, marker concordance is excellent.

The importance of Purcell's famous ghost picture lies not in its depiction of the physical landscape of the battlefield, however. It is far more significant for what it tells us of the people who were drawn to the site, and the mythology that already surrounded this special place even before the nineteenth century had ended. Whether by accident, as he claimed, or by design, Frank Purcell created a remarkable photograph.

TOP: *14.20A. "On June 24, 1876, at Custer's Battlefield," photo by Frank Purcell, 1897. Courtesy of James Brust.*

BOTTOM: *14.20B. 2000.*

In a lengthy explanation on the reverse of the photo mount, Purcell explains that he first took the view of Custer Hill, then inadvertently double exposed the image as he photographed an Indian playing the role of Bloody Knife in a war-dance reenactment in the valley below.

"Was it mere chance or did the camera see more clearly than eyes of man?" asked Purcell as he melodramatically mused over the meaning of this photo. His text is filled with not only historical inaccuracies, but also racial and ethnic stereotypes and prejudices that provide an interesting glimpse into attitudes of the time.[72] Trick photography of this type was popular in the 1890s, and Purcell may have purposely tried to achieve this effect. Regardless of the photographer's intent or interpretation, clearly he created a striking image, with the ghostly warrior raising his knife above the monument on Custer Hill as an American flag flutters in the background.

This picture was reissued without the text by another Billings photographer, A. B. Rumsey, though his rectangular cabinet card format cropped out the flag above the warrior's upraised arm. Many years later, Little Bighorn researcher John Carroll generated renewed interest in this image when he issued a small brochure titled "The Custer Battlefield Ghost Picture," reproducing both the photograph and Purcell's original text.[73]

Plate 14.21A, an 1898 view by Fred E. Miller, shows the wear and tear on Custer's wooden cross a few years after it was erected.[74] The inscription, "Here Fell Custer, June 25 1876," is still readable but less distinct. Both the top and the bottom edges of the horizontal piece show deterioration caused either by man or by nature. Part of the left side of the upper segment has been chipped off. The bottom section, and consequently the entire cross, is shorter than it was originally, likely the result of its having been broken off at the base and later reset into the ground without the lowermost portion. A comparison with the original 1894 appearance of the cross (plate 14.13A) readily shows these changes.

The comparison photo shows Custer's modern stone in the same place the cross had been. Some of the marble markers behind Custer's are blocked from view by its greater width, but the concordance between those visible in both photos is excellent. Beyond the markers we see the lower section of the four-foot fence. The cemetery is now surrounded by trees, and increased vegetation along the river blocks any view of the water. Aside from these changes, the landscape has changed little.

Lee Moorhouse took photo 14.22A, an extremely sharp photo of the markers on the slope of Custer Hill, in 1901. The original wooden cross erected for Custer in 1894 is still in place, but it has deteriorated further. The inscription is now barely visible, and the entire top section has broken off and is lying on the ground at the base of the cross. In the center foreground is what appears at first glance to be one heavily chipped marker. It is inscribed only "U.S. Soldier," as are most of the anonymous stones in the view, but it seems to be in the spot where Captain Tom Custer's marker was in other early photos. Only on careful examination can the viewer make out a second marker visible just behind the right edge of the unnamed one. That is the Tom Custer stone, and its entire right edge is heavily damaged. Also chipped are the markers for Lieutenant Smith on the far left and for Lieutenant Reily just to the right of it. All of these findings are consistent with reports of early vandalism to the markers on Custer Hill.[75]

The most important feature of this photograph, however, is the continued presence of the taller, thinner, wooden headboards and footboards for Boston Custer and Autie Reed. These are plainly visible in the right background of the hillside marker group. It has been written, and become accepted fact, that these early wooden markers were replaced with marble ones in 1896.[76] This photograph proves otherwise; the original wooden markers for Boston Custer and Autie Reed were still present in 1901. Yet another photograph, taken by the Wanamaker-Dixon expedition but not illustrated in this book, shows the two wooden headboards and one of the footboards still in place in 1909.[77] Hence, the replacement of the early wooden memorials for Boston Custer and Autie Reed with marble markers matching the others on Custer Hill did not take place until a still-unknown date at least a decade into the twentieth century.

In the modern comparison photo, taken from a somewhat higher camera position, one can easily see why the Tom Custer marker was hidden behind the one in the center foreground in the Moorhouse image. If the viewer were to imagine kneeling down to see our modern scene from a lower angle, as Moorhouse's camera did, the Tom Custer marker would go out of sight behind the one directly in front of it. The dark-faced stone for General Custer is in the same spot where the wooden cross once stood. The two markers for Lieutenants Smith and Reily are on the far left, just where they were in 1901. The stones that commemorate Boston Custer and Autie Reed are at the lower right corner of the fenced hillside marker group, where their

taller wooden headboards stand in the vintage view. They are of the same design as all the other markers and no longer have footboards.

The 1901 Moorhouse view shows thirty-six burials, including the Custer cross, the Boston Custer–Autie Reed headboards, and the Tom Custer stone that is almost completely hidden. Our modern photo shows only thirty-five in the same area. The spurious stone for Lieutenant Harrington is not an issue in this pair because it is out of the field of view on the left of the modern photo. A marker in the 1901 photo appears to be one that does not have a counterpart today (arrow). One of the Christian Barthelmess photos presented earlier (plate 14.18A) also has an extra

ABOVE: *14.22A. View of the markers on Custer Hill, photo by Lee Moorhouse, 1901. Image courtesy of the Division of Special Collections and University Archives, University of Oregon Library System, #2275.*

LEFT: *14.22B. 1994.*

TOP: *14.23A. "The Three Scouts," photo by Richard Throssel, 1908. Courtesy of Little Bighorn Battlefield National Monument, National Park Service, #427.*

BOTTOM: *14.23B. 1996.*

marker in the vintage view. We do not know when or why this marker disappeared. Aside from that, the overall marker concordance is again good.

Richard Throssel artistically posed three of Custer's Crow scouts (14.23A) amid the markers on Last Stand Hill in 1908.[78] On horseback facing the Little Bighorn Valley with rifles at the ready are, from left to right, White Man Runs Him, Hairy Moccasin, and Goes Ahead.

The wooden cross originally placed for Custer in 1894 progressively deteriorated and was in ruins by 1901. In this 1908 view we see a new cross for Custer that had been placed a few years before.[79] It is clearly visible, its top at the crook of Hairy Moccasin's arm. Also noteworthy, between Hairy Moccasin's horse and that of Goes Ahead, Weir Point can be seen in the distance.

The modern comparison photo was taken from a spot slightly uphill from the original

camera position. Nonetheless, Custer's modern dark-faced stone is in the same relative position that the wooden cross occupies in the original view. A precise marker count in the vintage photo is impossible because the horses block some of the markers from sight. Of those visible, though, the concordance appears to be good between the old photo and the new. Even from this distance, the deeper notch where the road was cut through Weir Point is evident.

As in the previous view, plate 14.24A shows the three Crow scouts posed on Custer Hill, although this time from a hilltop camera position with the Little Bighorn River and valley to their backs. The scouts flank the tall

wooden replacement cross for Custer. Immediately in front of the cross is the heavily chipped marker for Captain Tom Custer, and to the left is a stone with its top completely broken off, underscoring the problem of vandalism. Past the hillside group, the South Skirmish Line markers trail off toward Deep Ravine, with the familiar landscape of the Little Bighorn Valley beyond.

In the modern photo, the dark-faced stone for Custer and the marker for his brother Tom are both in the same relative positions. Exact marker comparison between the two views is difficult. The historical photo was taken from a camera position a bit farther uphill, which accentuates the tendency for

LEFT: *14.24A. "The Custer Battlefield," photo attributed to Joseph Dixon, 1909, but probably the work of Richard Throssel, 1908. Courtesy of National Anthropological Archives, Smithsonian Institution, #95-9805.*

RIGHT: *14.24B. 1998.*

This image of the three Crow scouts (14.24A) appeared as a plate in *The Vanishing Race,*[80] and hence would be considered the work of Joseph Dixon or his associates during the Wanamaker-Dixon expedition of 1909. A comparison with the prior 1908 photo by Richard Throssel, however, shows that the three Crows are dressed and equipped identically, right down to the feather on the rifle held by Goes Ahead. These two photographs were evidently taken at the same time and not a year apart.

What are we to make of this discrepancy? A relationship between Throssel and Dixon is known to have

existed. The first Dixon-led Wanamaker expedition did visit Crow Agency in 1908, the year the prior Throssel photo was taken, though not until their second stay there in 1909 were the images for *The Vanishing Race* taken. Throssel sold forty-two pictures to Dixon in 1908, and these became part of the Wanamaker collection. However, this photo was not known to be among them, and although Throssel and Dixon also worked together in 1909, none of Throssel's images was thought to have appeared in *The Vanishing Race.*[81]

Throssel took three other photographs of these Crow scouts in identical

attire, posed on Custer Hill. The original glass plates are at the American Heritage Center, University of Wyoming. One is a variant of "The Three Scouts." More important, another is an alternative version of this image, with the three Crow scouts in similar location and pose.[82] While possibly one of Dixon's staff was with Throssel as he made this series of photographs in 1908, and took this one himself, it is far more likely that this is Throssel's work. Hence, we credit this photograph from *The Vanishing Race* to Richard Throssel in 1908 and not to Joseph Dixon and his staff in 1909.[83]

TOP: *14.25A. "My glove on Custer's marker," photo by Elsa Spear, 1912. Courtesy of Paul and Teresa Harbaugh Collection.*

BOTTOM: *14.25B. 1998.*

OPPOSITE TOP: *14.26A. "An Anniversary Ceremony at Custer Battlefield," photographer and date unknown. Courtesy of Jack E. Haynes collection, Montana Historical Society.*

OPPOSITE BOTTOM: *14.26B. 1998.*

markers to go out of sight down the steep slope. In addition, the three scouts block some of the stones in the early view. The four-foot fence surrounds the hillside markers in the modern photo, and more trees appear along the river, but overall the background landscape is unchanged.

Custer's original marble marker, set in 1890 and replaced by a large wooden cross in 1894, was apparently never photographed. Plate 14.25A is the earliest dated photo we have located that shows a marble marker rather than a wooden cross used to commemorate General Custer; it shows that the transition had taken place by 1912. Shooting from a position below the hillside markers, Elsa Spear first placed her glove on Custer's stone to distinguish it from the others, a technique we have employed with a black drape in this pair and others. Identified in that fashion, the current Custer marker stands in the same spot where it was in 1912.

The ten-foot fence surrounds the monument in the vintage view but not in the modern picture. The recent photo shows the upper section of the four-foot fence that encloses the hillside markers. Lack of sharpness in the 1912 photo makes the distinguishing of individual markers from partly overlapping ones problematic, hence an exact count is difficult. The marker on the far right of the early photo is out of the field of view of our comparison image. Aside from that, marker concordance, including the Custer stone, is good with one exception. A marker near Custer's (arrow) does not have a current counterpart. Interestingly, the same "extra" stone can be seen in the 1901 view by Lee Moorhouse (plate 14.22A). The fate of that marker is not known.

Plate 14.26A shows a busy and diverse group, including uniformed soldiers, civilian visitors, and two Indians in full regalia, all gathered under flying flags during an observance on Custer Hill. The flags are a clue to dating this image, but even with careful study under magnification, both in this picture and in another taken at the same time, counting the number of stars precisely is difficult.[84] Clearly, however, these are not the forty-eight-star flags that came into use in 1912, but instead seem to be forty-six-star flags of the type used between 1908 and 1912.[85] Because the wooden cross for Custer, which was still in place in 1909, is no longer seen, this photo likely dates between 1910 and 1912. It may predate the previous photo (plate 14.25A), but because that image is dated and this one is not, we consider the prior picture to be the earliest dated photo showing a marble marker rather than a wooden cross for Custer.

In the early photo of this pair, the monument and ten-foot fence around it are seen atop the hill. For the purpose of comparison in the modern photo, a uniformed National Park Service ranger stands on the corner of the old concrete footing where the right corner fencepost had been. In our recent picture, Custer's marble marker is draped with a black cloth. We presume that a corresponding stone in the early view is the Custer marker. The fact that the soldier with his back to the camera, who seems to be directing the others, stands in front of that marker is further evidence that

it had special significance and is likely the one that commemorated Custer.

In the vintage photograph, a stone just downhill and partly obscuring the right side of the Custer marker has no modern counterpart. This is the "extra" marker seen in other views (plates 14.22A and 14.25A). Aside from that, concordance is good between the old and new images for those markers not blocked from view by the people on the hill in the early photo.

Plate 14.27A, a 1916 view of Custer Hill by L. A. Huffman, is the earliest dated image we have that shows marble markers rather than wooden head- and footboards for Boston

Custer and Autie Reed. It would be reasonable to speculate that they were erected between 1909 and 1912, at the same time as Custer's marble marker, but lacking proof we can only say that the stones for the two young civilians were placed sometime between 1909 and 1916. In Huffman's photograph, the marble markers for Boston Custer and Autie Reed are the two closest to the left edge of image. Their appearance matches the others on Custer Hill. The one for Boston Custer is on the far left, below the horse, while the other, for Autie Reed, is on the right of the pair in line with the left side of the ten-foot fence surrounding the monument. The cur-

rent marble markers for Boston Custer and Autie Reed are in the same spots and can be seen in the left foreground of our modern photo between the posts of the lower section of the four-foot fence that encloses the hillside marker group.

To locate Custer's marker in the early picture, we worked backward from the modern comparison photo. In our recent image, we placed a black drape on Custer's stone and had a uniformed National Park Service ranger stand on the concrete footing of the old ten-foot fence where the far right corner post had been. The marker in Huffman's vintage photograph that matches the location of the current Custer stone is indicated with an arrow, and we presume that this is the one that commemorates the general. To the right of the Custer marker in the 1916 view is another that has no modern counterpart. We believe that this is the same "extra" marker that is visible in several earlier historical photos (plates 14.22A, 14.25A, and 14.26A). Aside from that, marker concordance is good between the old and new photos. This 1916 Huffman view is the first of our historical images to show the spurious marker for Lieutenant Harrington, placed in 1910. That stone is the third from the right in both the vintage and the modern photographs.

The four-foot fence around the hillside group, originally proposed in 1915 to protect the markers, was erected on Custer Hill in 1930.[86] Along its uphill or eastern edge, it abutted the ten-foot fence around the monument until the latter was removed in 1963.[87] Both enclosures are clearly seen in this 1937 amateur photo by Charles Kuhlman (14.28A).

The four-foot fence remains to this day, standing alone on Custer Hill without the taller enclosure around the monument. However, it was modified slightly in about 1975. At that time, the section of the eastern or uphill edge in front of the monument was moved about eight feet forward (i.e., west), and a paved walkway was put in to allow visitors a better view of the hillside marble markers.[88] This change can be seen along the uphill side of the fence in the modern photo, to the left of the gate. Aside from those alterations in the fences and the presence of a pathway alongside the left edge of the enclosure, the scene has changed little.

Fifty-two marble markers stand within the four-foot fence on Custer Hill, according to a count made at the time this 1993 modern comparison photograph was taken. But because they are of such small scale in these photos and so closely grouped, one can block another, and discerning each one can be impossible. Nevertheless, marker concordance is good between the old and new photos and reinforces the conclusion that the marker placements within the hillside enclosure are virtually unchanged since the 1930s.

TOP: *14.28A. "Last Stand Area," photo by Charles Kuhlman, 1937. Courtesy of Little Bighorn Battlefield National Monument, National Park Service, #5996.*

BOTTOM: *14.28B. 1993.*

In 1888, the bodies of the men killed in the Fetterman fight of December 21, 1866, along with other burials from Fort Phil Kearny, Wyoming, were moved to the Custer Battlefield. The present cemetery area had not yet been plotted, and they were reburied on the battlefield just south of the monument on Custer Hill.[89] For a number of years thereafter, more than one hundred marble markers arranged in three rows stood on the site.

Photos of this marker group have an unfamiliar look to the modern viewer because all of these stones were later relocated to the cemetery and no longer stand on Custer Hill. The vintage view featured in this pair is even more unusual because it shows a fence around the Fetterman markers. We have included a more typical view as well, from another undated postcard, in which the Fetterman markers are not enclosed (plate 14.30). That one likely dates from the second decade of the twentieth century.

Plate 14.29A shows the top section of the four-foot fence surrounding the hillside marker group, which we know was built in 1930. Hence, this photo proves that the Fetterman markers were standing on Custer Hill until 1930 or later. Moreover, the presence of the two fences, similar in style, leads to speculation that the enclosures around the Custer Hill and Fetterman markers were erected at the same time.

Photographs showing this fence around the Fetterman stones are rare. Our research

LEFT: *14.30. "No. 16 Scene at Custer Battlefield, Hardin, Mont.," photographer and date unknown, circa 1910s, real photo postcard. Courtesy of James Brust.*

has turned up a number of images of these markers, but this is the only one in which they are enclosed. The scarcity of pictures of the fence point toward its having been in place for only a brief time.

The modern comparison photo shows that the Fetterman/Fort Phil Kearny markers sat where the parking area just south of the Custer monument is now located. In an aerial photograph taken between 1931 and 1934 (see plate 15.5), these markers are no longer present. Hence we know that the Fetterman markers were off Custer Hill by the latter date.

The relocation of these bodies of the Fetterman dead was only the start of a series of such removals from former frontier army posts of the Indian Wars era. The subsequent arrivals, though, were interred in the main cemetery area. As early as 1896, a request was made to move the Fetterman/Fort Phil Kearny graves into the cemetery as well, but action on this request was delayed for decades.[90]

The exact date on which the Fetterman/Fort Phil Kearny graves were moved into the main cemetery area is not known. Former battlefield historian Don Rickey wrote that they remained on Custer Hill until at least 1926, speculating that they were moved into the cemetery about 1930.[91] The paired photographs of the Fetterman stones support Rickey's premise.

Interest in the Fetterman/Fort Phil Kearny reburials at the Little Bighorn Battlefield was dramatically rekindled on July 17, 2002, when human remains were unearthed during a construction project in the parking area south of the monument on Custer Hill. While excavating to create traffic islands for the new Indian Memorial, workers discovered human bone fragments, nineteenth-century square nails, wooden coffin fragments, and clay brick of the type used to place government headstones. John Doerner and other National Park Service officials concluded that the human bones and other artifacts were originally from the Fetterman/Fort Phil Kearny burials, left behind in the ground when those remains were moved to the main cemetery in the 1930s. Evidence used to reach that conclusion included a comparison of the discovery site to historical photographs of the Fort Phil Kearny markers when they stood on Custer Hill.[92]

TOP: *14.31A. "National Cemetery at Custer Battlefield," photo by Christian Barthelmess, circa 1896. Courtesy of Montana Historical Society, #PAc 95-68, C-420.*

BOTTOM: *14.31B. 1997.*

Plate 14.31A is an earlier photograph of the Fetterman/Fort Phil Kearny markers on Custer Hill, taken by Christian Barthelmess about 1895 or 1896. Barthelmess stood with the Custer monument at his back, facing south toward the Keogh area and Calhoun Hill, and created this image, which is 180 degrees reversed from the prior views. The ruts of the old wagon road can be seen just above the far end of the line of markers to the right. Weir Point is in the background, with the distant mountains beyond.

This pair shows even more clearly than the prior one that the Fetterman/Fort Phil Kearny markers were located where the modern road and parking area are, just south of the monument on Custer Hill. The current roadway follows the same route as its rutted nineteenth-century predecessor.

15

THE CEMETERY

To facilitate the care of the graves of those killed at Little Bighorn, the Custer battlefield was declared a National Cemetery in 1879.[1] When the boundaries were officially set in 1886 by executive order of President Grover Cleveland, the entire battlefield area was a cemetery.[2] This explains the initial reburial of the Fetterman/Fort Phil Kearny dead in 1888 on what is now considered to be the main battlefield (see plates 14.29A, 14.30A, 14.31A). In 1889, proposals were set forth to create a fenced cemetery plot and to replace the wooden-stake burial markers still on the field with marble headstones.[3] This led both to Captain Sweet's 1890 expedition to place the marble markers on the Custer battlefield and to the creation of the burial area north of Custer Hill that is now identified as the cemetery.

When subsequent groups of Indian Wars–era reburials began arriving in 1890, their bodies were placed in this newly plotted sector. No pattern was established until 1894, but most were buried in the southern end of the present cemetery, first in what is now known as Section A, and later in Section B.[4] The men killed in the Hayfield fight near Fort C. F. Smith in 1867 were among those from a number of abandoned posts that were moved to the Custer Battlefield National Cemetery in 1892. Their graves, along with a larger monument that had originally been placed near Fort C. F. Smith to commemorate them in 1868, now rest in Section B, as do many of the others from that era.[5] Interestingly, their initial reburial in 1892 was in a different spot. The Fort C. F. Smith graves and monument were originally in what is now Section F, adjacent to the site of the Stone House (which was built two years later).

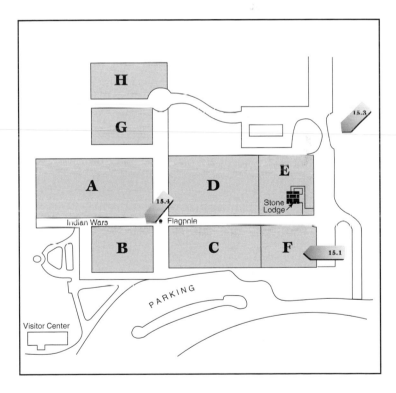

Map 15.1. National Cemetery

We are unaware of any written source that documents the initial placement of the Fort C. F. Smith graves, but this 1901 photograph by Lee Moorhouse (plate 15.1A) shows it clearly. The view is to the south, with Weir Point visible in the distance and the Wolf Mountains on the horizon. Beyond and to the right of the flagpole, the gravestones of Section A are seen row on row. Standing isolated in the right foreground is a single row of markers and a large stone obelisk. These are the graves of the Hayfield fight casualties, and the shaft is the memorial built for them at Fort C. F. Smith. The Stone House is just outside the field of view on the right side of the photograph.

In addition to this Moorhouse photograph, we have included a view of the Fort C. F. Smith marker and associated gravestones in place next to the Stone House, printed from an original glass-plate negative attributed to Christian Barthelmess and in the Robert C. Morrison collection at the Montana Historical Society (plate 15.2). The shadow of the Stone House roof is clearly visible in the foreground of the photo, with the photographer and his camera perched next to the chimney. This same monument is also visible next to the Stone House in the far left background of an earlier photo of Calhoun Hill by Christian Barthelmess (see plate 11.1A).

In the modern comparison photo (plate 15.1B), the foreground is filled with stones running in continuous lines through what are now Sections F and C beyond. The uniquely

TOP: *15.1A. View in the Custer Battlefield National Cemetery, photo by Lee Moorhouse, 1901. Image courtesy of the Division of Special Collections and University Archives, University of Oregon Library System, #2274.*

CENTER: *15.1B. 1995.*

RIGHT: *15.2. View of Fort C. F. Smith marker, printed from an original glass-plate negative attributed to Christian Barthelmess, circa 1896. Courtesy of Montana Historical Society, #PAc 95-70, box 14.*

Custodian's House, Custer Battlefield National Cemetery.

Herbert A. Coffeen, Publisher, Sheridan, Wyo.

shaped Fort C. F. Smith marker is no longer where it was in 1901, however. Instead it can now be seen in the middle distance on the left side of the image, in Section B of the cemetery. We do not know why the Fort C. F. Smith marker and graves were placed apart originally, or when they were set among the other abandoned post reburials, but without the historical photographic record, the fact that they were moved would be lost completely.

Also of note is the flagpole. Moorhouse's 1901 photo shows the original wooden staff, built in 1896. It was destroyed by lightning on June 21, 1907, then replaced in the same spot a year later in 1908 by the steel flagpole that still stands.[6]

Photo 15.3A of the Stone House and associated outbuildings is undated, but we can place it within a narrow time range. Throssel came to the Crow Reservation in 1902.[7] The flagpole visible in the image is the old wooden staff, destroyed by lightning in 1907. Hence this photo dates between 1902 and 1907. On the far left, the Fort C. F. Smith marker can be seen at the site of its original relocation in Custer Battlefield National Cemetery. The marker's proximity to the Stone House at that time can readily be seen. Between the Fort C. F. Smith obelisk and the Stone House, the Custer monument and surrounding ten-foot fence are visible in the background.

The Stone House, completed in 1894, and the several outbuildings and stables built the following year were the only structures at the battlefield in that era. This Throssel photo provides a good view of the entire complex. The Stone House served as the lodging for the superintendent and his family.

Turning to the modern photo, we see the Stone House structure in the same spot, its appearance relatively unchanged. It is no longer a residence, however, and now houses the White Swan Memorial Library, part of the research facilities of the Little Bighorn Battlefield National Monument. The flagpole is also in the same place, but it is the taller steel structure built in 1908. In every other way, though, the scene has changed consider-

The Cemetery 165

TOP: *15.4A. "Custer Battlefield," photographer and date unknown, real photo postcard. Courtesy of Paul and Teresa Harbaugh Collection.*

BOTTOM: *15.4B. 1998.*

ably. The outbuildings are gone, removed in 1965 to make room for more gravesites.[8] The Fort C. F. Smith marker can no longer be seen, because it was moved to another part of the cemetery. Many more gravestones now fill Sections E and F on both sides of the Stone House. The other obvious change is the dramatic increase in vegetation. In Throssel's early photo no trees appear. Starting in the late 1920s, however, trees and other plants were gradually added to enhance the cemetery's appearance.[9] Tall trees are now common in the cemetery and visitors center area. In our modern photo, they block the view of the

monument on Custer Hill and all terrain details beyond the cemetery, but they relieve the harshness of the early landscape.

Though undated, photo 15.4A of Section B of the cemetery and Custer Hill beyond was probably taken in the 1930s. Visible are both the four-foot fence surrounding the hillside markers placed in 1930 and the iron fence built around the cemetery in 1931.[10] No trees are seen, and this image likely predates the planting of 140 evergreen trees in the cemetery in 1941.[11] On the far right edge of the photo stands the Fort C. F. Smith marker. It is no longer in its initial spot near the

Stone House, but rather in its current location in Section B, proving that relocation had occurred by the time this photograph was taken. The large, blocklike monument in the left foreground commemorates the dead brought from Fort Keogh to the Custer Battlefield National Cemetery in 1924.

In the modern comparison photo, the markers in the cemetery are unchanged, but the overall appearance of the scene is different. The Fort C. F. Smith marker is on the far right, seen just inside the tree along the right border of the photo. It is in the same spot as in the vintage view, as are the Fort Keogh memorial on the left and nearly all the other markers in sight. Past the markers is a line of tall trees. Cars in the current parking area are visible just below the branches, but the thick foliage blocks the view of Custer Hill. Other landmarks of the modern battlefield, especially the visitors center, are also shielded from vision. This relative isolation of the cemetery has created a more solemn environment.

WE CLOSE with three aerial photos that we were unable to reshoot. All show not only the cemetery and the Stone House, but Custer Hill as well.

The aerial photo postcard titled "Scene of Custer Massacre 1876" is the earliest of the three. The view is toward the south, with the cemetery and the Stone House in the foreground and Custer Hill in the left middle distance. The photograph is undated, but evidence in the image places it within a three-year time frame. An iron fence built around the perimeter of the cemetery in 1931 is visible, but the speakers rostrum, constructed in the northeast (lower left) corner of the cemetery area in 1934 does not appear in the photo.[12] Hence, this photograph was taken between 1931 and 1934. The Fetterman/Fort Phil Kearny markers are no longer on Custer Hill, proving that they had been moved to the main cemetery by 1934. The road, initially dug in 1930, still has a freshly cut appearance.[13]

The Stone House is seen with all of its outbuildings. The old entrance road enters the view from the bottom margin of the image, converging in front of the Stone House with a smaller dirt path coming in from the right. No trees are visible anywhere in the cemetery area. The basic layout of the cemetery is easily seen. The area that is now Section A, in the southwest (upper right) corner of the burial area, is filled with neat rows of gravestones. The current Section B, in the upper left, is gradually filling in. A narrow paved path runs from the main walk to the Fort C. F. Smith marker, which has been moved from its initial location near the Stone House to its current spot in Section B, along with the individual gravestones of the dead from that post. Just below Section B and parallel to the main walkway through the burial area, a single row of graves appears in what would become Section C.

15.6. Aerial view of Custer Hill and the cemetery, photo by Charles Belden, September 1941. Courtesy of Little Bighorn Battlefield National Monument, National Park Service, #16979.

Next is Charles Belden's September 1941 aerial photo (plate 15.6), taken toward the northwest in a direction almost opposite to that of the previous image. The cemetery and Stone House are now in the background. The monument and mass grave on Custer Hill are in the foreground, surrounded by the ten-foot fence, while the hillside markers are encircled by the four-foot iron enclosure. This photograph shows how the two fences fit together until the taller one was removed in 1963. Just south (left) of the monument, two cars are parked in the area that used to contain the Fetterman/Fort Phil Kearny graves, which by that time had been moved into the cemetery. The entire roadway has a more finished appearance than in the prior photo, consistent with improvements that included grading in 1938 and placement of gravel a few months earlier in the summer of 1941.[14]

An open water tank, no longer present, is visible on the lower edge of the image, across the road to the east of the monument. On April 9, 1941, less than six months before this picture was taken, Superintendent Luce and his staff discovered a "horse cemetery"— a cache of horse bones and a few human remains—while digging a drainage pipeline from this water reservoir. These may have been the same horse bones originally interred in the Cordwood Monument in 1879. The "horse cemetery" was reopened in 1946, then largely forgotten until recently. In April and May 2002, to study the site prior to construction of improvements accompanying the new Indian Memorial, a team led by archaeologist Douglas Scott excavated the "horse cemetery" and documented its location.[15]

In the top right corner of the picture, the old entrance road runs past a small wooden building and through a decorative iron gate, features not seen in the earlier aerial view (plate 15.5). That road and a smaller path coming in from the west converge in front of the Stone House, which is seen with all of its outbuildings still standing and graced by a number of tall trees. The basic layout of the cemetery is plainly seen. The area that is now Section A, to the left of the flagpole and above the paved walkway, is filled with neat rows of gravestones. The current Section B, left of the flagpole on the near side of the walk, continues to fill in. As can be seen in the prior aerial photo, a narrow paved path runs from the main cemetery walk to the Fort C. F. Smith marker in Section B. To the right of Section B, the area that was to become Section C contains several rows of graves rather than just one. Despite the tall trees near the Stone House, overall vegetation is still sparse. Visible along the walkway and some of the cemetery boundary areas are the young evergreen trees planted the month this photo was taken, September 1941.[16]

The third aerial photo (plate 15.7) was taken by Kenneth Roahen during the seventy-fifth anniversary observance on June 25, 1951. It is oriented in a north-to-south direction similar to the early postcard view but opposite to Belden's 1941 picture. The Stone House and cemetery are in the foreground, and Custer Hill is in the left middle distance. The old entrance road enters on the right edge of the image, near the front of the Stone House,

which has at least one of its outbuildings intact. The basic configuration of the cemetery is unchanged, but it contains more gravestones because additional burials have taken place in the intervening decade. In this photograph, Section A is in the far right of the cemetery area, filled with neat rows of gravestones as it was in the earlier views. Section B, on the far left, has more graves than it did in 1941. It still features the Fort C. F. Smith marker, though the stone is difficult to see at this small scale. The Fort C. F. Smith marker is in the same spot as it was in 1941 and still is today, but the path that leads to it in the earlier views is no longer present. Section D, behind the Stone House, now has a few burials, and Section C on the near left has more than it did in the prior photo.

The trees along the cemetery walkways and boundaries, newly planted in the 1941 photo, have grown, and some new, smaller ones

have been added. In the lower left (northeast) corner of the cemetery is a small structure that is visible in the 1941 view but shows more clearly in this 1951 image. This was a rostrum, or speakers stand, built in 1934 and removed in 1965. Many of the ceremonial events of the seventy-fifth anniversary were carried out on this platform, which accounts for the large crowd standing in front of it in this 1951 photo.[17]

Perhaps the most important feature of Roahen's aerial photo is the view of the visitors center under construction. It is seen on the road between the cemetery and Custer Hill. Not until 1949 were funds finally appropriated to build a long-proposed visitors center that would house a museum and administrative offices. Ground was broken on July 17, 1950, and construction began shortly thereafter. The building was finally finished and dedicated in early July 1952.[18] The external

15.7. Aerial view of the Custer battlefield on the seventy-fifth anniversary of the battle, photo by Kenneth Roahen, June 25, 1951. Courtesy of Dennis Fox.

framework was complete when Roahen took this photo in 1951, but the cluster of small, temporary structures nearby suggest that work was still under way.

Roahen's photo is also interesting for the glimpse it provides of where visitors parked and how they moved about the battlefield in that era. Because the road brought cars in near the Stone House, parking was clustered in that area. The present parking area between the visitors center and the cemetery had not yet been created. Guests are seen walking from the Stone House to Custer Hill, where people are gathered, but only a single automobile is visible. Beyond the monument on Custer Hill, the road snakes through the landscape on its way to the Reno-Benteen defense site.

Significant changes were made in 1957. The current entrance road was built along the ridge that runs through the left-center foreground of the photo, and visitors now enter the national monument on the east side of the cemetery, bypassing the Stone House. The paved parking area between the cemetery and the visitors center was created in the same year.[19] With these revisions, the old entrance road fell into disuse and is barely noticed today.

16

UNMATCHED PHOTOGRAPHS ✑

I T HAS NOT always been easy to find the site at which a given historical photograph was taken. In some instances we searched for a spot during several battlefield visits before we located it, and at other times we had to go back and retake a modern comparison photo when the first effort turned out to be inaccurate. Given the fine state of preservation of the Little Bighorn Battlefield, though, each site could usually be found with enough searching. But not always. Despite our best efforts, a few of the images have eluded our attempts to match them. We present a trio of such pictures, partly as an example of how difficult this work can be but also in the hope that our readers will take up the challenge and help us finally match these photographs.

Plate 16.1 is one of a group of five photographs on identical, unidentified mounts. The companion images show Custer Hill as it appeared about 1895 and Crow people somewhere on their reservation. Hence, we have concluded that this photo of three well-dressed white women with what appear to be a group

16.1. *View of a group standing on a high point above the Little Bighorn Valley, photographer unknown, circa 1895. Courtesy of James Brust.*

of Indian boys in nonnative attire was taken in the same era and general location. They are standing on a high point, with what appears to be the Little Bighorn Valley in the distance, although we do not know that for sure. A river meanders on the valley floor, and the horizon line can be clearly seen. Despite these features, we were unable to find the spot at which this photograph was taken.

16.2. *"Slaper in water detail ravine,"*
photographer unknown, taken at the
fiftieth anniversary of the battle, June
25, 1926. Courtesy of Little Bighorn
Battlefield National Monument,
National Park Service, #6694.

Private William C. Slaper of Company M was one of the brave troopers besieged at the Reno-Benteen defense site who made the dangerous sortie to the river to get water for the wounded. Slaper attended the fiftieth-anniversary observance at the battlefield on June 25, 1926, and was photographed a number of times that day. Plate 16.2 is inscribed "Slaper in water detail ravine." Because of the uncertainty about which route or routes the water carriers used to reach the river, this photo is potentially of great historical significance. Here one of the soldiers who actually went for water poses in the ravine he said he used. If this spot could be located, Slaper would

be telling us, as he told the 1926 photographer, exactly which route he followed to the river. Alas, despite a number of strenuous walks up and down the various gullies leading from the Reno-Benteen defense site to the Little Bighorn River, we were unable to find the place where Slaper stood, and this photograph could not be re-created. Perhaps the steep sandstone walls of the ravine have eroded, making this location unrecognizable now. Given the historical significance of this image, the search should go on.

Plate 16.3 shows Al Croonquist, the man on the right with the white shirt, who was a friend of Elsa Spear's. She photographed him

Custer Battlefield   Al Croonquist
,1936

with this group of Indian people, sitting on a hill during a visit to the battlefield in 1936. Finding the spot on which they sat has proved to be surprisingly difficult. This photograph appears to have been taken outside the battlefield, somewhere in the vicinity of Highway 212 and the entrance to the national monument. Between the two men with tall hats, an automobile is traveling up what seems to be the old entrance road. Farther into the middle distance, a large truck and other vehicles are likely driving along Highway 87, which was at that time the main road through the Little Bighorn Valley but is now the frontage road for Interstate 90. On the left side of the horizon may be the trees around the Stone House and national cemetery. Despite all of these clues, we could not find the spot on which this group perched in 1936. A fair amount of grading must have been done when the present entrance road was built in 1957, so this little hill may no longer exist. Although this photo is not of great historical significance, the challenge of matching it remains.[1]

16.3. "Custer Battle field, Al Croonquist, 1936," photo by Elsa Spear, 1936. Courtesy of Paul and Teresa Harbaugh Collection.

AFTERWORD

A GOOD DEAL OF the theorizing about the Battle of the Little Bighorn has flowed from the study of the terrain and the markers placed on it. A crucial consideration concerns how precisely current features match their historical appearance. We trust that this study of historical photographs has provided important information that will help answer that question.

Looking first at the topography, we find that it has changed little. With the notable exception of the notch in Weir Point that was deepened for road construction and the collapse of sections of the steep walls of Deep Ravine, the terrain has barely changed at all. Some commonly held notions about alterations in the field are not borne out. Despite changes to Custer Hill from the burial and removal of the Fort Phil Kearny graves, the horse cemetery, and the various generations of road and parking areas, the summit of the hill on which the monument rests has not been flattened significantly, as has often been asserted. Also, the markers on Calhoun Hill were not moved to accommodate the loop road. Similar construction on other parts of the field is obvious as well, but overall we have shown that the Little Bighorn Battlefield is in an excellent state of preservation.

Second, the earliest generations of wooden grave markers, replaced in 1890 by today's still-familiar stones, are documented only in the surviving early photos taken in the 1870s and 1880s. Many of those rare views are presented in this book. These stakes, easily felled or moved, had little permanence, and the marble markers placed by Captain Owen Sweet's detail did not always accurately mirror their locations, as our comparison photos verify.

But those 1890 stones, which have come to characterize the entire field, have heavily influenced generations of battle theorists. Are they still in their original locations? The modern photos show a remarkable concordance between the earliest photos of those markers and their counterparts today. A few spurious stones have been added over the years, and through this project we also determined that two of the original markers were missing. They have since been replaced. Overall, to an extraordinary degree, today's markers remain in the spots where the originals were placed in 1890. Modern battle students can study these marker placements with confidence that the pattern remains unchanged since 1890.

In some instances, the historical photos literally illustrate personal accounts of battle participants. Gall's description to D. F. Barry of Custer's skirmish line locations, the stories told to Edward Curtis by the three Crow scouts, Sergeant Daniel Kanipe standing next to Sergeant Edwin Bobo's marker—one can debate the accuracy of their information, but the photos put us right there with them as they describe the events.

Photographs undeniably place viewers "on the field" in a way that other descriptive accounts cannot match. Study of these images enhances the feeling of personal involvement with the events of 1876.

We are not the first to study vintage battlefield photographs as historical documents or to use the then-and-now comparison technique. William Frassanito and others have done this with Civil War imagery, and it has been applied to frontier history as well.

But serious investigation of these early photos still lags behind research into other primary sources. We hope this book will help change that. We also hope that our more than ten years of crisscrossing the Little Bighorn Battlefield National Monument and its surrounding countryside seeking to match up those long-ago images with today's ravines and ridges will ensure that the wonderful legacy left by these photographers will continue to be appreciated by today's students and motivate them to locate additional undiscovered views.

NOTES ON THE MAKING OF THE MODERN
COMPARISON PHOTOGRAPHS

ALL OF THE modern comparison photographs were taken by James Brust, using a Nikon F3 35mm single lens reflex camera with a 50mm f1.4 Nikkor lens. The camera was placed on a tripod for maximum sharpness. Kodak black-and-white 5052 TMX film was used to make all of the modern comparison photos, except for some of the 1999 shots and all of those in 2000, which were taken on Agfa APX. The film was professionally developed and printed.

APPENDIX ⋙

Stanley J. Morrow's 1879 Photographs of Little Bighorn

IN THE SPRING of 1879, frontier photographer Stanley J. Morrow took a series of pictures of the Little Bighorn Battlefield. They may be the most important group of photos ever taken of that storied site. Anyone with even a passing interest in the battle is certain to come across one or more of these early images. Yet despite their significance, they have rarely been studied comprehensively. Many appear elsewhere in this book, accompanied by modern comparison photos. We add this appendix to further highlight Morrow's important series of photos of the battlefield and to present all of them in the same place to provide a convenient reference and facilitate their study.

Morrow published his battlefield views in at least two different sets of stereo cards. While the images are the same, the numbers and titles vary. Both sets have the imprint "Photographed and Published by S. J. Morrow, Yankton, D.T." One set, titled "Photographic Gems of the Great Northwest," has all of the titles preprinted on the reverse, so we know the full scope of the series, twelve in all, numbered from 185 through 196. In addition to the battlefield photos, the numbers and titles of two other series are printed on the backs of the same cards. These are "Crook's Expedition Against Sitting Bull 1876" and "Local Series, Yankton."

The second Morrow stereograph series to include Little Bighorn photos was called "Photographic Views of the Great Northwest." These cards, however, do not have preprinted titles, but only the individual number and title on the reverse of each photo. The numbers range from 34 to at least 44.

The captions provided here include the number and full title Morrow gave to each view. Because of the preprinted information on the "Photographic Gems" set, our knowledge of those numbers and titles is more complete, and we use those preferentially, noting the alternate numbers in brackets.[1] Of the twelve overall views, four have variants, but these were never assigned separate numbers or titles. Morrow's numbering does not always follow a topical sequence in either series, so we discuss the photos by subject matter.

The full series can be divided into three sets of four photographs each.

The first of these groups (#185 [#34], #191 [#40], #192 [#41], and #193 [#42]) documents the gathering of bones from around the field on top of Custer Hill and the subsequent construction of a cordwood pyramid around them by Captain Sanderson's detail. This "Cordwood Monument" was the first memorial atop Custer Hill.[2] In addition, #185 [#34], both in its title and in its content, may be telling us that Custer actually died on top of the hill and not on the western slope as his present marble marker would indicate. For a more thorough discussion of Morrow's four views from the top of Custer Hill, including modern comparisons, see photo pairs 14.2 through 14.5 in the main text of this book.

In the background of #185 [#34], what may be a group of men can be seen along the South Skirmish Line near the head of Deep Ravine. A variant of this photo has two other clearly seen groups of men working along the South Skirmish Line. Also of note in the distance of #185 [#34] and #191 [#40], across the Little Bighorn River, are the four tents of Captain Sanderson's camp. A closer view of the campsite appears later in the series (#195 [#43]).

Four of Morrow's photographs show grave markers around the field. In #186 [#35], a wooden cross honoring Lieutenant Crittenden is being newly lettered. In a minor variant of this photo, the soldier's head and arm are held at slightly different angles, and the strings of his leather waist pouch are positioned differently. These differences are barely noticeable, and the Montana Historical Society, which owns the variant view, has not assigned a separate file number to it. The two versions are so similar that we have illustrated only one.

In #187 [#36], Morrow has captured the short-lived, spurious grave of Lieutenant Sturgis, erected for the benefit of his mother, who visited the field in 1878. Photo #189 [#38] features a large wooden memorial for Captain Keogh and thirty-eight soldiers of Company I. Two versions of this picture exist. Both show an officer, believed to be Sanderson, accompanied by a single soldier in one and several in the other. Keogh's gravesite is behind the large wooden marker honoring the entire group.

The final Morrow photo of grave markers is #190 [#39]. Taken on the western slope of Custer Hill, it shows a jumble of bones, with crude wooden stakes, one of which is marked "Unknown." Morrow may have intended this picture to illustrate the untidy state of the field before Sanderson's men did their work. It is of interest because a modern comparison of this view reveals some early burial stakes where no current marble markers stand (see plates 14.6A and B).

Turning to the final four views in the series, we find a dramatic picture of the bluffs along the Little Bighorn River below Custer Hill (#188 [#37]), at the foot of what has recently been referred to as "Cemetery Ravine."[3] Morrow's title seems to indicate that some of Custer's men were driven into the river and drowned there, but this is not verified by any other account.

Next is a picture of Captain Sanderson's "camp at the ford" (#195 [#43]). The campsite, visible in the distance in views #185 [#34] and #191 [#40], is around a bend in the river just upstream from the bluffs in #188 [#37]. The camp consists of four tents and two covered wagons. A variant shows one of the wagons in a different spot. We cannot be certain which ford Morrow was referring to in his title.

The series concludes with two rarely seen views. Photo #194 [#44] is a river ford where Morrow tells us Custer either tried to attack or "met his first reverse." This is probably Medicine Tail Coulee Ford, although the absence of permanent landmarks in this photograph makes it impossible to tell for sure. Another photo shows a wickiup still standing at the site of the Indian village, somewhere in the Little Bighorn Valley (#196 [#unknown]). Neither of these images could be matched to make modern comparison photos.

Stanley J. Morrow's views of Custer's battlefield are justly famous. Credit is due also to L. A. Huffman, however, because although he confused the attribution and the date of these photographs, he kept them in circulation. While Morrow's own glass plates were eventually destroyed by fire, his negatives of the Custer Battlefield obtained by Huffman survived, and seven are now in the collection of the Montana Historical Society. These pictures continue to fascinate and to teach us.

They are an enduring tribute to the man who took them.

On the following pages we present the full series—twelve views plus three variants, a total of fifteen images in all. Beneath each photo is the number and title used by Morrow in both the "Photographic Gems" series, followed, in brackets, by that from the "Photographic Views" set.

#185 "Bones on Custer's Battlefield showing spot where Custer made his last stand."
[#34—"Gen'l. Custer's last stand, looking in the direction of ford and Indian village."] Courtesy of W. H. Over Museum, #316.

Variant of #185 [#34] showing several groups of men working along the South Skirmish Line. Courtesy of Little Bighorn Battlefield National Monument, National Park Service, #672.

Photographed and Published by
S. J. MORROW, YANKTON, D. T.

Photographic Views of
THE GREAT NORTH-WEST.

OPPOSITE TOP: *#186 "Lieut. Crittenden's grave on the Custer Battle Field." [#35—"Custer's battle field. Lettering the head-boards."] Courtesy of Montana Historical Society, #981-346.*

OPPOSITE BOTTOM: *#187 "Supposed grave of Lieut. Sturgis." [#36—"Supposed grave of Lieut. Sturgis."] Courtesy of Montana Historical Society, #981-224.*

ABOVE: *#188 "Bluff where some of Custer's men were driven into the Little Horn and drowned." [#37—"Bluff on the Little Horn, where some of Custer's men were driven to a watery grave."] Courtesy of Montana Historical Society.*

ABOVE: *#189 "Decorating the graves on Custers Battle field. Col. Keogh and thirty eight men massacred, 1879." [#38—"Decorating the graves on Custer's Battle field."] Courtesy of W. H. Over Museum, #311.*

LEFT: *Variant of #189 [#38] showing four soldiers rather than one accompanying an officer believed to be Captain Sanderson. Courtesy of Montana Historical Society, #981-367.*

OPPOSITE TOP: *#190 "Bones and unknown graves." [#39—"Unknown, showing several graves and the ridge where the last stand was made."] Courtesy of Montana Historical Society, #981-347.*

OPPOSITE BOTTOM: *#191 "Bones gathered on Custer's hill before bur[y]ing them." [#40—"Bones gathered on Custer's hill previous to placing them in the monument."] Courtesy of Montana Historical Society, #981-368.*

90—Graves of Unknown, Custer Hill

1877 COPYRIGHT "Where Custer Fell." HUFFMAN

87—First Monument Custer Hill.

88—First Monume

PHOTOGRAPHIC GEMS OF THE GREAT NORTHWEST.

Photographed and Published by S. J. Morrow, Yankton, D. T.

154

OPPOSITE TOP: *#192 "Building the Monument on Custers Battle field." [#41—"Building monument on Custer's hill."] Courtesy of Montana Historical Society, #981-369.*

OPPOSITE BOTTOM: *#193 "Monument on Custers Battle field." [#42—"The monument on Custer's hill, containing all the bones found on the field."] Courtesy of Montana Historical Society, #981-349.*

ABOVE: *#194 "Ford on the Little Horn where Custer met his first reverse." [#44—"The ford, where Custer attempted to cross to attack the Indian village."] Courtesy of W. H. Over Museum, #307.*

PHOTOGRAPHIC GEMS OF THE GREAT NORTHWEST.

Photographed and Published by S. J. Morrow, Yankton, D. T.

OPPOSITE TOP: *#195 "Capt. Sanderson camp at the ford while gathering and burying bones." [#43—"Capt. Sanderson's camp at the ford, while gathering the bones and building the monument."] Courtesy of W. H. Over Museum, #305.*

OPPOSITE BOTTOM: *#Variant of #195 [#43] in which the men and one of the wagons are in different positions. Courtesy of Montana Historical Society.*

ABOVE: *#196 "Wick-up sort of temporary Indian Lodge, a portion of Sitting Bulls camp." [# unknown] Courtesy of W. H. Over Museum, #308.*

NOTES

Chapter 1. Historical Background

1. Graham, *Custer Myth,* xii.

2. Russell, *Custer's Last,* 3.

3. Terry to Sheridan, May 16, 1876, Record Group 393 (M1495), National Archives.

4. Gray, *Centennial Campaign,* 287.

5. Second Lieutenant Winfield Scott Edgerly wrote to his wife on July 4, "We were told that the Indians had undoubtedly discovered our presence as several had been seen on the bluffs and the only thing left for us to do was move on them at once." Clark, *Scalp Dance,* 24.

6. At the Reno Court of Inquiry, Moylan testified that Reno, Benteen, Keogh, and Yates were given command of battalions, noting, "Each of these battalions I have named consisted of three companies, except Captain Yates' which was two companies." Nichols, *Reno Court,* 213. Edgerly similarly informed Camp that Custer had divided the regiment "into four battalions, Benteen, Reno, Keogh and Yates and had McDougall rear guard for pack train. He took Keogh and Yates with him." Hammer, *Custer in '76,* 54. While other terminology appears in the literature to denote subregimental segments of the command, we use the term "battalion" to describe units of two or more companies. Although most battle historians, including the authors of this book, assume that Keogh commanded Companies C, I, and L and Yates E and F, the evidence is less than conclusive on that point and subject to interpretation. Earlier in the campaign, Keogh had commanded Companies B, C, and I, and Yates, E, F, and L.

7. *Gray, Centennial Campaign,* 296. Sills and Nichols concluded that the total number of men with Reno was 165, 141 of whom were officers and soldiers. Nichols, *In Custer's Shadow,* 184.

8. Graham, *Custer Myth,* 249; Hammer, *Custer in '76,* 92, 97.

9. Stands in Timber and Liberty, *Cheyenne Memories,* 197–98.

10. Gray, *Centennial Campaign,* 296, gives the loss as 40 killed, 13 wounded, and 17 abandoned in the timber. Nichols, *In Custer's Shadow,* 383, interprets the loss as 37 killed, 10 wounded, and 17 abandoned in the timber.

11. Two of the more thought-provoking analyses of the Weir Point episode are Taunton, "Enigma of Weir Point," and Sills, "Weir Point Perspective," 45–51.

12. Gray, *Centennial Campaign,* 206, gives a total of 12 killed—13, if one includes Vincent Charley—and 41 wounded during the two-day siege. Nichols, *In Custer's Shadow,* 384–85, places the loss at 15 killed and 55 wounded. The subsequent deaths from wounds brought the fatalities sustained in the siege to 20.

13. Taunton, *Custer's Field,* 26.

14. Wells, "Kanipe, Martin, and Benteen"; Nichols, *Reno Court of Inquiry,* 388–89, 395–97.

15. The Cheyenne Soldier Wolf recounted the flight of women and children to the east side of the river: "When these women were crossing the river, and some were going up the hills, they discovered more troops coming." Grinnell Papers, Braun Research Library. Another Cheyenne, Tall Bull,

described how "women going over east [of the river] to get on high ground to overlook Reno fight discovered Custer coming." Hammer, *Custer in '76,* 212. For an excellent summary of the location and findings at Luce and Nye-Cartwright Ridges, see Trinque, "Elusive Ridge."

16. According to testimony at the 1879 Reno Court of Inquiry, the closest slain soldier to the ford was found 200 to 800 yards east of the river, most accounts placing the body about 500 yards from the crossing point. Nichols, *Reno Court,* 66–67, 322, 328, 417, 495, 548.

17. John Stands in Timber asserted that "the Battle proper began below and west of the cemetery, [and] moved to Custer Ridge" in an interview, August 8, 1958, Little Bighorn Battlefield National Monument (LBBNM). Drawing on the oral history of Stands in Timber and other Cheyennes, this concept is developed in Fox, *Archaeology, History.*

18. Hardorff, *Lakota Recollections,* 147.

19. Godfrey Papers, Library of Congress.

20. Nichols, *Reno Court,* 417.

21. Hammer, *Custer in '76,* 121.

22. Stands in Timber, *Cheyenne Memories,* 201.

23. Graham, *Custer Myth,* 75.

24. Hardorff, *Hokahey!*

25. Nichols, *Reno Court,* 236; Taunton, *Custer's Field,* 12.

26. Nichols, *Reno Court,* 453–54; Hammer, *Custer in '76,* 58, 95; Taunton, *Custer's Field,* 16, 41.

27. Hammer, *Custer in '76,* 248; Taunton, *Custer's Field,* 8, 12–13.

28. Taunton, *Custer's Field,* 14–15; Hardorff, *Custer Battle Casualties II.* Stands in Timber stated, "The horses of the gray horse soldiers were frightened away by Indians coming up the big ravine. . . . Indians coming from the north and from the south forced these gray horse soldiers into the Big Ravine." Stands in Timber interview, August 8, 1958, LBBNM.

29. Barnard, "Mark Kellogg's Role." For a fuller treatment of Kellogg's role, see Barnard, *I Go with Custer;* also see Donahue and Moore, "Gibbon's Route" and Donahue, "Revisiting Col. Gibbon's Route."

30. Taunton, *Custer's Field,* 22. For details

of the soldiers' remains, see Hardorff, *Custer Battle Casualties* and *Custer Battle Casualties II.*

31. The most complete published record of the postbattle history of Little Bighorn is Rickey, *History of Custer Battlefield.* Another useful source recounting the burials, reburials, and ongoing forensic studies is Scott, Willey, and Connor, *They Died with Custer.*

32. Bourke Diary, quoted in Hardorff, *Custer Battle Casualties,* 54–55.

33. "Report on the Custer Battlefield Rendered by Capt. Owen J. Sweet, 25th Infty., May 15, 1890," LBBNM.

34. Sweet to Camp, November 24, 1912, Camp Collection, A312 C11329, LBBNM.

Chapter 2. Archaeological Digs

1. At the time of the fire and the dig projects of the 1980s, the National Park Service site still bore the official name of Custer Battlefield National Monument. In 1991, Congress approved legislation changing the battlefield's name to Little Bighorn Battlefield National Monument.

2. For further, more detailed insight into the battlefield archaeological projects, see the following works: Scott and Fox, *Archaeological Insights;* Scott et al., *Archaeological Perspectives;* Scott, Willey, and Connor, *They Died with Custer;* Fox, *Archaeology, History;* and Barnard, *Digging.*

3. Barnard, *Digging,* 103–104.

4. Barnard, *Digging,* vi.

5. Fox, *Archaeology, History,* 35.

6. Barnard, *Digging,* 117.

7. Scott et al., *Archaeological Perspectives,* 116–21.

8. Scott et al., *Archaeological Perspectives,* 121–22.

9. Scott et al., *Archaeological Perspectives,* 31–33.

10. Scott et al., *Archaeological Perspectives,* 87–88.

11. Scott, Willey, and Connor, *They Died with Custer,* 238.

12. Scott, Willey, and Connor, *They Died with Custer,* 9.

13. Scott, Willey, and Connor, *They Died with Custer,* 241, 259.

14. Scott, Willey, and Connor, *They Died with Custer,* 277–78.

15. Scott, Willey, and Connor, *They Died with Custer,* 296.

16. Scott, Willey, and Connor, *They Died with Custer,* 301.

17. Scott, "Cartridges, Bullets, and Bones."

Chapter 3. Important Photographers

1. Brust, "John H. Fouch"; Brust, letter to the editor, *Montana* 45 (Spring 1995), 90–91; and Brust, "Photojournalism, 1877."

2. Brust, "John H. Fouch," 7.

3. Hurt and Lass, *Frontier Photographer;* Hedren, *With Crook in the Black Hills;* Gray, "Photos, Femurs, and Fallacies"; and Brust, "Stanley J. Morrow's 1879 Photographs."

4. Though well established in the literature, the connection between Morrow and Mathew B. Brady is not solidly documented. Published versions of the story that Stanley J. Morrow learned photography from Mathew B. Brady appeared as early as 1938, when photo historian Robert Taft wrote that Morrow was "a veteran of the Civil War, said to have been trained by M.B. Brady" (Taft, *Photography and the American Scene,* 307, 495n333a). It is likely, though, that the story actually came from Morrow's widow, Isa Morrow. Taft cites a biographical sketch of Morrow in the Yankton (South Dakota) *Press and Dakotan,* June 6, 1936, and fellow photo historian Elmo Scott Watson, who made the same assertion a year later (Watson, "Way Out West," 148, 151). Watson corresponded with the photographer's son, Earl S. Morrow. In an undated letter to Watson, likely written in 1937, Earl Morrow copied a 1924 story his mother had written about her photographer-husband in an unnamed newspaper. Mrs. Morrow, who would have been seventy-nine years old in 1924, said that Morrow met Brady at Point Lookout and became interested in photography and that the two took pictures together. She even specifies a published image in *The Photographic History of the Civil War* (vol. 7, p. 63), which she says Morrow took under Brady's supervision (see Watson Papers, Newberry Library, MMS Watson, Box 42, Folder 643). The photo she mentions is a group portrait of General James Barnes and his staff at Point Lookout, with identification of the officers but no mention of Morrow or Brady. The tale of a connection with Mathew B. Brady was taken up by Morrow's biographers. They thought evidence to support it could be found in Morrow's own photographs in the collection of the W. H. Over Museum in Vermillion, South Dakota (Hurt and Lass, *Frontier Photographer,* 3). A review of the catalog of Morrow photos at the Over Museum reveals several that had been taken at Point Lookout Prison. Two in particular relate to a possible connection between Morrow and Mathew B. Brady. Number 77 is captioned "Photo made by Mathew B. Brady and S. J. Morrow at Point Lookout, Maryland (Federal Prison for confederate prisoners). Mr. Brady was the noted photographer with the Federal Army and taught Mr. Morrow photography. Taken about 1863–1864." It is not known when and by whom this caption was written, however, and there is no printed logo on the mount that would establish a firm attribution to Brady. A second view, number 80, is captioned "Prison Camp, Point Lookout, Maryland, 1864. Photograph gallery of Mathew B. Brady second building from left. This building is where Mr. Brady taught Mr. S. J. Morrow the photograph business. Photo-wet plate process." Lettering visible on the building in the photo does read "Picture Ga. . . ," but nowhere on the structure or in the picture does the name of Mathew B. Brady appear. Hence, these photos do not document an association between Morrow and Brady at Point Lookout, and we are still left without proof of a link between them. Morrow was at Point Lookout Prison and may have learned photography there, but we feel it is unlikely that Brady, a man who loved the spotlight, would have been present to teach him at this isolated outpost in Maryland. Interestingly, another photo in the Morrow collection may have been a source of confusion. Number 75 is a portrait of Major Allen G. Brady of the Twentieth Volunteer Relief Corps, who may have been stationed at Point Lookout. Perhaps those who subsequently studied Morrow's photographs simply got their Bradys mixed up. Future research may eventually yield more solid evidence that Mathew Brady or one of his associates did train Morrow, but for now, this story lacks convincing proof.

5. Hurt and Lass, *Frontier Photographer,* 2–3.

6. Watson, "Way Out West," 147–48; Watson, "Photographing the Frontier," 66.

7. Gray, "Itinerant Frontier Photographers," 8.

8. Earl S. Morrow to Elmo Scott Watson, undated letter likely written in 1937, Watson Papers, MMS Watson, Box 42, Folder 643, Newberry Library. Mrs. Morrow stated, "When General Custer left Yankton to round up Sitting Bull and his tribes, Mr. Morrow was to have gone with him but on account of his chemicals and glass plates not arriving from Chicago on time he did not go." But writing years after the event, Mrs. Morrow may have been confused. It was in 1873 that Custer and the Seventh Cavalry passed through Yankton on their way to join the Yellowstone Expedition that surveyed a route for the Northern Pacific Railroad, not in 1876 prior to the Little Bighorn. Her accuracy is further undermined by her statement that Morrow "accompanied General Crook as official photographer on his trip to catch the Indians who massacred General Custer and his men." While Morrow did photograph Crook's command in the field in 1876, he had not accompanied their campaign and had no official attachment.

9. Hurt and Lass, *Frontier Photographer,* 32–33.

10. Hurt and Lass, *Frontier Photographer,* 32–34; Hedren, *With Crook in the Black Hills,* 10.

11. Hedren, *With Crook in the Black Hills,* 16ff.

12. Gray, "Itinerant Frontier Photographers," 10.

13. Gray, "Nightmares to Daydreams," 37–38.

14. Brust, "John H. Fouch," 16.

15. Heski, *Little Shadow Catcher.*

16. Tilden, *Following the Frontier;* Montana Historical Society, *F. Jay Haynes.*

17. Brown and Felton, *Frontier Years;* Karson, *L. A. Huffman;* Brust, letter to the editor, *Montana* 48 (Spring 1998), 84.

18. Mautz, *Biographies of Western Photographers,* 382. Most of our information on Moorhouse, including the correct year of his death, was provided by Thomas Robinson of Portland, Oregon, in e-mail messages to James Brust between March 28 and April 1, 2001.

19. Visitors Register, Custer Battlefield National Cemetery, March 30, 1895 to September 20, 1910, LBBNM. Lee Moorhouse of Pendleton, Oregon, signed the register on September 14, 1901.

20. Hutchins, *Papers of Edward S. Curtis,* 14n2; Brust, "Curtis Photographs," 11n1.

21. Frink and Barthelmess, *Photographer on an Army Mule.*

22. Albright, *Crow Indian Photographer.*

23. O'Connor, *Fred E. Miller.*

24. Little information has been published on H. R. Locke. He is listed in Treadwell and Darrah, *Stereographers of the World.* Information gathered from Internet research sites led us to conclude that his full name was Henry Robinson Locke. He was born in Pennsylvania in 1867 and died in Sheridan, Wyoming, on August 22, 1927. See South Dakota Historical Society, Special Photograph Collections (www.sdhistory.org/arcspec.htm), and the U.S. GenWeb Project, Sheridan Municipal Cemetery (www.rootsweb.com/~wysherid/hj-ly.htm).

25. Mitchell, "William Richard Cross." Additional information on Cross was provided by his great-grandson, Milton Miller, in telephone interviews and correspondence with James Brust, October 2002. William Richard Cross was born in Shaftsbury, Vermont, on November 24, 1839, and died in Hot Springs, South Dakota, on December 23, 1907. During his career he operated galleries in Omaha and Niobrara, Nebraska, and Hot Springs, South Dakota, specializing in scenic views and Indian portraits.

26. Information on Kenneth Roahen is from the *Billings (Montana) Gazette,* January 2, 1955, and from his niece, Mrs. Elaine Ooley of Bridgeton, Missouri, in numerous conversations with Brian Pohanka and James Brust, and in an e-mail message to Brian Pohanka dated May 6, 2001.

27. Spear, *Bozeman Trail Scrapbook.* Additional information was provided by Elsa Spear's daughter, Marilyn Bilyeu (interviews with James Brust, May 26, 2002, and July 10, 2002); her long-time friend Mary Ellen McWilliams (e-mail message to James Brust, May 25, 2002); and University of Wyoming American Heritage Center archivist Leslie Shores (e-mail message to James Brust, May 22, 2002).

28. Spear, *Bozeman Trail Scrapbook,* 89.

Chapter 4. The Approach to the Valley

1. Smalley, "Where Was the Crow's Nest?" 77–88.

2. Graham, *Custer Myth,* 112.

3. Wiebert and Wiebert, *Sixty-six Years,* x–xi, xvi–xvii.

4. Hardorff, *On the Little Bighorn,* 73.

5. Darling, *Benteen's Scout to the Left,* 35–39. In this carefully researched and thought-out study, Darling believed that uncertainties of up to one mile existed and that he could only estimate the location of the morass.

6. We believe the Camp view of the morass reproduced here (plate 4.2A) has never been published before. For Camp's other picture of the morass, see Donahue, "Knipe's Recollections," 8. Kanipe's name is spelled both ways in the historical record.

7. Donahue, "Knipe's Recollections," 8.

8. Donahue, "Knipe's Recollections," 6–7, 12–13.

Chapter 5. Reno's Valley Fight

1. Ryan, "One of Custer's First Sergeants." For Ryan's fuller accounting of the Little Bighorn fight, see Barnard, *Ten Years.*

2. Barnard, *Ten Years,* 291.

3. Nichols, *Reno Court,* 84.

4. Nichols, *Reno Court,* 561. Precisely what was stated in the way of orders to Reno has been variously reported and remains a point of debate among students of the battle. For example, Lieutenant Wallace at the Reno Court of Inquiry testified that he heard, "The Indians are about two miles and a half ahead, on the jump, follow them as fast as you can and charge them wherever you find them and we will support you" (p. 21). Scout Fred Girard testified that he heard it as, "You will take your battalion and try and overtake and bring them to battle and I will support you" (p. 86). At another point, Girard stated, "Major Reno, you will take your battalion and try to overtake the Indians and bring them to battle and I will support you" (p. 112). In his official report of July 5, 1876, Reno stated, "Lieutenant Cooke, Adjutant, came to me and said the village was only two miles ahead and running away; to move forward at as rapid a gait as prudent, and to charge afterward, and that the whole outfit would sup-

port me. I think those were his exact words." At the time Custer issued his orders to the major, neither man may have known for certain that the village was still standing in the valley.

5. The first messenger was Private Archibald McIlhargey and the second was Private John E. Mitchell. Both men remained with Custer's command and died with it. Hammer and Nichols, *Men with Custer,* 232, 245.

6. Barnard, *Ten Years,* 291–93.

7. See Barnard, *Digging,* 127–28. For more details about O'Hara's remains and those of other soldiers, see Scott, Willey, and Connor, *They Died with Custer,* 55, 164–65, 322.

8. See Barnard, *Digging,* 149–63, based on a lengthy series of formal interviews with Jason Pitsch, Glen Swanson, and Doug Scott, and further discussions with Douglas McChristian, Neil Mangum, John Doerner, Richard A. Fox Jr., Brian C. Pohanka, James S. Brust, Joe Sills Jr., and Michael A. Donahue.

9. McIntosh had been buried where he fell on the Reno retreat route in 1876. A year later, his remains were exhumed and moved to the national cemetery at Fort Leavenworth, Kansas. In 1909, McIntosh was reburied in Arlington National Cemetery. In correspondence with Camp, Captain Sweet reported, "I found a board over a mound with Lieut. McIntosh's name on it. In digging into the grave some parts of a skeleton were found, hence to the memory of that gallant officer I placed his headstone on the spot where he fell." That suggests that some of McIntosh's bones were still there in 1890. Sweet to Camp, November 24, 1912, Camp Collection, A312 C11329, LBBNM.

10. Hutchins, *Papers of Edward S. Curtis,* 332, and facing foldout. Reno's fording place is several river meanders downstream in the original version of the map.

11. Wiebert and Wiebert, *Sixty-six Years,* 20–21.

12. Bookwalter, "Photographs Described," 16.

13. Brininstool, *Troopers with Custer,* 129. Thomas O'Neill was promoted to first sergeant in the army and eventually became a captain in the Washington, D.C., park police.

14. Hammer, *Custer in '76,* 106.

15. Graham, *Custer Myth,* 34.

16. Hammer and Nichols, *Men with Custer,* 45–46. A lonely and embittered man after his discharge from the army, Burkman lived the last thirty years of his life in Billings, Montana, before he committed suicide in 1925.

17. Hardorff, *Custer Battle Casualties,* 150–51, and *Custer Battle Casualties II,* 125–26.

18. Brust, "Adventurous Detour," 11, and "Norris Drew Early On-site Map," 14–15.

19. Rickey, *History of Custer Battlefield,* 142n150.

20. A strikingly similar but not identical view, taken on September 17, 1928, appears in an album compiled by Albert W. Johnson and presented to Elizabeth B. Custer, now in the LBBNM archives.

21. Barnard, "Ken Hammer," 20.

22. Jason Pitsch began metal detecting in 1990 and was aided in his research by Glen Swanson. See Brust, "Where Was the Timber?" 7–8. At the time of its 1938 installation the Reynolds marker was taller than it is now (see photo in Barnard, "Ken Hammer," 20). It was initially embedded in concrete, so when the local farmers moved it out of the field, they had to cut it off at ground surface level, thus shortening it (Glen Swanson to James Brust, telephone interview, May 27, 2002).

23. After replacing the original wooden marker for Lieutenant McIntosh with a marble stone in 1890, Captain Sweet suggested that a fence be placed around the new marker to protect it from the horse herds and cultivation activities of the local Crow Indians. See "Report on the Custer Battlefield Rendered by Captain Owen J. Sweet, 25th Infty., May 15, 1890," LBBNM. It is unclear exactly when the fence was erected.

24. Brust, "Learning about the Little Big Horn," 51, 68n2.

25. Wiebert and Wiebert, *Sixty-six Years,* 28–29, 99, 104, 137, and accompanying map.

26. Brust, "Lt. Oscar Long's Early Map," 7, 11–12, 13n35.

27. Brust, "Where Was the Timber?" 5–11.

Chapter 6. Reno-Benteen Defense Site

1. Most books dealing with this subject focus on the Custer segment of the Battle of Little Bighorn and may neglect the story of the valley and bluff fights. Readers seeking further information on those segments of the battle should review Stewart, *Custer's Luck;* Gray, *Centennial Campaign;* Utley, *Cavalier in Buckskin;* and Sklenar, *To Hell with Honor.*

2. Martin gave Camp two different statements. See Hammer, *Custer in '76,* 101, 105.

3. Sklenar, *To Hell with Honor,* 312.

4. For excellent maps on troop dispositions on June 25 and June 26 at the Reno-Benteen defense site, see Nichols, *In Custer's Shadow,* 199.

5. Stewart, *Custer's Luck,* 413.

6. Stewart, *Custer's Luck,* 413.

7. Barnard, *Ten Years,* 298, 300.

8. Rickey, *History of Custer Battlefield,* 36, 64–65.

9. Rickey, *History of Custer Battlefield,* 113.

10. One photograph in LBBNM group D66, taken in the summer of 1963 but not reproduced in this book, shows the Reno-Benteen monument in its original spot, but with the fence no longer around it. Another series of photos, LBBNM D22, documents the various construction projects done at the battlefield between April and December 1965. While park records make no mention of the moving of the Reno-Benteen memorial, they do reveal that the construction at the Reno-Benteen defense site was done between September and November. This dates the two views documenting the movement of the memorial to the fall of 1965.

11. Hardorff, *Custer Battle Casualties,* 130, and *Custer Battle Casualties II,* 97.

12. Nichols, *Reno Court,* 554.

13. The official transcript of the Reno Court of Inquiry, now at the National Archives in Washington, D.C., has been widely available only since 1992 (Nichols, *Reno Court*). For twenty years before that, researchers relied on an earlier published version of the Reno Court testimony, taken from the contemporary newspaper coverage in the *Chicago Times,* as access to the Reno Court transcript was limited. See Utley, *Reno Court,* ii.

14. Utley, *Reno Court,* 395.

15. Hammer and Nichols, *Men with Custer,* 306; Hardorff, *Custer Battle Casualties II,* 96.

16. Hammer, *Custer in '76,* 72.

17. Hardorff, *Custer Battle Casualties II*, 95–96.

18. Hammer, *Custer in '76*, 62.

19. Hardorff, *Custer Battle Casualties*, 129–30, *Custer Battle Casualties II*, 96–97, and *On the Little Bighorn*, 131.

20. Tuttle, "Who Buried Lieutenant Hodgson?" 11–15.

21. Hardorff, *Custer Battle Casualties II*, 98.

22. Superintendent Oscar Wright to Quartermaster General, June 13, 1910, Record Book—Letters sent 1893–1925, LBBNM. Wright stated: "I have the honor to report the arrival of the enclosed list of head-stones from Capt. R. H. Rolf, Quartermaster U.S.A. Lee, Mass. These headstones have all been set in brick and concrete foundations at their proper places, as near as was possible to ascertain." According to Wright's letter, head-stones were received for Lieutenants Harrington, Hodson [*sic*], Porter, and Sturgiss [*sic*].

23. Edward Luce to Ralph Cartwright, December 22, 1943, document #20, Edward S. Luce folder, Cartwright Collection, Phoebe Apperson Hearst Memorial Library.

24. Rickey, *History of Custer Battlefield*, 88.

25. Hardorff, *Custer Battle Casualties*, 147–48, and *Custer Battle Casualties II*, 121–24.

26. Hardorff, *Custer Battle Casualties II*, 124–25. Sweet set only two markers for the dead on Reno's field—the one for DeWolf and a second for McIntosh.

27. Hardorff, *Custer Battle Casualties*, 147–48.

28. Hardorff, *Custer Battle Casualties II*, 107.

29. Nichols, *Reno Court*, 278, 335.

30. For a summary of the conflicting accounts of the fate of Private Clear, see Hardorff, *Custer Battle Casualties*, 135–36, and *Custer Battle Casualties II*, 106–108.

31. Hammer, *Custer in '76*, 66; Nichols, *Reno Court*, 281. In the various versions of the Reno court testimony, Hare stated, "The man I had with me was killed near the river." Since Clear was Hare's orderly, it has been assumed that he was the man referred to, but we can-not be certain that this is what Hare meant.

32. Hardorff, *Custer Battle Casualties II*, 107.

33. Chris Pendle to Camp, July 14, 1919. Camp Collection, Brigham Young University, MSS 57, box 2, folder 5. See also Hammer and Nichols, *Men with Custer*, 1.

Chapter 7. Weir Point

1. Trinque, "It's About Time." For the purposes of this study, we use Wallace's times, which formed the basis for the battle chronologies developed by John Gray.

2. Wallace put Benteen's arrival at ten minutes after Reno gained the bluff (Nichols, *Reno Court*, 36) as did Hare (Hammer, *Custer in '76*, 66) and Roy (Hammer, *Custer in '76*, 113).

3. Hammer, *Custer in '76*, 62.

4. Clark, *Scalp Dance*, 9.

5. Ghent Papers, Library of Congress; Taunton, "Enigma of Weir Point," 24.

6. Nichols, *Reno Court*, 290.

7. Nichols, *Reno Court*, 642.

8. Nichols, *Reno Court*, 371. In his testimony Reno stated that Hare was sent to the pack train after the major returned from Hodgson's body. This seems impossible when weighed against the accounts of other veterans, Hare in particular. Godfrey noted that Reno went on his foray after Hare departed and while the command was awaiting the pack train. Graham, *Custer Myth*, 141.

9. Nichols, *Reno Court*, 373.

10. Hammer, *Custer in '76*, 70.

11. Edgerly to Godfrey, January 17, 1886, Hagner Collection, New York Public Library.

12. Clark, *Scalp Dance*, 9. Camp, who interviewed and corresponded with Edgerly, noted, "Weir afterwards told Edgerly that he did not have permission and did not ask for any." Hammer, *Custer in '76*, 55.

13. Nichols, *Reno Court*, 445.

14. Nichols, *Reno Court*, 408–409.

15. Nichols, *Reno Court*, 180. See also Herendeen's account in Graham, *Custer Myth*, 264.

16. Hare, who arrived with Reno's order to open communications, was of the opinion that "Custer was fighting them." Hammer, *Custer in '76*, 67.

17. Nichols, *Reno Court*, 408; Taunton, Weir Point, 29.

18. John Gray places their arrival at 5:42 P.M., Charles Kuhlman at 5:45 P.M., and Francis Taunton at 5:45–5:50 P.M.

19. Hammer, *Custer in '76,* 76.

20. Nichols, *Reno Court,* 144, 218–19.

21. Hammer, *Custer in '76,* 70.

22. Hammer, *Custer in '76,* 81.

23. Nichols, *Reno Court,* 410.

24. Nichols, *Reno Court,* 485, 567.

25. Nichols, *Reno Court,* 445–46.

26. Hammer, *Custer in '76,* 130.

27. Nichols, *Reno Court,* 446; Hardorff, *Camp, Custer, and the Little Bighorn,* 63–64.

28. Clark, *Scalp Dance,* 25.

29. Graham, *Custer Myth,* 219.

30. Godfrey, "Cavalry Fire Discipline."

31. Nichols, *Reno Court,* 446.

32. Ghent Papers, Library of Congress.

33. Graham, *Custer Myth,* 220.

34. Nichols, *Reno Court,* 161.

35. Godfrey, "Custer's Last Battle," 374.

36. Nichols, *Reno Court,* 162–63.

37. Rickey, *History of Custer Battlefield,* 36, 98. The road from Custer Hill to the Reno-Benteen area was initially cut in 1930, graded in 1938, and surfaced at a later date.

38. Kuhlman, *Legend into History,* 96, 101–102.

39. Carroll, "Little Big Horn Medals of Honor," 23–29. The Medal of Honor water carriers, grouped by company, were Private Neil Bancroft, Private David Harris, and Sergeant Stanislas Roy (Company A); Private Thomas Callan, Sergeant Rufus Hutchinson, and Private James Pym (Company B); Private Peter Thompson (Company C); Private Abram Brant, blacksmith Frederick Deetline, Private William Harris, Private George Scott, Private Thomas Stevens (Stivers), Private Frank Tolan, and Sergeant Charles Welch (Company D); Private Theodore Golden (Company G); Sergeant George Geiger, blacksmith Henry Mechlin (Mechling), saddler Otto Voit (Frank May) and Private Charles Windolph (Company H).

40. Carroll, "Little Big Horn Medals of Honor," 26–27; Hammer and Nichols, *Men with Custer,* 280–81. Pym left the army in late 1879, only to be murdered in Miles City, Montana, in 1893. Photographer L. A. Huffman was from Miles City and may have known Pym there prior to his murder. Thus, he may have had a special interest in seeing the site of Pym's heroics.

41. The other three were saddler Michael Madden of Company K and Privates William Slaper and James Weeks of Company M. See Hammer and Nichols, *Men with Custer,* 213, 322, 367; Brininstool, *Troopers with Custer,* 57, 59.

42. Marquis, *Wooden Leg,* 259–60.

43. Godfrey, "Custer's Last Battle," 378.

44. Nichols, *In Custer's Shadow,* 199.

45. Stewart, *Custer's Luck,* 425–26.

46. Hutchins, *Papers of Edward S. Curtis,* 37.

47. Hutchins, *Papers of Edward S. Curtis,* 45–46.

48. Hutchins, *Papers of Edward S. Curtis,* 25–26.

49. Curtis, *North American Indian,* 43–50.

50. Hutchins, *Papers of Edward S. Curtis,* 33.

51. Brust, "Curtis Photographs," 10.

52. Brust, "Letting the Photos Speak," 168–69.

53. Nichols, *Reno Court,* 423; Kuhlman, *Legend into History,* 96, 102.

Chapter 8. Custer's Approach

1. Hammer, *Custer in '76,* 92, 97.

2. Hammer, *Custer in '76,* 94.

3. Nichols, *Reno Court,* 397.

4. Nichols, *Reno Court,* 395.

5. Hammer, *Custer in '76,* 94, 97; Graham, *Custer Myth,* 249.

6. Hammer, *Custer in '76,* 92–94.

7. Nichols, *Reno Court,* 440.

8. Graham, *Story of the Little Big Horn,* xxxvi; Hammer, *Custer in '76,* 75.

9. Nichols, *Reno Court,* 480.

10. Camp Collection, Brigham Young University, box 6, folder 6.

11. Wells (in "Kanipe, Martin and Benteen") computes Kanipe's departure in the 3:09 to 3:12 P.M. time frame, and Martin at 3:20 to 3:25.

12. Nichols, *Reno Court,* 390.

13. Hammer, *Custer in '76,* 101.

14. Nichols, *Reno Court,* 390, 404.

15. Nichols, *Reno Court,* 441.

16. Hutchins, *Papers of Edward S. Curtis,* 46–47, 50, 53, 75, 101–102, 132, 150, 158.

17. Hammer, *Custer in '76,* 178–79; Graham, *Custer Myth,* 13.

18. Graham, *Custer Myth,* 23.

19. Hammer, *Custer in '76,* 176–77; Graham, *Custer Myth,* 25.

20. Hammer, *Custer in '76,* 175.

21. Libby, *Arikara Narrative,* 160.

22. Camp to Gen. Charles Woodruff, March 3, 1910, in Hutchins, *Papers of Edward S. Curtis,* 143.

23. Wells, "Custer's Arrival Time"; Sills, "Crow Scouts."

24. For various versions of Curley's story, see Graham, *Custer Myth,* 10–19; Hammer, *Custer in '76,* 159–73; Hutchins, *Papers of Edward S. Curtis,* 62–65.

25. Graham, *Custer Myth,* 12–14; Sills, "Crow Scouts," 14.

26. Hammer, *Custer in '76,* 181, 184.

27. Libby, *Arikara Narrative,* 116.

28. Magnussen, *Peter Thompson's Narrative,* 117, 120–21.

29. Hammer, *Custer in '76,* 126. It is possible that a fifth trooper, Private Gustav Korn of Company I, also dropped back from Custer's column. Camp's informants were divided in their opinions on this; five veterans of the fight thought that Korn's runaway horse took him to Reno's command, while three others believed Korn had been assigned to the pack train. See Hardorff, *Walter M. Camp's Little Bighorn Rosters,* 166.

30. Hammer, *Custer in '76,* 98, 126.

31. Fox, "West River History," 155–58.

32. If Custer had been incapacitated at the ford, Adjutant Cooke and the headquarters staff would have reported to the next senior officer with the command, Captain Keogh. In fact, Cooke and others of the staff were later found near Custer's body, not with Keogh. The 1938 narrative of Joseph White Cow Bull describing the shooting of a "soldier chief" at the ford is inconsistent with other Native American accounts. See Michno, *Lakota Noon,* 123–24.

33. Nichols, *Reno Court,* 495.

34. Nichols, *Reno Court,* 322, 328.

35. Hammer, *Custer in '76,* 134; Hardorff, *Camp, Custer, and the Little Bighorn,* 79.

36. Tall Bull in Hammer, *Custer in '76,* 212; He Dog in Hardorff, *Lakota Recollections,* 74; Soldier Wolf in Hardorff, *Cheyenne Memories,* 43.

37. Liddic and Harbaugh, *Camp on Custer,* 122.

38. Foolish Elk in Hammer, *Custer in '76,* 198; Good Voiced Elk in Hardorff, *Camp, Custer, and the Little Bighorn,* 84.

Artifact findings in the vicinity of the ford suggest that some firing occurred there but do not indicate a pitched battle; periodic flooding has doubtless compromised the area nearest to the ford. Greene, *Evidence and the Custer Enigma,* 16–18.

39. Hardorff, *Lakota Recollections:* Nicholas Ruleau, 41; Lights, 166.

40. Hardorff, *Camp, Custer, and the Little Bighorn,* 90.

41. Hardorff, *Lakota Recollections,* 143–45.

42. Trinque, "Elusive Ridge," 3–8.

43. Cartwright put the number of expended shells discovered in his initial survey as 103 and noted that they lay in groups of three. Anders Papers, University of North Dakota, OGL#43-6-5.

44. Stands in Timber and Liberty, *Cheyenne Memories,* 197–98.

45. Marquis, *Wooden Leg,* 229.

46. Brust, "Letting the Photos Speak," 173–75.

47. Fox, *Archaeology, History,* 139, 279, 284, 291, 313, 333.

48. The photographs in *The Vanishing Race* are frequently misdated and misattributed. When the book was published in 1913, it contained 80 gravure illustrations, each marked "[Copyright] by Rodman Wanamaker 1913." The expedition that produced the images was one of three financed by Philadelphia department store magnate Rodman Wanamaker and led by Doctor Joseph K. Dixon. The pictures were actually taken in 1909, not 1913, but were marked with the latter year because that was the date of their publication. Wanamaker, as financier of the project, copyrighted them in his own name, even though he was not present when they were taken. The title page states that the book was "Written and Illustrated by Dr. Joseph K. Dixon," implying that he had taken the photos. This was not the only place in which Dixon claimed to be the photographer. James Brust owns an original photographic print (not a gravure) of one of the pictures in the book. The vintage typewritten label on the back of the frame says "Photographed by Dr. Joseph K. Dixon, August 1909." Despite Dixon's assertions, though, it is doubtful that Dixon actually took the photos. In his acknowledgment section (p. vii), Dixon said,

"My staff—Rollin Lester Dixon, W. B. Cline and John D. Scott rendered intelligent assistance." Left unstated by Dixon but pointed out by Crawford Buell in his introduction to the 1973 reprinted edition was the fact that all three of these men were photographers. Buell believed that these three actually took most of the photos.

Western art expert Brian Dippie made us aware of a small booklet, copyright 1909, titled on the cover *Wanamaker Primer on the North American Indian, Hiawatha Produced in Life, Wanamaker-Originator*. The booklet contains two separately paged pamphlets. The second is a program for the Wanamaker film of Hiawatha. The first deals with the expedition photographs. It states, "The leader of the expedition, Dr. Joseph K. Dixon, who for years has been absorbed with the study of the North American Indian, took with him his son as color artist and two photographers as assistants" (38, 40). The text goes on to discuss the use of color slides, and Dixon is known to have used colored lantern slides in lectures he gave at the Panama-Pacific International Exposition in 1915, and presumably at other times as well. So it appears that Rollin Lester Dixon colored lantern slides and that W. B. Cline and John Scott were the expedition photographers.

Dippie agrees that Joseph Dixon took few if any pictures (Brian Dippie to James Brust, July 14, 2000, and September 24, 2001). So, with the exception of a few plates that may have been taken by Richard Throssel in 1908 (one of which we have used in this book; plate 14.23A), the correct year for any of the photos in *The Vanishing Race* is 1909. The photographer was certainly not Wanamaker, could possibly have been Joseph Dixon, but most likely was either Cline or Scott. Without any way to tell which of the photographers present in 1909 actually took a given image, we have continued to credit them to Joseph Dixon as overall on-site director of the project.

49. Fox, "West River History," 144–49.

Chapter 9. The Butler Marker and Deep Coulee

1. Hardorff, *Custer Battle Casualties,* 110.

2. Hammer, *Custer in '76,* 116; Hardorff, *On the Little Bighorn,* 40.

3. Hardorff, *Custer Battle Casualties,* 110, *Custer Battle Casualties II,* 51.

4. Rickey, *History of Custer Battlefield,* 53, 139n102.

5. Clipping from unknown New York newspaper, December 8, 1905, E. B. Custer Collection, #19-44-59, LBBNM. The article reads,

Such was the case recently when one of Reno's men was dug up, somewhere in the wild stretch of country between Custer hill and the bluffs where Reno's command held their savage foe at bay. This man was a sergeant, a crack shot, who had been dispatched by Reno to find out what had happened to Custer and to carry news of Reno's own desperate plight. The sergeant was caught midway between the two commands and was finally killed, but not until he had reckoned with many of his savage foes. When he was found his body was literally surrounded with shells and his comrades knew enough of his ability as a shot to swear that every shell represented a casualty on the Indian side. A comrade who assisted in burying the man where he fell only a short time ago headed a party to the spot, and the remains were disinterred and brought to Custer Cemetery.

While this story is similar to Godfrey's version of Butler's death, we are told that this was one of Reno's men, not Custer's (as Butler was). No specific location on the battlefield is given, and the man is unnamed. Information is too lacking here to conclude that this news piece describes the discovery of Butler's body in Deep Coulee. For further analysis of this matter, see Scott, Willey, and Connor, *They Died with Custer,* 124–25.

6. Scott, Willey, and Connor, *They Died with Custer,* 126–29; Scott and Willey, *Osteological Analysis,* xii–xiii, 90–105. Forensic study of the remains indicates that the body was not Sergeant Butler's.

7. Greene, *Evidence and the Custer Enigma,* 59 (and associated map).

8. Godfrey, "Custer's Last Battle," 370.

9. Hardorff, *Custer Battle Casualties,* 59–65.

10. "Report on the Custer Battlefield Rendered by Capt. Owen J. Sweet, 25th Infty., May 15, 1890," LBBNM.

11. Wessinger to Depot Q[uarter]. M[aster]. Omaha, Nebraska, October 15, 1916,

Letters Received and Sent, 1916–1930, LBBNM. If the stone Wessinger speaks of had no inscription at all, it would not have been one set by Sweet.

12. Wessinger, October 15, 1916, Letters Received and Sent, 1916–1930, LBBNM.

13. Godfrey to Camp, January 1, 1920, LBBNM #11834.

14. Camp to Godfrey, November 13, 1919, LBBNM #11833.

15. Wessinger to Q[uarter].M[aster]. G[eneral]. Washington, D.C., Through D.Q.M. Omaha, Nebraska, September 7, 1917, Letters Received and Sent, 1916–1930, LBBNM.

16. Q.M.G. to Wessinger, September 18, 1917, and Wessinger to Q.M.G., September 22, 1917, Letters Received and Sent, 1916–1930, LBBNM.

17. Camp to Godfrey, November 13, 1919, LBBNM #11833.

18. Quartermaster General to Wessinger, January 24, 1920, Letters Received and Sent, 1916–1930, LBBNM.

19. Quartermaster General to D.Q.M., Omaha, Nebraska, February 12, 1920, Letters Received and Sent, 1916–1930, LBBNM. The copy of this letter in the record book of letters received is dated February 12, 1921, but it is evident from the sequence that the true date was 1920.

20. The original negative of our photo (plate 9.1A) was one of 1,695 Huffman negatives donated to the Montana Historical Society (MHS) in 1982. Prior to their donation to the society, the negatives were in the possession of the Coffrin Gallery in Miles City, Montana, for almost fifty years. The Huffman negative collection included many images from the 1916 Custer Trail Expedition on which Huffman had accompanied General Godfrey and Walter Camp. When the Huffman negatives were cataloged by the historical society, every effort was made to identify those negatives that had been taken by Huffman on the 1916 expedition.

At the time it was cataloged, this view of the Butler marker in Deep Coulee (MHS #981-195), along with five other negatives, was stored in an envelope labeled "General Godfrey and a bunch of old timers," with an additional notation "at the Custer Monument, 1916." One of the negatives in this Coffrin envelope (MHS #981-192) was sleeved in what MHS staff assumed was a vintage, Huffman-era negative envelope with the handwritten inscription, "No. 11, Gen. Godfrey and a bunch of old timers at the monument, 1916." This negative is a verifiable 1916 image of Godfrey and others at the monument. It was issued by Huffman as postcard #11 in his series of cards of the 1916 expedition with Godfrey and Camp. Of the other five negatives in this envelope (MHS #981-193 to #981-197), two show crowds at the Custer monument during an observance, but they seem to have been taken in a different year than 1916. The other three negatives, including this image of the Butler marker, are views not taken at the monument. Therefore, although these six negatives were filed together in the same Coffrin envelope, it appears to the authors that not all the negatives were taken at the same time, and only one of them (#981-192) fits the description on the Coffrin sleeve. Huffman negative collection information from Lory Morrow, Montana Historical Society photograph archives supervisor, to James Brust, September 14, 2001, January 31 and February 14, 2002, e-mail messages in the possession of the author). As discussed in the text, the photograph of the inscribed Butler stone in Deep Coulee must have been taken by Huffman later than June 1916. Huffman was very likely at the battlefield in 1926, and he may have taken this photograph then.

21. Trinque, "Elusive Ridge," 3.

22. Trinque, "Elusive Ridge," 3–5.

23. Luce to Graham, October 19, 1943, LBBNM.

24. Haines to Brust, June 6, 1994, letter in possession of the author. It is worth noting that despite Luce's assertion that a first sergeant rode at the rear of a cavalry company, in fact, that position was generally occupied by the company second sergeant. The first sergeant would be near the company commander at the front of the column.

25. Trinque, "Elusive Ridge," 5–7.

26. Luce to George Osten, February 26, 1947, LBBNM.

27. "Memorandum Of Conference Held June 24–25, 1947 at Custer Battlefield, Montana," LBBNM. This report was probably

prepared in September 1947 to bolster Luce's request to move the Butler marker. It mentions the surveying of the 1891 site by Aubrey Haines, which did not take place until late August.

28. Haines to Brust, June 6, 1994.

29. Edmund Rogers to Luce, September 1, 1947, LBBNM.

30. Howard W. Baker, Associate Regional Director, to NPS Director, September 25, 1947, LBBNM; and Baker to Rogers, October 6, 1947, LBBNM.

31. "Minutes of a Meeting at Custer Battlefield, Montana, July 21 and 22, 1949," submitted by George H. Zacherle, August 3, 1949, LBBNM. See also [Superintendent's] Monthly Narrative Report for July 1949, LBBNM. Those attending the meeting and participating in the Butler marker relocation were Edward S. Luce, Custer Battlefield National Monument superintendent; Colonel Elwood L. Nye, U.S Army, Rtd., and professor of veterinary medicine at Colorado A and M College, Fort Collins; Major George H. Zacherle, Veterinary Corps, U.S. Army, assistant professor of military science and tactics, Colorado A and M College; Floyd Cross, dean of Division of Veterinary Medicine, Colorado A and M College; Lloyd C. Moss, professor of veterinary medicine, Colorado A and M College; George G. Osten, Billings, Montana; Casey E. Barthelmess, Miles City, Montana; and Dan Bowman, Miles City.

32. Kuhlman, *Legend into History*, 230n58.

33. Nelson, "Sergeant Butler's 'Travelling' Marker," 7.

34. Hardorff, *Custer Battle Casualties II*, 54.

35. "Minutes of a Meeting at Custer Battlefield, Montana, July 21 and 22, 1949," LBBNM.

36. Nine maps used by Luce to map artifact finds are in the archives of Little Bighorn Battlefield National Monument. Each is based on an enlargement of the 1891 USGS topographical map, with the relic locations added by hand. None shows any artifacts at the Butler marker site. LBBNM #15991–#15999.

37. Haines to Brust, telephone interview, December 21, 1995, memo of the conversation in the possession of the author.

38. Hammer to Brust, interview, June 27, 1998, memo of the conversation in the possession of the author.

39. Osten to Brininstool, June 17, 1948, quoted in Osten to William Henry, February 4, 1969, LBBNM.

40. Camp to Godfrey, November 13, 1919, LBBNM #11833.

41. Hammer, *Custer in '76*, 116.

42. Doug Scott to Brust, e-mail messages, January 29 and October 6, 2001.

Chapter 10. Finley-Finckle Ridge

1. Nichols, *Reno Court*, 494–95.

2. Wengert and Davis, *That Fatal Day*, 8, 18; Hammer, *Custer in '76*, 95. Camp noted that veteran Charles Windolph confirmed Kanipe's account, having seen "Finckle's body sticking full of arrows, just as Kanipe says." Camp Collection, Brigham Young University, box 6, folder 6.

3. Harrington commanded Company C on the Reno scout and his daughter later informed W. J. Ghent that the family was told he had also commanded the company in the Custer fight. Grace A. Harrington to W. J. Ghent, April 19, 1938. Ghent Papers, Library of Congress. For insight into Captain Custer's and Lieutenant Harrington's assignments, see Nichols, *Reno Court*, 132; Hammer, *Custer in '76*, 128; and Magnussen, *Peter Thompson's Narrative*, 52.

4. Carroll, *Benteen-Goldin Letters*, 27–28.

5. Fox, *Archaeology, History*, 149–54. For a somewhat different interpretation of this action, see Michno, *Lakota Noon*, 181–82.

6. Hardorff, *Lakota Recollections*, 147. Born a Ute, as a boy Yellow Nose was captured and adopted into the Cheyenne. His seizure of the guidon is often placed on Calhoun Hill, but Brave Bear's recollections seem to tie in well with the events on Finley-Finckle Ridge. The fact that warriors in the environs of Deep Ravine witnessed Yellow Nose flaunting the trophy lend further credence to this interpretation. The ridge is visible from much of the terrain south of the ravine, while the western flank of that elevation largely obscures the soldier position on Calhoun Hill.

7. Hardorff, *Custer Battle Casualties*, 112.

8. Taunton, *Custer's Field*, 23.

9. The contract for construction of the

Stone House was signed on May 18, 1894. Excavation began on June 24, and the building was completed and passed inspection on November 12, 1894. The cost was $4,330. On June 22, 1895, another contract was sought to construct the outbuildings and stables. These structures were completed and accepted on October 29, 1895. See journal entries dated June 27 and November 12, 1894, and June 22, August 20, and October 29, 1895, Journal, Custer Battlefield National Cemetery, folder 224, White Swan Library, LBBNM.

10. *Big Horn County News,* Montana, August 30, 2000, 2; John Doerner to James Brust, December 4, 2001, e-mail message in the possession of the author. The replacement marker is designated #258.

Chapter 11. Calhoun Hill

1. Nichols, *Reno Court,* 453, 548; Maguire to General A. A. Humphreys, July 2, 1876, pp. 150–57 in "Tombstones for Bluecoats: New Insights into the Custer Mystery," by W. Kent King, unpublished ms. on file, LBBNM; Taunton, *Custer's Field,* 11. Edgerly informed Camp that "Calhoun's men lay in remarkably good line, with their officers in their proper positions for a coolly planned resistance." Hammer, *Custer in '76,* 58. It should be noted that despite many descriptions of men in proper defensive alignment, relatively few soldier markers are emplaced on Calhoun Hill. Without a significant number of fallen troopers on Calhoun Hill, how did witnesses know the battle positions? They may have viewed accumulations of cartridge cases that indicated skirmish line firing; archaeological evidence of shells in skirmish formation was found on Calhoun Hill. See Fox, *Archaeology, History,* 104–109.

2. Nichols, *Reno Court,* 236; Taunton, *Custer's Field,* 12; Frost, *General Custer's Libbie,* 246.

3. Hardorff, *Camp, Custer, and the Little Bighorn,* 90; Hardorff, *Lakota Recollections,* 143. See also Sills, "Were There Two Last Stands?" 13–21.

4. Hardorff, *Camp, Custer, and the Little Bighorn,* 99; Hardorff, *Lakota Recollections,* 166.

5. Fox, *Archaeology, History,* 102–103.

6. Wells, "Little Big Horn Notes," 10.

7. Archaeological findings reveal that some of the same weapons fired from Greasy Grass Ridge, likely against Company C, were later fired from the Henryville position. Wells has postulated that the soldiers on Calhoun Hill were able to hold their ground some twenty to twenty-five minutes after the rout of Company C; see Wells, "Fight on Calhoun Hill."

8. Graham, *Custer Myth,* 89, 95.

9. Fox, *Archaeology, History,* 101–11.

10. Frost, *General Custer's Libbie,* 246; Hardorff, *Custer Battle Casualties II,* 15.

11. The lieutenant was the son of Civil War general Thomas Leonidas Crittenden and grandson and namesake of Senator John Jordan Crittenden of Kentucky. Jerry Cecil, "Lt. Crittenden," 32, 35; Hardorff, *Custer Battle Casualties,* 104, *Custer Battle Casualties II,* 17, and *On the Little Bighorn,* 188.

12. Hardorff, *Custer Battle Casualties II,* 17–18.

13. Cecil, "Lt. Crittenden," 35–36.

14. Cecil, "Lt. Crittenden," 35–36.

15. Rickey, *History of Custer Battlefield,* 70.

Chapter 12. The Keogh Sector

1. Hammer, *Custer in '76,* 95; Liddic and Harbaugh, *Camp on Custer,* 96; Carroll, *Benteen-Goldin Letters,* 32.

2. Nichols, *Reno Court,* 453–54; Edgerly to Godfrey, March 28, 1927, Godfrey Papers, Library of Congress; Hammer, *Custer in '76,* 130; Frank Anders to E. A. Brininstool, November 7, 1942, Anders Papers, University of North Dakota. The guidon and gauntlets were recovered in the wake of the September 9, 1876, engagement at Slim Buttes, Dakota Territory.

3. Mrs. Eliza Porter to Lieutenant Colonel M. V. Sheridan, May 22, 1877, Sheridan Papers, Library of Congress; Hardorff, *Custer Battle Casualties II,* 42; Simon Snyder letter, July 30, 1876, LBBNM; Owen Sweet to Walter Camp, November 24, 1912, Camp Collection, A312 C11329, LBBNM.

4. Nichols, *Reno Court,* 67–68, 453–54; Bourke Diary, USMA Library; Fox, *Archaeology, History,* 111–13.

5. Dixon, *Vanishing Race,* 176; Michno, *Lakota Noon,* 233; Hardorff, *Lakota Recollections,* 51; Hammer, *Custer in '76,* 199, 201.

6. Hammer, *Custer in '76,* 207; Wells, "Little Big Horn Notes," 13–14; Hardorff, *Lakota Recollections,* 157,159. Long honored by a traditional stone cairn, in 1999 the site of Lame White Man's death was commemorated with a red granite stone, similar to the soldiers' markers. A second stone was erected nearby in honor of another Cheyenne fatality, Noisy Walking.

7. Visitors Register, Custer Battlefield National Cemetery, March 30, 1895, to September 20, 1910, LBBNM. Daniel A. Kanipe and W. M. Camp signed the register on September 17, 1908, with no mention of Mrs. Kanipe, but on August 6, 1909, D. A. Kanipe's signature is followed by that of M. A. Kanipe. Camp is known to have accompanied the Kanipes on this 1909 visit; see Donahue, "Knipe's Recollections," 13.

8. Hammer and Nichols, *Men with Custer,* 29, 180.

9. Scott et al., *Archaeological Perspectives,* 65–69.

10. The Christian Barthelmess views of the Little Bighorn battlefield have presented puzzles in both attribution and dating. One major repository of Barthelmess's work is the Montana Historical Society, which houses a collection donated by the photographer's descendants. This Barthelmess collection consists of both copy prints and vintage photographs but only eleven original negatives. The copy prints, made by the family prior to the donation to the MHS, were organized into three sections: A, B, and C. Groups A and B were copy prints made from photographs located in two separate albums belonging to the Barthelmess family. The descendants felt confident that all the photographs in these two albums had been taken by Christian Barthelmess. The group C images were copy prints made from loose, individual, vintage photographs that also belonged to the Barthelmess family. There was some question whether all the group C photographs had been taken by Barthelmess or if some might have been the work of other photographers that had been acquired by Christian Barthelmess or his son Casey. Each copy print was designated by a letter A, B, or C, followed by a number, but the numbers were sequential over the entire collection and did not begin anew with each change in letter.

At some point in his career, Christian Barthelmess prepared a handwritten list of photos titled "Thirty Years in the Army, A Story in Pictures without Words." The numbers on this list correspond to the numerals assigned to the copy prints, though there are no letter designations. The list seems to cover those images in the two albums, A and B, but not the loose or C photos. Barthelmess's "Thirty Years in the Army" lists four Little Bighorn photos, numbers 99 through 102, all described merely as "Views of Custer's Battleground." These images would have appeared in the Barthelmess families' album A, but that volume is lost. Unfortunately, in 1982 the two albums belonging to the Barthelmess family were stolen and apparently thrown in the Yellowstone River. Album B washed up on the bank and was recovered and is now at the Montana Historical Society. Album A never resurfaced.

However, the collection does contain individual vintage prints of two of the four images on Barthelmess's list. A-101 is the view of the Keogh markers in plate 12.4A, and the title used in the main text of this book was inscribed on the reverse of the vintage print by the photographer's son, Casey Barthelmess, Sr. The other surviving battlefield image from the lost album is A-99, a view of Custer Hill that includes a dog sleeping among the markers. That picture is not reproduced in this book, but the same dog appears in other battlefield photographs attributed to Christian Barthelmess (plates 14.18A and 14.19A). In addition to A-99 and A-101, the C section of the Barthelmess collection contains a number of Custer battlefield views, some of which appear in this volume.

The Montana Historical Society photograph archives also contains an interrelated collection of vintage photographs and negatives donated by the family of Robert Clelland Morrison (1850–1938) of Miles City, Montana. Morrison was making photographs in the area by the early 1880s, a number of years before Barthelmess arrived at nearby Fort Keogh (see Hoopes, *This Last West,* 259). Documents in the MHS files reveal both a personal and a professional relationship between the Barthelmess and Morrison families. Morrison, who was an artist as well as a photographer, retouched photos for Christian

Barthelmess. After Barthelmess's tragic death in 1906, Morrison obtained a number of his negatives from Mrs. Barthelmess, who later, after her remarriage, moved into a small house behind the Morrisons. The Morrison collection at the MHS contains virtually no written information that might provide attribution of the images. Some of the vintage photographs bear Morrison's logo, but most do not. Most of the negatives are not identified or labeled in any way. In a number of instances, the same image appears in both the Barthelmess and the Morrison collection. There are no Little Bighorn views among the Morrison vintage prints, but there are glass-plate negatives of the battlefield in the Morrison collection. Some of these correspond to images in the C section of the Barthelmess collection, but others do not. A detailed study of the two collections has been made by Lory Morrow, MHS photograph archives supervisor, and Casey Barthelmess, Jr., grandson of photographer Christian Barthelmess. The material was also reviewed by author James Brust in an on-site visit to the Montana Historical Society on June 23–24, 2003. In many instances it is simply impossible to be sure which of the two photographers created a given image, and we cannot exclude the possibility that Robert C. Morrison took some of the Little Bighorn views that appear in the two collections. But the firmest attribution belongs to those photos in the two albums, A and B, that belonged to the Barthelmess family. If we accept these as the work of Christian Barthelmess, then we know he visited and photographed the Little Bighorn, as documented by the surviving photos A-99 and A-101. Also, we know he had a dog with him that seems not to appear in any other photographer's work. Given the presence of the same dog in other battlefield views taken in the same era, both in the C section of the Barthelmess collection and in glass-plate negatives in the Morrison material, and knowing that Morrison eventually acquired some of Barthelmess's negatives, we will credit all Little Bighorn views in either the Barthelmess or the Morrison collection at the MHS to Christian Barthelmess, although in fact some could have been taken by Morrison.

These Barthelmess views are undated, but the large wooden cross placed for the general on Custer Hill in 1894, still in good condition, is seen in some, while others show the Stone House, completed in November 1894, and its outbuildings, which were finished in October 1895. This would tend to place Christian Barthelmess at the battlefield in late 1895 or in 1896. While it is possible that he made more than one visit, we will date the Barthelmess views of the Little Bighorn battlefield ca. 1896.

11. Scott et al., *Archaeological Perspectives*, 65.

12. Taunton, *Custer's Field*, 8, 9, 20, 35. Taunton's description of the Keogh marker relocation is accurate except for the distance; the misplaced stone was about eighty yards north of the correct site, not sixty feet.

13. Hammer, *Custer in '76*, 95n15.

14. Camp's battlefield map, heavily influenced by Kanipe's descriptions, showed Bobo's body on the north end of the group immediately around Keogh, just as this marker is. Taunton, *Custer's Field*, 20.

15. John Doerner to James Brust, March 23, 2001, e-mail message in the possession of the author.

16. Hardorff, *Custer Battle Casualties*, 16, 105–106, and *Custer Battle Casualties II*, 42–44.

17. Superintendent Oscar Wright to Quartermaster General, June 13, 1910, Record Book—Letters sent 1893–1925, LBBNM.

18. That photograph, not reproduced in this book, was by Lee Moorhouse, #2267, University of Oregon Library System.

19. Doerner to Brust, August 16, 2001, e-mail message in the possession of the author; Doerner to Brust, Pohanka, and Barnard, October 11, 2001. The replacement marker is designated #259.

20. Hammer, *Custer in '76*, 252; Barnard, *I Go with Custer*, 148. The wooden headboard that Sweet placed for Kellogg in 1890 had been constructed by the First U.S. Cavalry regimental quartermaster, First Lieutenant Jacob G. Galbraith. See "Report on the Custer Battlefield Rendered by Capt. Owen J. Sweet, 25th Infty., May 15, 1890," LBBNM.

21. Barnard, *I Go with Custer*, 140–50, contains a detailed review of all historical evidence regarding the site of Kellogg's death. See also Rickey, *History of Custer Battlefield*, 69.

22. Barnard, *I Go with Custer*, 149.

Chapter 13. Below Custer Hill

1. First Sergeant Frederick Hohmeyer, Sergeant John S. Ogden, Corporals George C. Brown and Albert H. Meyer, and Privates Richard Farrell, William Huber, Andy Knecht, and William H. Rees. See Hardorff, *Custer Battle Casualties,* 15, *Custer Battle Casualties II,* 66-69.

2. McDougall to E. S. Godfrey, May 19, 1909, in Graham, *Custer Myth,* 377.

3. Nichols, *Reno Court,* 535.

4. Nichols, *Reno Court,* 237.

5. Nichols, *Reno Court,* 323, 328.

6. Nichols, *Reno Court,* 418.

7. Graham, *Custer Myth,* 95.

8. Godfrey to Quartermaster General, January 7, 1921. Godfrey Papers, Library of Congress. The heads were those of Privates John E. Armstrong of Company A and John J. McGinnis of Company G, both killed in Reno's valley fight. It should be remembered that the Indian village had moved north on the evening of the battle.

9. Hardorff, *Custer Battle Casualties II,* 47. Additional evidence that Sturgis's head was identified can be found in Taunton, *Custer's Field,* 23, 44.

10. Hardorff, *Custer Battle Casualties II,* 134–35.

11. Hammer, *Custer in '76,* 72; Hardorff, *Custer Battle Casualties II,* 135–36.

12. Hardorff, *Camp, Custer, and the Little Bighorn,* 66.

13. Hardorff, *Camp, Custer, and the Little Bighorn,* 100.

14. Hammer, *Custer in '76,* 95. See also manuscript for an 1879 lecture delivered at West Point, N.Y., Godfrey Papers, Library of Congress.

15. Scott et al., *Archaeological Perspectives,* 72–74, 123–24.

16. Hardorff, *Camp, Custer, and the Little Bighorn,* 84.

17. Hardorff, *Lakota Recollections,* 87; Hammer, *Custer in '76,* 213.

18. Hardorff, *Lakota Recollections,* 32.

19. Hardorff, *Lakota Recollections,* 157.

20. Hardorff, *Lakota Recollections,* 168; Hammer, *Custer in '76,* 210.

21. Hardorff, *Lakota Recollections,* 52, 55.

22. Wells, "Little Big Horn Notes," 18.

23. Charles Corn to William O. Taylor, September 15, 1909, Camp Collection, LBBNM. Corn's statement is not completely clear but seems to imply that Custer's soldiers were operating in proximity to noncombatants who were moving near the river. Taken in context with other Cheyenne accounts, this action appears to have occurred north and west of Custer Hill.

24. Hardorff, *Lakota Recollections,* 31–32.

25. Hardorff, *Hokahey!* 72.

26. Stands in Timber and Liberty, *Cheyenne Memories,* 198–99. For additional Northern Cheyenne oral history recounting an engagement in the northern sector of the battlefield, see Trinque, "Fight in Fishing Woman Ravine." Trinque places this action north of Deep Ravine and west of Custer Hill. Relying on the same Cheyenne accounts, Michael Donahue believes that the fight with Companies E and F occurred somewhat farther north. Donahue presented his interpretation in "Beyond Custer Hill."

27. Boyes, "Don Rickey interview with John Stands in Timber."

28. Hardorff, *Cheyenne Memories,* 200–201.

29. Boyes, "Don Rickey interview with John Stands in Timber," 3.

30. Some confusion exists about the date of this photograph, as the Montana Historical Society has it cataloged as having been taken in 1916. But as noted elsewhere, some Huffman images taken in other years were inadvertently cataloged as 1916. The negative for this photo of the cavalry parade on the battlefield, like the earlier misdated view of the Butler marker in Deep Coulee, was in an envelope labeled "General Godfrey and a bunch of old timers at the Custer Monument," an obvious error. A photograph similar to this one is in the Edward S. Godfrey Collection at the U.S. Army Military History Institute, Carlisle, Pennsylvania (RG48S, Box 2.79), catalogued as 1926; the Seventh Cavalry marched at the fiftieth anniversary observance (see Rickey, *History of Custer Battlefield,* 80–83). For these reasons we date this Huffman photo to 1926.

31. Rickey, *History of Custer Battlefield,* 81.

32. Hammer and Nichols, *Men with Custer,* 339.

33. Hardorff, *Custer Battle Casualties II,* 45–47.

34. Hardorff, *Custer Battle Casualties,* 66, and *Custer Battle Casualties II,* 48; Michno, *Mystery of E Troop,* 201–203; Brust, "Lt. Oscar Long's Early Map," 5. In some of these references, Mrs. Sturgis's first name was mistakenly given as Mamie. In fact Mamie Sturgis was a later descendant of the family. Mrs. Sturgis's first name was Jerusha. See Hammer and Nichols, *Men with Custer,* 338.

35. Superintendent Oscar Wright to Quartermaster General, June 13, 1910, Record Book—Letters sent 1893–1925, LBBNM.

36. Brust, "Learning about the Little Big Horn," 52, 67.

37. For good reviews of the historical accounts of bodies in Deep Ravine see Scott et al., *Archaeological Perspectives,* 39, and Fox, *Archaeology, History,* 203–13. For a contrasting interpretation of the evidence of bodies in the ravine, see Michno, *Mystery of E Troop,* 39ff.

38. Nichols, *Reno Court,* 237.

39. Carroll, *Benteen-Goldin Letters,* 27; Hardorff, *On the Little Bighorn,* 40–41, 131.

40. Scott et al., *Archaeological Perspectives,* 224–42. The archaeology team used a similar pair of a 1937 photo and a 1987 comparison (p. 239).

41. Fox, *Archaeology, History,* 176–80.

42. Rickey, *History of Custer Battlefield,* 72–73; Upton, *Fort Custer on the Big Horn,* 100–112.

43. D. F. Barry to William A. Graham, November 7 [no year but probably late 1920s], letter in the possession of and used courtesy of Glen Swanson.

44. This viewpoint has been put forth most strongly in Fox, *Archaeology, History,* 173–94. Also see Donahue, "Revisiting Col. Gibbon's Route," and Trinque, "It's About Time."

45. Stands in Timber and Liberty, *Cheyenne Memories,* 200.

Chapter 14. Custer Hill

1. Hammer, *Custer in '76,* 236–37.

2. Barnard, *Ten Years,* 305.

3. Nichols, *Reno Court,* 68; Hardorff, *Custer Battle Casualties II,* 28; Graham, *Custer Myth,* 364.

4. Graham, *Custer Myth,* 377; Taunton, *Custer's Field,* 8.

5. Hardorff, *Custer Battle Casualties,* 115–16. Lieutenant (later General) George A. Woodruff, Seventh Infantry, noted Sharrow's remains. As previously recounted, Tom Custer appears to have been acting as aide to his older brother. While some witnesses placed Voss's body closer to the river, several who knew him well identified his remains on Custer Hill. Vickory (whose real name was John H. Groesbeck) was detailed from Company F as regimental color bearer, but because the flag was carried with the pack train, he likely served as an orderly on the staff. Thomas O'Neill said that Voss lay across Vickory. Some evidence suggests that Sergeant Robert Hughes, bearer of Custer's personal guidon, was killed near the river; the bloodstained waistband of his trousers was discovered in the abandoned village. Hardorff, *Custer Battle Casualties, II,* 66–67, 81–82.

6. Hardorff, *Custer Battle Casualties,* 112, 114–16, and *Custer Battle Casualties II,* 66, 68, 80.

7. E. S. Godfrey Diary, Godfrey Papers, Library of Congress.

8. Pickard described finding his bunkie "Le Roche" on the hillside (*Portland Journal,* August 2, 1923). Lynch mentioned Liemann (Camp Collection, Brigham Young University, box 4, folder 2) and a man named "Donovan" who was probably Dohman, as no Donovan died in the battle. Hammer, *Custer in '76,* 139. Lynch, in fact, may not have been attached to the pack train detail as he later claimed, but assigned to the steamer Far West. However, he certainly learned details of the scene from his fellow troopers. Hardorff, *Camp, Custer, and the Little Bighorn,* 41–42.

9. Nichols, *Reno Court,* 454.

10. Nichols, *Reno Court,* 68.

11. Kanipe to Camp, July 20, 1908, Camp Collection, Brigham Young University, box 5, folder 7.

12. Taunton, *Custer's Field,* 14.

13. Hammer, *Custer in '76,* 87.

14. Nichols, *Reno Court,* 549.

15. Nichols, *Reno Court,* 68.

16. Hardorff, *Custer Battle Casualties II,* 20.

17. Barnard, *Ten Years,* 304; Taunton, *Custer's Field,* 29.

18. Ryan to Camp, December 17, 1908, Camp Collection, Brigham Young University, box 1, folder 41.

19. Hardorff, *Custer Battle Casualties II*, 15–16, 38–40; Hammer, *Custer in '76*, 87, 102. In 1890, Captain Sweet erected a marker for Lord on the lower portion of the south skirmish line where he discovered staff buttons and remnants of fabric in context with some human remains. Sweet was apparently unaware of the earlier identification of Lord on Custer Hill.

20. Graham, *Custer Myth*, 220, 345. See also manuscript for an 1879 lecture delivered at West Point, N.Y., Godfrey Papers, Library of Congress.

21. October 13, 1912, Camp Collection, Brigham Young University, box 2, folder 8; Hardorff, *Camp, Custer, and the Little Bighorn*, 94–95.

22. Barnard, *Ten Years*, 304.

23. Nichols, *Reno Court*, 68.

24. Nichols, *Reno Court*, 307.

25. Nichols, *Reno Court*, 307, 322; Barnard, *Ten Years*, 303.

26. Hardorff, *Lakota Recollections*, 75.

27. Hardorff, *Lakota Recollections*, 67.

28. Fox, *Archaeology, History*, 116–17; Scott and Bleed, *Good Walk around the Boundary*, 42–43.

29. Hardorff, *Lakota Recollections*, 146–49.

30. Hardorff, *Lakota Recollections*, 185; Hammer, *Custer in '76*, 207, 210.

31. Hammer, *Custer in '76*, 202.

32. Hardorff, *Hokahey!* 72–73. Marquis credited the recollection of this incident to Wooden Leg, but both Hardorff and Gregory Michno more accurately ascribe the story to Big Beaver, as related to Joe Blummer. See Michno, *Lakota Noon*, 256–58, for an examination of this phase of the battle.

33. Graham, *Custer Myth*, 110.

34. Hardorff, *Hokahey!* 75.

35. Hammer, *Custer in '76*, 210.

36. Neihardt, *Black Elk Speaks*, 104.

37. For details of the discovery of the John Fouch photograph of the Custer Battlefield, see Brust, "Into the Face of History," 104–10.

38. For details on Fouch's visit to the Little Bighorn Battlefield, see Brust, "Fouch Photo May Be the First," 4, "John H. Fouch," 7, and "Adventurous Detour," 10–12.

39. Military authorities seemed in general agreement that Custer died on top of the hill.

In a letter dated October 29, 1878, George D. Ruggles, acting adjutant general, Department of Dakota, directed Lieutenant Colonel G. P. Buell, commanding officer of Fort Custer, to send an expedition to the Little Bighorn to secure all human bones within a cone or pyramid of stones, adding, "The Department Commander thinks that the most suitable location for the grave is the highest point of the ridge just in rear of where General Custer's body was found." This directive led to the reburial expedition of early April 1879, led by Captain Sanderson, who would create the Cordwood Monument and state in his report that it was located "immediately in rear of where General Custer's body was found." See Gray, "Photos, Femurs, and Fallacies," 50.

40. Hardorff, *Custer Battle Casualties*, 35, 71; Brust, "Fouch Photo May Be the First," 10n16.

41. Barnard, *Custer's First Sergeant*, 3, and *Ten Years*, 303–304.

42. Gray, "Nightmares to Daydreams," 36–38; Hedren, "Holy Ground," 197–98.

43. Gray, "Nightmares to Daydreams," 37.

44. Gray, "Nightmares to Daydreams," 37.

45. Rickey, *History of Custer Battlefield*, 98.

46. Hardorff, *Custer Battle Casualties*, 69–71; Hedren, "Holy Ground," 201–202.

47. Hardorff, *Custer Battle Casualties*, 70–71; Charles Roe to Assistant Adjutant General, Department of Dakota, St. Paul, Minnesota, August 6, 1881, LBBNM #11319.

48. Rickey, *History of Custer Battlefield*, 63.

49. Hardorff, *Custer Battle Casualties*, 43–50. Two of the eyewitnesses quoted by Hardorff made it clear that the remains finally identified as General Custer's consisted of far less than a full skeleton (45, 50).

50. "Report on the Custer Battlefield Rendered by Capt. Owen J. Sweet, 25th Infty., May 15, 1890," LBBNM.

51. The identification of the subjects in the group photo is based on photographer D. F. Barry's handwritten inscription on the reverse of another print of this image in the archives of the Little Bighorn Battlefield National Monument (LBBNM #422). This version is reproduced in Frost, *Custer Album,*

176. However, Frost misread the name of the man second from the left, calling him "Sergeant Horn" rather than Ham. In a 1914 letter to artist Joe Scheuerle, provided by Brian Dippie, Barry relates that Ham was not in the Little Bighorn battle but joined the Seventh Cavalry in 1877 and was a member of Captain McDougall's Company B. For more information on the wounds received by White Swan during Reno's valley fight and his rescue by fellow Crow scout Half Yellow Face, see Cowdrey, "Crows Who Scouted for Custer," 41–44.

52. Hammer and Nichols, *Men with Custer,* 78, 287. Both were civilians. Boston Custer, twenty-seven years old, had earlier served in the Seventh Cavalry as forage master and on the 1876 Sioux campaign was a citizen guide. Autie Reed, only eighteen, had no official role. The name of Custer's nephew is mistakenly inscribed on both the monument and his individual marker as "Arthur Reed." His correct name was "Harry Armstrong Reed."

53. Hardorff, *Custer Battle Casualties,* 23, 34, 44, 55, 99, 121–22, and *Custer Battle Casualties II,* 90. Sheridan's 1877 exhumation party did not attempt to recover the remains of the two young civilians. The bodies were secured some months later, however, through the compassionate efforts of the families of Lieutenant James Calhoun (General Custer's brother-in-law) and Captain George Yates, both of whom also died in the battle. The coffins of Boston Custer and Autie Reed were shipped to Monroe, Michigan, and buried at Woodlawn Cemetery in January 1878. See Hardorff, *Custer Battle Casualties II,* 86–87, 90; Hammer and Nichols, *Men with Custer,* 78, 287.

54. The wooden headboards had been constructed by the First U.S. Cavalry regimental quartermaster, First Lieutenant Jacob G. Galbraith; see "Report on the Custer Battlefield Rendered by Capt. Owen J. Sweet, 25th Infty., May 15, 1890," LBBNM. Sweet's report makes no mention of footboards.

55. Superintendent Oscar Wright to Quartermaster General, June 13, 1910, Record Book—Letters sent 1893–1925, LBBNM. The body of Second Lieutenant Henry M. Harrington, Company C, could not be identified after the battle. No historical account places Harrington on Custer Hill, and it is more likely that he died fighting with his company in the region of Finley-Finckle Ridge.

56. Rickey, *History of Custer Battlefield,* 69; Journal, Custer Battlefield National Cemetery, folder 224, White Swan Library, LBBNM. Journal entry dated August 6, 1906, states, "Supt. Grover erected wooden cross at General Custer place 12 years ago," which would have been 1894, a fact confirmed by this Haynes photo showing the cross in virtually new condition in that year. Another journal entry, dated February 1, 1896, says, "Gen'l Custer stone entirely carried away." It would seem from Haynes's 1894 photo that the original marble marker for Custer was gone by 1894.

57. Hardorff, *Custer Battle Casualties,* 25, 33, 100.

58. Hardorff, *Custer Battle Casualties,* 34, 100–101.

59. Journal, Custer Battlefield National Cemetery, folder 224, White Swan Library, LBBNM. Journal entry, dated April 7, 1895, states, "Report many markers on battlefield have fallen or about to due to freezing at bases."

60. For detailed information on Adams, Becker, and the creation of "Custer's Last Fight," see Taft, "Pictorial Record," 377–85.

61. Otto Becker to Ethan Shepley, November 17, 1939, Anheuser-Busch Companies' Archives, courtesy of archivist William Vollmar. Shepley was a member of the board of directors of Anheuser-Busch and a Busch family attorney. Becker was eighty-five years old at the time he wrote this letter and confused about some details. He cited James McLaughlin's 1910 book, *My Friend the Indian,* as a source of "much information on the country surrounding the battlefield and background which I made after photos showing the Little Big Horn River in the distance." Becker realized his mistake, telling Shepley in another letter the next day that he had obtained *My Friend the Indian* many years after he painted "Custer's Last Fight." But though he was confused on the source, that he used one or more photographs to create the background landscape is almost certainly an accurate fact.

62. The other photographic images Becker might have used include the 1877

John Fouch view (plate 14.1A in this book) and Stanley J. Morrow's "Where Custer Fell" (plate 14.3). The more likely candidates, in addition to this 1894 Haynes view (plate 14.13A), are a ca. 1882 view attributed to D. F. Barry (LBBNM #1389) and a ca. 1894 photo attributed to H. R. Locke (LBBNM #14351), neither of which is reproduced in this volume.

Further indirect evidence that this 1894 Haynes view of Custer Hill was the image Becker used to create the background of "Custer's Last Fight" has been pointed out to the authors by Brian Dippie. Anheuser-Busch distributed a pamphlet titled "Custer's Last Battle," ca. 1896, prepared by Arthur Koenig, a close friend of Adolphus Busch and owner of the Milwaukee Lithographic and Engraving Company, which employed Otto Becker. Koenig's pamphlet contained a number of narratives about the Little Bighorn battle, including quotes from Olin D. Wheeler's 1893 booklet *6,000 Miles through Wonderland*, written for the Northern Pacific Railroad and "illustrated from photos by Haynes." Since that publication predates Haynes's 1894 trip to the Little Bighorn, it is an earlier Haynes battlefield image taken ca. 1882 that appears on page 100, showing Curley at the unfenced monument on Custer Hill (a variant of plate 14.7A in this book, reproduced in Tilden, *Following the Frontier*, 191). Even more convincingly, this same Haynes picture of Curley at the monument appears as a vignette in the lower margin of the earliest printings of "Custer's Last Fight," though reversed as would be expected when copied onto a lithograph stone.

Finally, in a 1901 Northern Pacific Railroad annual titled *Wonderland*, Olin Wheeler reproduces our Haynes photo (plate 14.13A). All of these factors point to this Haynes view from atop Custer Hill as the likely source of Becker's background landscape for "Custer's Last Fight."

63. Journal, Custer Battlefield National Cemetery, folder 224, White Swan Library, LBBNM. Journal entry, dated July 11, 1893, states, "Supt. A. N. Grover took charge of cemetery"; that of November 12, 1894, reads, "Lodge [Stone House] completed." (See chapter 10, note 9.)

64. Rickey, *History of Custer Battlefield*, 41.

65. Journal, Custer Battlefield National Cemetery, folder 224, White Swan Library, LBBNM. Journal entry, dated April 28, 1896. See also Rickey, *History of Custer Battlefield*, 63.

66. Hardorff, *Custer Battle Casualties*, 35.

67. Sanderson to Post Adjutant, Fort Custer, April 7, 1879, LBBNM file 218.

68. Charles Roe to Assistant Adjutant General, Department of Dakota, St. Paul, Minnesota, August 6, 1881, LBBNM #11319.

69. Hardorff, *On the Little Bighorn*, 121.

70. Hardorff, *On the Little Bighorn*, 121; Carroll and Price, *Roll Call*, 165.

71. Hardorff, *On the Little Bighorn*, 126.

72. The full text on the reverse of Purcell's photo reads

On June 24, 1876, at Custer's Battlefield. Overlooking the Little Horn river, in Montana, the Sioux Indians under Chiefs Gaul and Rain-in-the-Face massacred Gen. George A. Custer and 263 officers and men of his command. Not a white man escaped to tell the tale. The government has made the battlefield a national cemetery. The dead were buried where they fell, a white marble slab marking each grave. A white cross stands where Custer's body was found. Near it is an imposing monument on which is inscribed the names and rank of the dead heroes.

On Decoration Day 1897, nearly 21 years after the battle, memorial exercises were held on the battlefield. The first exposure for this photo was made at the battlefield where Custer fell and the second exposure was made by accident to catch "Bloody Knife" as he appeared in war costume; he with over 200 other Crow and Cheyenne Indians were holding a war dance in the valley just below the battlefield.

Was it mere chance or did the camera see more clearly than eyes of man? Does the weird spectre of paganism hate in heart, and knife in hand, forever hover over this spot casting its shadow dark and grim, emblem of murder and unrest and savage cruelty across the fair white shafts that tell of peace and faith and the "White Christ's endless reign?" Or on this anniversary day, where for the last time, on the vast continent that once was theirs, dark eyes glowed with triumph, and dark brows were crowned with glory, came some red prophet of the long ago invoking the great spirit's vengeance for centuries of wrong?

Who can tell?

Copyrighted, June, 1897, by Frank Purcell, Billings, Montana.

73. Carroll, *Custer Battlefield Ghost Picture.*

74. This Fred Miller photograph was obtained from the archives of the Montana Historical Society. It has a copy print of the image, acquired in 1970 from Jean Castles and inscribed "photo taken in 1898." Castles, in turn, had received captioning information from Hulda Miller Fields, daughter of the photographer Fred E. Miller, and mother of Miller's biographer Nancy Fields O'Connor (Lory Morrow, Montana Historical Society photograph archives supervisor, to James Brust, February 8 and 13, 2002, e-mail messages in the possession of the author). Hulda Miller Fields had not yet been born in 1898, and the source of her information is not known, but her dating of this image is reasonably accurate. Miller was active on the Crow reservation from 1898 to about 1912 (O'Connor, *Fred E. Miller,* 11). By 1901, the top of the Custer cross had broken off. Hence, this photo must have been taken between 1898 and 1901.

75. Rickey, *History of Custer Battlefield,* 69.

76. Rickey, *History of Custer Battlefield,* 69.

77. That 1909 photo, LBBNM #2468, is one of a large number of Wanamaker-Dixon photographs in the LBBNM archives that were not used in *The Vanishing Race.* It is not illustrated in this book; however, it appears, along with a modern comparison photo, in Brust, "Learning about the Little Big Horn," 56–57; and Brust, "Photo Essay of Historical Views of the Little Big Horn Battlefield," in Hardorff, *Custer Battle Casualties II.*

78. The title and date of this photograph are from Albright, *Crow Indian Photographer,* 126–27. Throssel's original negative of this image is in the collection of the American Heritage Center, University of Wyoming (Negative TP633, Throssel #6944). Archivist Leslie Shores confirms that the plate is marked with the copyright year 1908 (Leslie Shores to James Brust, April 23, 2002, e-mail message in the possession of the author).

79. A photo titled "Custer Monument" by Edward S. Curtis, copyright 1905, which appears in *The North American Indian,* shows a replacement wooden cross for Custer. Although most of the known Curtis views of the Little Bighorn were taken in 1907 (Brust, "Curtis Photographs," 10), he did visit the field in 1905 (Hutchins, *Papers of Edward S. Curtis,* 16; Albright, *Crow Indian Photographer,* 9), and likely 1905 is the correct date of "Custer Monument." Hence, the sadly deteriorated cross of 1901 had been replaced by 1905. Another early view showing a replacement cross for Custer was taken by Julia Tuell (1886–1960) in 1907 (Aadland, *Women and Warriors,* 114). Neither of these photographs is reproduced in this book.

80. Dixon, *Vanishing Race,* opposite page 144.

81. Albright, *Crow Indian Photographer,* 30–35; Peggy Albright to James Brust, April 2, 2002, e-mail message in possession of the author.

82. American Heritage Center negatives numbered TP634 through TP636 are original glass plates by Richard Throssel that show the three Crow scouts on Custer Hill in the same attire as "The Three Scouts" (plate 14.23A) and "The Custer Battlefield" (plate 14.24A). TP635 is a variant of "The Three Scouts," while TP634 is an alternative version of "The Custer Battlefield." The only one dated is "The Three Scouts" (TP633), which is marked 1908, but the identical setting, clothing, and equipment indicate that all five images were made at the same time.

83. Following the same logic, two other photographs in *The Vanishing Race* may be attributed to Richard Throssel. "Custer Scouts" (facing page 130) and "Here Custer Fell" (facing page 142) both show the three Crow scouts on Custer Hill, attired and equipped just as they are in the documented Throssel images. Curley also appears in these two plates, though unmounted and wearing everyday clothing rather than traditional native attire. A well-known antagonism existed between Curley and the other three Crow scouts, and his presence in these photos may have required some diplomacy on the part of the photographer. Throssel, a resident of Crow Agency and an adopted member of the tribe, would have been a more likely candidate to convince all four scouts to pose together than an outsider such as Dixon.

84. The other image is titled "Crowds at an anniversary ceremony at Custer Battlefield. Headstones show where the soldiers fell at Custer's Last Stand." It is also an unnumbered item in the Jack E. Haynes collection at the Montana Historical Society and is not reproduced in this book.

85. After the admission of Oklahoma in 1907, the flag contained forty-six stars of no fixed design from 1908 until New Mexico and Arizona joined the union in 1912. The American flag was then changed to a mandated pattern of six rows of eight stars each. That forty-eight-star design remained in use until 1959, when Alaska achieved statehood.

86. Rickey, *History of Custer Battlefield,* 112.

87. Rickey, *History of Custer Battlefield,* 113.

88. Brust, "Learning about the Little Big Horn," 68.

89. Some references state that the Fetterman/Fort Phil Kearny reburials at the Custer Battlefield National Cemetery took place in 1888, while others give the date as 1889. All remains were exhumed from the Fort Phil Kearny cemetery in October 1888, although one witness later said they were initially moved to Fort McKinney in Buffalo, Wyoming, before eventually being reinterred at the Little Bighorn (Spear, *Bozeman Trail Scrapbook,* 77–78). Lieutenant George S. Young, who was then post quartermaster at Fort McKinney, later told Camp that he recalled that the reinterment on Custer Hill, in which he participated, also took place in October 1888 (Hardorff, *On the Little Bighorn,* 120–21). Rickey, in *History of Custer Battlefield,* at one point gives the reburial date as 1888 (p. 51) but in another section implies that it was in 1889 (pp. 63–64). *Custer National Cemetery* gives 1889 as the date of the Fetterman/Fort Phil Kearny reburials (p. 23). Camp, in various letters and notes, vacillated as to the correct date but did uncover documents stating that the reburial took place during the fiscal year ending June 30, 1889, which means the actual reinterment might have been in either calendar year 1888 or 1889 (Hardorff, *On the Little Bighorn,* 122, 148–49, 159, 197). Recognizing the uncertainty, we use 1888 as the correct year, on the strength of the recollection of Lieutenant Young, who took part in the event.

90. Rickey, *History of Custer Battlefield,* 53.

91. Rickey, *History of Custer Battlefield,* 53, 117.

92. Doerner, "Human Bones Discovered," 1, 14–15.

Chapter 15. The Cemetery

1. Rickey, *History of Custer Battlefield,* 29.

2. Rickey, *History of Custer Battlefield,* 30, 36. Initially, only the Custer section of the field was preserved. The Reno-Benteen site was added in 1930.

3. Rickey, *History of Custer Battlefield,* 64, 68.

4. Rickey, *History of Custer Battlefield,* 56. For a map of the cemetery and a list of abandoned military post reinterments, see *Custer National Cemetery,* 9, 23. After the Fetterman/Fort Phil Kearny reburials on Custer Hill, the next to be transferred were the dead from Fort Sisseton, Dakota Territory, in 1890, followed by Fort Stevenson, Dakota Territory, in 1891, and then remains from a number of posts in 1892.

5. *Custer National Cemetery,* 8, 11–12, 23; Rickey, *History of Custer Battlefield,* 51–52.

6. Rickey, *History of Custer Battlefield,* 57; Journal, Custer Battlefield National Cemetery, folder 224, White Swan Library, LBBNM. Journal entries, dated June 21, 1907 and June 28, 1908.

7. Albright, *Crow Indian Photographer,* 1, 7.

8. Rickey, *History of Custer Battlefield,* 102.

9. Rickey, *History of Custer Battlefield,* 59, 99, 111; Journal, Custer Battlefield National Cemetery, folder 224, White Swan Library, LBBNM.

10. Rickey, *History of Custer Battlefield,* 58, 112. The cemetery had been fenced since 1891, but prior to 1931, wooden materials were used.

11. Rickey, *History of Custer Battlefield,* 99.

12. Rickey, *History of Custer Battlefield,* 57–58.

13. Rickey, *History of Custer Battlefield,* 36.

14. Rickey, *History of Custer Battlefield,* 98.

15. Rickey, *History of Custer Battlefield,* 125–26; Doerner, "Seventh Cavalry Horse Cemetery Excavated," 1, 18–19.

16. Rickey, *History of Custer Battlefield*, 99.

17. Rickey, *History of Custer Battlefield*, 57, 59, 102. For a photo of the rostrum in use during the seventy-fifth anniversary observance, see Rickey, *History of Custer Battlefield*, 92.

18. Rickey, *History of Custer Battlefield*, 101–102. Rickey provides contradictory information about the visitors center construction, saying at one point that it began in July 1950, and then two sentences later giving a start date of July 1951. If the latter date were accurate, this 1951 Roahen aerial photo would not show the visitors center. Likely, the 1950 date is correct for the start of construction.

19. Rickey, *History of Custer Battlefield*, 98–99.

Chapter 16. Unmatched Photographs

1. Elsa Spear discussed this photograph in a videotaped interview made at the battlefield and supplied to the authors by her daughter, Marilyn Bilyeu. The video is undated but probably was made in the mid-1980s. Spear explained that Croonquist was "secretary of the dude ranchers," so likely he served in an organization of people in that business, as her family was. She speaks of the number of cars parked on the nearby ridges, so evidently some large-scale event had brought Croonquist and the Spears to the area, perhaps the sixtieth anniversary of the battle. The people in the photo were perched on this hilltop to watch the proceedings. Interestingly, when asked by the interviewer where the cars were parked and where these observers sat, Elsa Spear, usually quite sharp even in her eighties and nineties, was unsure of the exact location. She pointed in the general direction of the park entrance and beyond, which seems to match our thoughts on the approximate photo site. But her inability to pinpoint this exact location underscores our own difficulties and reinforces our speculation that the spot may have been altered in some fashion between 1936 and the 1980s, perhaps by road grading. Sadly, Al Croonquist perished in a plane crash near Bozeman, Montana, in January 1938.

Appendix.
Stanley J. Morrow's 1879 Photographs

This text and the biography of Morrow in chapter 3 have been adapted from a presentation by James Brust at the 9th Annual Symposium of the Custer Battlefield Historical and Museum Association, held at Hardin, Montana, on June 23, 1995.

1. L. A. Huffman used his own numbers and titles when he reprinted and published Morrow's Little Bighorn battlefield negatives, but we have not catalogued them in this book. For a listing of the Huffman titles and numbers, see Brown and Felton, *Frontier Years*, 46.

2. Gray, "Nightmares to Daydreams," 36–38.

3. Michno, *Mystery of E Troop*, 60–61.

BIBLIOGRAPHY ✑

Archival Sources

Frank L. Anders Papers, OGL#43-5-1, Elwyn B. Robinson Special Collections, Chester Fritz Library, University of North Dakota, Grand Forks.

Anheuser-Busch Companies' Archives, St. Louis, Mo.

John G. Bourke Diary, Volume 21, July 21, 1877, U.S. Military Academy Library, West Point, N.Y.

Walter M. Camp Collection, Brigham Young University, Provo, Utah.

Ralph G. Cartwright Collection, Phoebe Apperson Hearst Memorial Library, Lead, S.Dak.

W. J. Ghent Papers, Library of Congress, Washington, D.C.

Edward S. Godfrey Papers, Library of Congress, Washington, D.C.

G. B. Grinnell Papers, Braun Research Library, Southwest Museum, Los Angeles.

Francis R. Hagner Collection, Manuscripts and Archives Division, New York Public Library.

Little Bighorn Battlefield National Monument (LBBNM), Crow Agency, Mont.

Lee Moorhouse materials, Division of Special Collections and University Archives, University of Oregon Library System.

Record Group 393, Headquarters Military Division of the Missouri, National Archives, Washington, D.C.

Philip H. Sheridan Papers, Library of Congress, Washington, D.C.

Elmo Scott Watson Papers, Newberry Library, Chicago, Ill.

Newspapers

Big Horn County News (Montana), August 30, 2000, p. 2.

Portland Journal, August 2, 1923.

Hardin (Montana) Tribune, June 22, 1923.

Books and Journal Articles

Aadland, Dan. *Women and Warriors of the Plains: The Pioneer Photography of Julia E. Tuell.* Missoula, Mont.: Mountain Press Publishing, 2000.

Albright, Peggy. *Crow Indian Photographer: The Work of Richard Throssel.* Albuquerque: University of New Mexico Press, 1997.

Barnard, Sandy. *Custer's First Sergeant John Ryan.* Terre Haute, Ind.: AST Press, 1996.

_____. *Digging into Custer's Last Stand.* Terre Haute, Ind.: AST Press, 1998.

_____. *I Go with Custer: The Life and Death of Reporter Mark Kellogg.* Bismarck, N.Dak.: Bismarck Tribune Publishing, 1996.

_____. "Ken Hammer, Looking for Walter Camp." *Greasy Grass* 11 (May 1995): 20, 25–29.

_____. "Mark Kellogg's Role during the 1876 Campaign." In *1st Annual Symposium, Custer Battlefield Historical & Museum Association, Inc.,* 9–11. Hardin, Mont.: CBHMA, 1988.

_____. *Ten Years with Custer: A Seventh Cavalryman's Memoirs.* Terre Haute, Ind.: AST Press, 2001.

Bookwalter, Thomas. "The Photographs Described." In R. Norvelle Wathen, *The Custer Battlefield: An Aerial Perspective.* Louisville, Ky.: R. N. Wathen, 1976.

Boyes, William, ed. "Don Rickey Interview with John Stands in Timber," August 8, 1956. Little Big Horn Associates, 1991.

Brininstool, Earl. *Troopers with Custer.* Harrisburg, Pa.: Stackpole, 1952.

Brown, Mark, and William Felton. *The Frontier Years: L. A. Huffman, Photographer of the Plains.* New York: Bramhall House, 1955.

Brust, James. "Adventurous Detour to Battlefield," *Greasy Grass* 10 (May 1994): 8–12.

_____. "Curtis Photographs Offer Unique Glimpse of Custer's Crow Scouts." *Greasy Grass* 13 (May 1997): 10–16.

_____. "Fouch Photo May Be the First." *Greasy Grass* 7 (May 1991): 2–10.

_____. "Into the Face of History." *American Heritage* 43 (November 1992): 104–13.

_____. "John H. Fouch, First Post Photographer at Fort Keogh." *Montana, The Magazine of Western History* 44 (Spring 1994): 2–17.

_____. "Learning about the Little Big Horn Battle from Photos Old and New." In *8th Annual Symposium, Custer Battlefield Historical & Museum Association, Inc.,* 50–69. Hardin, Mont.: CBHMA, 1995.

_____. Letter to the editor. *Montana, The Magazine of Western History* 45 (Spring 1995): 90–91.

_____. Letter to the editor. *Montana, The Magazine of Western History* 48 (Spring 1998): 84.

_____. "Letting the Photos Speak." In *The Papers of Edward S. Curtis Relating to Custer's Last Battle,* edited by James Hutchins, 161–85. El Segundo, Calif.: Upton and Sons, 2000.

_____. "Lt. Oscar Long's Early Map Details Terrain, Battle Positions." *Greasy Grass* 11 (May 1995): 5–13.

_____. "Norris Drew Early On-site Map of Battle." *Greasy Grass* 10 (May 1994): 13–15.

_____. "Photojournalism, 1877, John H. Fouch, Fort Keogh's First Post Photographer." *Montana, The Magazine of Western History* 50 (Winter 2000): 32–39.

_____. "Stanley J. Morrow's 1879 Photographs of the Custer Battlefield." In *9th Annual Symposium, Custer Battlefield Historical & Museum Association, Inc.,* 47–78. Hardin, Mont.: CBHMA, 1996.

_____. "Where Was the Timber?" In *11th Annual Symposium, Custer Battlefield Historical & Museum Association, Inc.,* 5–12. Hardin, Mont.: CBHMA, 1998.

Carroll, John, ed. *The Benteen-Goldin Letters on Custer and His Last Battle.* New York: Liveright, 1974.

_____. *The Custer Battlefield Ghost Picture.* Bryan, Tex.: privately published, 1978.

_____. "The Little Big Horn Medals of Honor." *Research Review: The Journal of the Little Big Horn Associates* 4 (January 1990): 20–32.

Carroll, John, and Byron Price. *Roll Call on the Little Big Horn, 28 June 1876.* Fort Collins, Colo.: The Old Army Press, 1974.

Cecil, Jerry. "Lt. Crittenden, Striving for the Soldier's Life." *Greasy Grass* 11 (May 1995): 30–36.

Clark, George M. *Scalp Dance: The Edgerly Papers on the Battle of the Little Big Horn.* Oswego, N.Y.: Heritage Press, 1985.

Cowdrey, Mike. "Crows Who Scouted for Custer." *Greasy Grass* 14 (May 1998): 39–44.

Curtis, Edward. *The North American Indian, Being a Series of Volumes Picturing and Describing the Indians of the United States and Alaska.* Vol. 3. Cambridge, Mass.: The University Press, 1908.

Custer National Cemetery. Little Bighorn Battlefield National Monument, Mont.: Southwest Parks & Monuments Association, 1999.

Darling, Roger. *Benteen's Scout to the Left: The Route from the Divide to the Morass, June 25, 1876.* El Segundo, Calif.: Upton and Sons, 1987.

Dixon, Joseph. *The Vanishing Race: The Last Great Indian Council.* Glorieta, N.Mex.: Rio Grande Press, 1973.

Doerner, John. "Human Bones Discovered during Indian Memorial Construction." *The Post Dispatch of the Frontier Army of the Dakota* 17 (July 2002): 1, 14–15.

_____. "Seventh Cavalry Horse Cemetery Excavated at Little Bighorn Battlefield." *The Post Dispatch of the Frontier Army of the Dakota* 17 (July 2002): 1, 18–19.

Donahue, Michael. "Beyond Custer Hill." In *17th Annual Symposium, Custer Battlefield Historical & Museum Association, Inc.,* 26–51. Hardin, Mont.: CBHMA, 2004.

_____. "Knipe's Recollections Help Camp Reconstruct Custer's Final Hours." *Greasy Grass* 14 (May 1998): 2–17.

_____. "Revisiting Col. Gibbon's Route." *Greasy Grass* 19 (May 2003): 12–20.

Donahue, Michael, and Michael Moore. "Gibbon's Route to Custer Hill." *Greasy Grass* 7 (May 1991): 22–32.

Fleming, Paula, and Judith Luskey. *The North American Indians in Early Photographs.* New York: Dorset Press, 1986.

Fox, Richard A., Jr. *Archaeology, History, and Custer's Last Battle: The Little Big Horn Reexamined.* Norman: University of Oklahoma Press, 1993.

_____. "West River History." In *Legacy: New Perspectives on the Battle of the Little Bighorn,* edited by Charles Rankin, 139–65. Helena: Montana Historical Society Press, 1996.

Frink, Maurice, and Casey Barthelmess. *Photographer on an Army Mule.* Norman: University of Oklahoma Press, 1965.

Frost, Lawrence. *The Custer Album: A Pictorial Biography of General George A. Custer.* New York: Bonanza Books, 1984.

_____. *General Custer's Libbie.* Seattle, Wash.: Superior Publishing, 1975.

Godfrey, Edward S. "Cavalry Fire Discipline." *Journal of the Military Service Institution* 19 (September 1896), 252–79.

_____. "Custer's Last Battle." *Century Monthly Illustrated Magazine* 43 (January 1892): 358–84.

Graham, William. *The Custer Myth: A Source Book of Custeriana.* New York: Bonanza Books, 1953.

_____. *Story of the Little Big Horn, Custer's Last Fight.* New York: Bonanza Books, 1926.

Gray, John. *Centennial Campaign: The Sioux War of 1876.* Norman: University of Oklahoma Press, 1988.

_____. "Itinerant Frontier Photographers and Images Lost, Strayed or Stolen." *Montana, The Magazine of Western History* 38 (April 1978): 2–15.

_____. "Nightmares to Daydreams." *By Valor and Arms* 1 (Summer 1975): 30–39.

_____. "Photos, Femurs, and Fallacies—Part II." *The (Chicago) Westerners Brand Book* 20 (September 1963): 49–51, 56.

Greene, Jerome. *Evidence and the Custer Enigma: A Reconstruction of Indian-Military History.* Golden, Colo.: Outdoor Books, 1986.

Hammer, Kenneth, ed. *Custer in '76: Walter Camp's Notes on the Custer Fight.* Provo, Utah: Brigham Young University Press, 1976.

Hammer, Kenneth, and Ron Nichols, eds. *Men with Custer: Biographies of the Seventh Cavalry.* Hardin, Mont.: CBHMA, 1995.

Hardorff, Richard G. *Camp, Custer, and the Little Bighorn.* El Segundo, Calif.: Upton and Sons, 1987.

_____. *Cheyenne Memories of the Custer Fight.* Spokane, Wash.: Arthur H. Clark, 1995.

_____. *The Custer Battle Casualties, Burials, Exhumations, and Reinterments.* El Segundo, Calif.: Upton and Sons, 1989.

_____. *The Custer Battle Casualties, II: The Dead, the Missing, and a Few Survivors.* El Segundo, Calif.: Upton and Sons, 1999.

_____. *Hokahey! A Good Day to Die! The Indian Casualties of the Custer Fight.* Spokane, Wash.: Arthur H. Clark, 1993.

_____. *Lakota Recollections of the Custer Fight.* Spokane, Wash.: Arthur H. Clark, 1991.

_____, ed. *On the Little Bighorn with Walter Camp: A Collection of W. M. Camp's Letters, Notes, and Opinions on Custer's Last Fight.* El Segundo, Calif.: Upton and Sons, 2002.

_____. *Walter M. Camp's Little Bighorn Rosters.* Spokane, Wash.: Arthur H. Clark, 2002.

Hedren, Paul. "Holy Ground: The United States Army Embraces Custer's Battlefield." In *Legacy: New Perspectives on the Battle of Little Bighorn,* edited by Charles Rankin, 189–206. Helena: Montana Historical Society Press, 1996.

_____. *With Crook in the Black Hills: Stanley J. Morrow's 1876 Photographic Legacy.* Boulder, Colo.: Pruett Publishing Company, 1985.

Heski, Thomas. *The Little Shadow Catcher: D. F. Barry, Celebrated Photographer of Famous Indians.* Seattle, Wash.: Superior Publishing, 1978.

Hoopes, Lorman. *This Last West.* Helena, Mont.: Falcon Press Publishing, 1990.

Hurt, Wesley, and William Lass. *Frontier Photographer: Stanley J. Morrow's Dakota Years.* Lincoln: University of Nebraska Press, 1956.

Hutchins, James, ed. *The Papers of Edward S. Curtis Relating to Custer's Last Battle.* El Segundo, Calif.: Upton and Sons, 2000.

Karson, Terry. *L. A. Huffman, Pioneer Photographer* (exhibition catalog). Billings, Mont.: Yellowstone Art Center, 1990.

Libby, O. G. *Arikara Narrative of the Campaign against the Hostile Dakotas.* New York: Sol Lewis, 1973.

Liddic, Bruce, and Paul Harbaugh, *Camp on Custer: Transcending the Custer Myth.* Spokane, Wash.: Arthur H. Clark, 1995.

Kuhlman, Charles. *Legend into History.* Fort Collins, Colo.: The Old Army Press, 1977.

Magnussen, Daniel O., ed. *Peter Thompson's Narrative of the Little Bighorn Campaign.* Glendale, Calif.: Arthur H. Clark, 1974.

Marquis, Thomas, trans. *Wooden Leg: A Warrior Who Fought Custer.* Lincoln: University of Nebraska Press, 1931.

Mautz, Carl. *Biographies of Western Photographers.* Nevada City, Calif.: Carl Mautz Publishing, 1997.

Michno, Gregory. *Lakota Noon.* Missoula, Mont.: Mountain Press Publishing, 1997.

———. *The Mystery of E Troop: Custer's Gray Horse Company at the Little Bighorn.* Missoula, Mont.: Mountain Press Publishing, 1994.

Mitchell, Lynn. "William Richard Cross, Photographer on the Nebraska–South Dakota Frontier." *South Dakota History* 20 (Summer 1990): 81–95.

Montana Historical Society. *F. Jay Haynes, Photographer.* Helena: Montana Historical Society Press, 1981.

Neihardt, John G. *Black Elk Speaks.* Lincoln: University of Nebraska Press, 1995.

Nelson, R. L. "Sergeant Butler's 'Travelling' Marker." *Research Review: The Journal of the Little Big Horn Associates* 8 (Spring 1974): 5–9.

Nichols, Ronald. *In Custer's Shadow: Major Marcus Reno.* Fort Collins, Colo.: The Old Army Press, 1999.

———, ed. *Reno Court of Inquiry.* Crow Agency, Mont.: Custer Battlefield Historical & Museum Association, 1992.

O'Connor, Nancy. *Fred E. Miller, Photographer of the Crows.* Missoula: University of Montana, 1985.

Rickey, Don. *History of Custer Battlefield.* Billings, Mont.: Custer Battlefield Historical & Museum Association, 1967.

Russell, Don. *Custer's Last.* Fort Worth, Tex.: Amon Carter Museum of Western Art, 1968.

Scott, Douglas D. "Cartridges, Bullets, and Bones: A Look Back at the Archaeology of the Little Bighorn Battle." unpublished manuscript, Lincoln, Nebr.: Midwest Archaeological Center, National Park Service, 2000.

Scott, Douglas, and Peter Bleed. *A Good Walk around the Boundary: Archaeological Inventory of the Dyck and Other Properties Adjacent to Little Bighorn Battlefield National Monument.* Lincoln: Nebraska Association of Professional Archeologists and Nebraska State Historical Society, 1997.

Scott, Douglas, and Richard A. Fox. *Archaeological Insights into the Custer Battle: An Assessment of the 1984 Field Season.* Norman: University of Oklahoma Press, 1987.

Scott, Douglas, Richard A. Fox, Melissa Connor, and Dick Harmon. *Archaeological Perspectives on the Battle of the Little Bighorn.* Norman: University of Oklahoma Press, 1989.

Scott, Douglas, and P. Willey. *Osteological Analysis of Human Skeletons Excavated from the Custer National Cemetery.* Technical Report No. 50. Lincoln, Nebr.: Midwest Archaeological Center, 1997.

Scott, Douglas, P. Willey, and Melissa Connor. *They Died with Custer: Soldiers' Bones from the Battle of the Little Bighorn.* Norman: University of Oklahoma Press, 1998.

Sills, Joe, Jr. "The Crow Scouts: Their Contribution in Understanding the Little Big Horn Battle." In *5th Annual Symposium, Custer Battlefield Historical & Museum Association, Inc.,* 11–18. Hardin, Mont.: CBHMA, 1992.

———. "Weir Point Perspective." In *7th Annual Symposium, Custer Battlefield Historical & Museum Association, Inc.,* 45–51. Hardin, Mont.: CBHMA, 1994.

———. "Were There Two Last Stands?" In *2nd Annual Symposium, Custer Battlefield Historical & Museum Association, Inc.,* 13–21. Hardin, Mont.: CBHMA, 1989.

Sklenar, Larry. *To Hell with Honor: Custer and the Little Bighorn.* Norman: University of Oklahoma Press, 2000.

Smalley, Vern. "Where Was the Crow's Nest?" In *13th Annual Symposium, Custer Battlefield Historical & Museum Association, Inc.,* 77–90. Hardin, Mont.: CBHMA, 2000.

Spear, Elsa. *Bozeman Trail Scrapbook: The books and photos of Elsa Spear.* Banner, Wyo.: The Fort Phil Kearny/Bozeman Trail Association, and the family of Elsa Spear, 1993.

Stands in Timber, John, and Margot Liberty. *Cheyenne Memories* Lincoln: University of Nebraska Press, 1967.

Stewart, Edgar. *Custer's Luck.* Norman: University of Oklahoma Press, 1955.

Taft, Robert. *Photography and the American Scene: A Social History, 1839–1889.* New York: Dover Publications, 1938.

_____. "The Pictorial Record of the Old West, IV. Custer's Last Stand—John Mulvaney, Cassilly Adams, and Otto Becker." *Kansas Historical Quarterly* 14 (November 1946): 361–90.

Taunton, Francis. *Custer's Field: A Scene of Sickening Ghastly Horror.* London: Johnson-Taunton Military Press, 1986.

_____. "The Enigma of Weir Point." In *No Pride in the Little Big Horn.* London: English Westerners' Society, 1987.

Tilden, Freeman. *Following the Frontier with F. Jay Haynes, Pioneer Photographer of the Old West.* New York: Knopf, 1964.

Treadwell, T. K., and William Darrah. *Stereographers of the World.* National Stereoscopic Association, 1994.

Trinque, Bruce. "Elusive Ridge." *Research Review: The Journal of the Little Big Horn Associates* 9 (January 1995): 2–8.

_____. "The Fight in Fishing Woman Ravine." *Custer and His Times, Book Four.* Little Big Horn Associates, 2002.

_____. "It's About Time: Time, Watches, and Events—June 25, 1876." In *17th Annual Symposium, Custer Battlefield Historical & Museum Association, Inc.,* 16–25. Hardin, Mont.: CBHMA, 2004.

Tuttle, Jud. "Who Buried Lieutenant Hodgson?" In *4th Annual Symposium, Custer Battlefield Historical & Museum Association, Inc.,* 9–16. Hardin, Mont.: CBHMA, 1991.

Upton, Richard. *Fort Custer on the Big Horn, 1877–1898: Its History and Personalities as Told and Pictured by Its Contemporaries.* Glendale, Calif.: Arthur H. Clark, 1973.

Utley, Robert. *Cavalier in Buckskin.* Norman: University of Oklahoma Press, 1988.

_____, ed. *The Reno Court of Inquiry.* Fort Collins, Colo.: The Old Army Press, 1972.

Watson, Elmo. "Photographing the Frontier." *The (Chicago) Westerner's Brand Book* 4 (January 1948): 66.

_____. "Way Out West: The Story of Stanley J. Morrow, a Pioneer Photographer in Every Sense of the Word." *Coronet* 5 (April 1939): 147–53.

Wells, Wayne. "Custer's Arrival Time at the River." In *1st Annual Symposium, Custer Battlefield Historical & Museum Association, Inc.,* 76–87. Hardin, Mont.: CBHMA, 1988.

_____. "The Fight on Calhoun Hill." In *2nd Annual Symposium, Custer Battlefield Historical & Museum Association, Inc.,* 22–34. Hardin, Mont.: CBHMA, 1989.

_____. "Kanipe, Martin, and Benteen." *Research Review: The Journal of the Little Big Horn Associates* 2 (Spring 1988): 10–15, 31.

_____. "Little Big Horn Notes: Stanley Vestal's Indian Insights." *Greasy Grass* 5 (May 1989): 9–19.

Wengert, James W., and E. Elden Davis, eds. *That Fatal Day: Eight More with Custer.* Howell, Mich.: Powder River Press, 1992.

Wiebert, Henry, and Don Wiebert. *Sixty-six Years in Custer's Shadow.* Billings, Mont.: Falcon Press, 1985.

INDEX